A Sociology of Mystic Practices

A Sociology of Mystic Practices

Use and Adaptation in the Emergent Church

Dann Wigner

FOREWORD BY
Mathew Guest

PICKWICK *Publications* · Eugene, Oregon

A SOCIOLOGY OF MYSTIC PRACTICES
Use and Adaptation in the Emergent Church

Copyright © 2018 Dann Wigner. All rights reserved. Except for brief quotations in critical publications or reviews, no part of this book may be reproduced in any manner without prior written permission from the publisher. Write: Permissions, Wipf and Stock Publishers, 199 W. 8th Ave., Suite 3, Eugene, OR 97401.

Pickwick Publications
An Imprint of Wipf and Stock Publishers
199 W. 8th Ave., Suite 3
Eugene, OR 97401

www.wipfandstock.com

PAPERBACK ISBN: 978-1-5326-3687-5
HARDCOVER ISBN: 978-1-5326-3689-9
EBOOK ISBN: 978-1-5326-3688-2

Cataloguing-in-Publication data:

Names: Wigner, Dann, author. | Guest, Mathew, foreword.

Title: A sociology of mystic practices : use and adaptation in the emergent church / Dann Wigner. Foreword by Mathew Guest.

Description: Eugene, OR: Pickwick Publications, 2018 | Includes bibliographical references and index.

Identifiers: ISBN 978-1-5326-3687-5 (paperback) | ISBN 978-1-5326-3689-9 (hardcover) | ISBN 978-1-5326-3688-2 (ebook)

Subjects: LCSH: Mysticism. | Mystics. | Emerging church movement. | Christianity—21st century. | Postmodernism—Religious aspects—Christianity.

Classification: LCC BR121.3 E45 2018 (print) | LCC BR121.3 (ebook)

Manufactured in the U.S.A.   06/07/18

To Leann

Contents

Foreword by Mathew Guest | ix
Preface | xiii
Acknowledgments | xxi

Chapter One: Introduction | 1
Chapter Two: The Emergent Church in the United States of America | 21
Chapter Three: Literary Evidence of Emergent Church Use of Mystic Practices | 54
Chapter Four: Empirical Methodology | 95
Chapter Five: Phenomenological Appropriation of Mystic Practices | 129
Chapter Six: Theological Reinterpretation of Mystic Practices | 193
Chapter Seven: Conclusions, Contributions, and Recommendations | 241

Appendix A: Spiritual Practices Questionnaire | 255
Appendix B: Interview Questions | 256
Appendix C: Participant Information Sheet | 260
Appendix D: Ethical Consent Form | 261

Bibliography | 263
Index | 273

Foreword

IT IS NOW OFTEN assumed without question that strict or conservative religious traditions exist in a relationship of counter reaction to modern culture. Indeed, sociologists of religion have often assumed that such movements—whether they be fundamentalist Muslims, orthodox Jews or the Southern Baptists of the USA - achieve an enhanced identity by sustaining strong opposition to the more permissive cultures that surround them. Conservative groups subscribe to what sociologist Peter Berger calls "deviant bodies of knowledge"; that is, their belief systems are antithetical to the dominant norms and values of western culture, most commonly associated with religious and ethnic tolerance, gender equality, liberal morality and a division of religion from the state. They survive, and in some cases thrive, by keeping modernity out. The paradigm of postmodernity appears to pose an even greater problem for these traditions, as it challenges notions of an unchanging, absolute truth; stresses social contingency; and elevates the value of individual freedom. If the humanistic optimism of modernity is disturbing to religious conservatives, then we might expect the hyper-consumerism and individualism of postmodernity to be even more so.

And yet there have been developments in recent decades that challenge this understanding, developments that suggest that religion may exist in a positive relationship of engagement with western culture. In the USA, the history of evangelicalism since the 1940s has been one of ever-more innovative strategies of engagement with popular culture, media, politics and education, all in an effort to spread the good news more effectively and maintain relevance among emerging generations. Cultural resources have been successfully appropriated for the evangelical cause; the rise of the megachurches is perhaps the most striking recent example, merging the convenience ethos of the shopping mall with an accessible, essentialist Christian message. What's the sense in being constrained by tradition when your market niche is moving in a different direction?

The Emerging Church Movement (ECM) has emerged from this crucible of cultural and religious factors. Borne of an evangelical spiritual entrepreneurship but also a deep-felt disillusionment with the conventions of the evangelical mainstream, it has been preoccupied with the challenges of embodying Christian identity whilst embracing the culture in which we live. While sharing with the megachurches a positive orientation to cultural resources, the ECM has been altogether more cerebral, reflective and self-consciously egalitarian, engaging in ritual experimentation without a desire for a settled liturgy, and theological conversation without a desire for its final resolution. Since its inception in the 1990s its direction of travel has been complex, simultaneously inspired by the global networks that make up the broader ECM, while also profoundly localised, each ECM group typically shaped by a set of concerns and practices steered by its own membership. In an important recent volume on the movement, Gerardo Marti and Gladys Ganiel emphasize its tendency to foster a "strategic religiosity," oriented to a perpetual process of re-examining and reconfiguring the traditions that most shape their identities. It is fitting that their book is entitled *The Deconstructed Church*.

Insofar as the ECM is a movement marked by innovation and creativity, it is correctly called progressive. Its tendency to promote traditionally leftist causes, challenge patriarchal structures and question the doctrinal norms of more conservative Christianity reinforces this impression. But if it has one eye firmly on the future, it has another on the distant past. Recent research has identified in the ECM a keen interest in the mystical and contemplative traditions, emerging as a major source of spiritual sustenance among those yearning for an experience of antiquity and deep authenticity that can only be derived from a sense of the ancient. This trend—exemplified most vividly in the renewed interest in monastic forms of Christian piety—is perhaps especially pronounced within emerging churches in the USA. The US ECM is marked by a counter-reaction to the highly visible models of church promoted by the megachurches, viewed as contrived, superficial and overly indebted to the social norms of hyper-consumerism. By seeking meaning in mystical traditions, the ECM embraces a resource that recaptures a sense of the wisdom and quiet seriousness many believe has been lost from contemporary Christianity.

This appropriation of the mystical by the Emerging Church is the focus of this welcome book by Dann Wigner. As scholarship on the ECM grows and develops, we are finding out more about its local variations and about how it uses the spiritual sources at its disposal. As Wigner demonstrates, the crucial issue here is not the nature of the sources themselves—be they meditation, online media or postmodern philosophy—rather, it is the way they are appropriated into the religious lives of ECM members. Wigner draws from new research into ECM groups in the southwestern USA, focusing on how they engage in mystical practices they take to be derived from long-standing Christian traditions. By using ethnographic methods that explore how ECM members embody and make sense of these practices, he offers a nuanced, empirically robust analysis of an important strand in the movement's development. This is an important contribution to our understanding of one of the most intriguing and unpredictable movements in contemporary Christianity.

Mathew Guest

Reader in the Sociology of Religion
Durham University, UK.

Preface

What is the Emergent Church?

I FOCUS MY BOOK ON the subject of spiritual borrowing, specifically on the borrowing of mystic practices from the Catholic, Orthodox, and Anglican traditions by participants in the emergent church. However, the emergent church itself may be a relatively unknown subject for many, so a few opening definitions and descriptions are in order. In the first chapter, I will offer some conceptual definitions of the emergent church that I have gleaned from other studies along with an operating definition of my own, but these definitions require background familiarity with the emergent church for full comprehension. In this light, I would like to emphasize that defining the emergent church is not easy. In fact, it can be likened to the frustrating activity of nailing Jell-O to a wall.[1] Every answer to this question must first travel through a matrix of subjective interpretation on the part of the answerer. It may be tempting to approach this question conceptually. In this sense, I could define the emergent church according to particular beliefs or practices that are typical of their theology, philosophy, or ethics. Conversely, it is tempting to approach the question phenomenologically. In this sense, I could define the emergent church according to observed behaviors and defined social structure that is visible in specific local churches or larger institutional associations. Each approach only deals with a piece of the problem of describing the emergent church accurately. As a result, I will briefly outline a fourfold approach to defining the emergent church through presenting (1) what it is not, (2) what it is, (3) what theological and sociological characteristics it has, and (4) what local emergent churches look like.

It is much easier to say what the emergent church is *not* rather than what it is. So, let's begin by contrasting the emergent church with some

---

1. DeYoung and Kluck, *Why We're Not Emergent (by Two Guys Who Should Be)*, 16-17.

standard definitions of religious groups. First, the emergent church is not a denomination. "The word *denomination* was adopted as a neutral and nonjudgmental term that implied that the group referred to was but one member, denominated by a particular name, of a larger group to which other Protestant denominations belonged. It was an inclusive term conveying the notion of mutual respect and recognition."[2] Denominations have discrete boundaries, but they are involved with and generally accepted by the larger society. The emergent church reaches across denominational boundaries of organization, and, as a group, the emergent church is suspicious of the level of organization necessary to create a unit as coherent and institutional as a denomination based on particular beliefs and/or religious practices. There are certain denominational markers that are present within the emergent church, but these markers are vestiges of the denominational contexts from which local emergent churches have "emerged." Next, this reasoning extends to the term *sect* as equally inapplicable for the emergent church. In fact, this term might be even more distasteful to participants in the emergent church. *Denomination* and *sect* are quite analogous terms when applied to formal religious institutions with the important distinction that denominations recognize the coexistence and potential validity of other denominations. Sects view religious boundaries as more rigid and tend to view faith in exclusive terms, according to which members of a particular sect would see themselves as the only bearers of truth. While levels of exclusivity vary among sects, even when "an established sect has lost its appearance of opposition to the rest of the society and other religious groups, . . . it remains doctrinally or theoretically exclusive."[3] Any hint of exclusivity is questioned and often rejected by participants in the emergent church. So, the emergent church is stridently critical of the institutional structure of both denominations and sects as well as of their propensity for strict rules of belief and behavior.

Shifting focus from impersonal structures, the emergent church similarly rejects definition in terms that emphasize central leaders or obedience to group norms. This group does not fall under the category of new religious movement, or the more pejorative and obsolete term *cult*, chiefly because they do not find their definition and cohesion around a single person's doctrinal beliefs.[4] While there are many notable leaders in the emergent church who write voluminously, they often disagree, deal with disparate contexts, or only write to describe the changes which they view already happening

2. Hudson, "Denominationalism," 2286.
3. Introvigne, "Cults and Sects," 2084.
4. Wessinger, "New Religious Movements: An Overview," 6513.

in emergent church groups. Lastly, the emergent church does not bear the marks of a religious order: "Popularly, religious orders are thought to include any and all men or women who profess public vows of poverty, chastity, and obedience; follow a common rule of life; engage in a specific kind of work (e.g., teaching, nursing, missionary endeavor); and submit to the directions of superiors who may be either appointed by higher ecclesiastical authority or elected in some manner by the order's members."[5] Pointedly, the emergent church has unequivocally rebelled against matters of social hierarchy and corporate adherence to standards of behavior, yet they have shown an interesting, though uneven, engagement with intentional community. To this end, I will discuss some intentional communities that are present in the emergent church in chapter four, but the emergent church is a much larger entity than these specific communities. So, from this basis of what the emergent church is *not*, we can now proceed to engage with what the emergent church actually is.

According to those within the emergent church, the best designation for it is as a *conversation*.[6] While I do not wish to contradict that label, a more helpful designation for the emergent church is to view it as a composite of a theological school of thought and a social movement. From the side of theology, the emergent church is a conversation about faith, belief, and religious practice. "Considered in its own proper nature, theology has some constituent parts . . . for example, doctrines concerning the Trinity, Christology, the sacraments, ecclesiology, and Mariology."[7] With regard to such "constituent parts" of theology, the emergent church can be compared to other theological schools of thought such as Protestant Liberalism or Neo-Orthodoxy. In comparison, these schools of thought never came to be centered in a single denomination; rather, they delineated a particular method for theological interpretation. The emergent church does value statements about specific doctrines but only as propositions to be questioned. To contrast, both Protestant Liberalism and Neo-Orthodoxy represented a top-down approach to theology, according to which academic theology filtered down level by level to the common Christian. Conversely, the emergent church approaches theology with greater emphasis on a bottom-up approach, beginning at the popular or "grass roots" level. Additionally, while most theological schools of thought are bound together conceptually by particular answers to standard theological questions (e.g., "What do you believe about God?"), the emergent church is bound by *the act of questioning* standard theological

---

5. Mitchell, "Religious Communities: Christian Religious Orders," 7721.
6. Kimball, "The Emerging Church and Missional Theology," 86.
7. Congar, "Theology: Christian Theology," 9139.

answers, or, at least, what they perceive to be standard theological answers. So, while the emergent church is in part a theological school of thought, that label does not fully define it.

The other principal piece of defining the emergent church is as a social movement. It is this aspect which is often given the greater emphasis by researchers while the theological aspect is given preeminence by those participants within the emergent church. In fact, many studies refer to the emergent church as the emergent church *movement* and leave it at that. Simply defined, a social movement is a "loosely organized but sustained campaign in support of a social goal, typically either the implementation or the prevention of a change in society's structure or values."[8] The emergent church does share many markers with other social movements, but the crux of any social movement is the common goal which has drawn the movement into being. The emergent church is notably lacking on this front. There is no defined goal. In fact, participants stress that they have no goal; rather, they are a collective conversation about *the search* for a goal. Still, the emergent church can be defined by common ritual actions or a few (very few) shared beliefs. From this perspective, the emergent church could be compared and contrasted with the neo-charismatic movement. The neo-charismatic movement was similarly trans-denominational and amorphous; however, they did share the common defining traits of the baptism of the Holy Spirit (i.e., speaking in tongues, prophecy, dreams, healing, etc.). The emergent church lacks such a common core of experience. As a result, the emergent church is a hybrid: part social movement and part theological school of thought. This composition does make description quite difficult, but there are some common theological and sociological characteristics of the emergent church that help to flesh out a more accurate portrait.

My study is qualitative in nature, aiming at thick description of specific churches, so there are not too many generalizations concerning the emergent church in most of this book. Yet, there are a few general characteristics, both theological and sociological, that hold true for the purposes of presenting a basic portrait of the conversation. As noted above, the theological nature of the emergent church does not center on particular doctrines or beliefs but on questioning and doubt. With this perspective, it is unsurprising that theological characteristics are indistinct. For instance, the emergent church puts a very high value on cultural relevance, but they are quite open that a large part of the process is figuring out exactly what "cultural relevance" is. Closely related, the theology of the emergent church displays an abiding concern for postmodernism and postmodernity as a trait. I will tackle the

---

8. *Encyclopaedia Britannica* (online), "Social Movement."

definition of *postmodernism* in chapter two, but it is an ambiguous term that can often only be approached by listing what it is against. This negative process of definition is indicative of the emergent church as well, and it is likely a result of how deeply they engage with postmodernism. A final typical theological characteristic of the emergent church, thankfully with a little more tangibility, is their common heritage in evangelicalism. While not all participants in the emergent church emerged from an evangelical context, the majority of them did, including the most respected voices in the conversation. As a result, the emergent church is consciously shaping its theology in distinction from evangelical theological markers. These primary markers to which the emergent church reacts ambivalently are "*conversionism*, the belief that lives need to be changed; *activism*, the expression of the gospel in effort; *Biblicism*, a particular regard for the Bible; and what may be called *crucicentrism*, a stress on the sacrifice of Christ on the cross."[9] In light of this origin point, the bulk of chapter two is devoted to sketching out the relationship between evangelicalism and the emergent church. While common theological characteristics of the emergent church can be frustratingly vague, common sociological traits offer a little firmer ground.

Churches that identify with the emergent church conversation typically have multiple traits in common. To begin, one theological trait also manifests through sociological traits in the emergent church: cultural relevance. Cultural relevance as a theological value shows up sociologically through a strong emphasis on inclusion of all races, ethnicities, sexual orientations, genders, and lifestyles within the typical emergent church setting. Additionally, social justice issues figure prominently in the emergent church conversation as well as in emergent church action. Other characteristics have less of a direct link with a theological emphasis. As a third trait, my book shows that the emergent church places a high value on experimentation within the ritualistic/cultic aspect of religion. As a result, the religious-spiritual practices of each individual emergent church can vary widely. Coupled with an attitude of experimentation, participants are explicit about the informal and impermanent nature of the emergent church. They do not intend to set up a new denomination or sect. The emergent church is a conversation of transition with all emphasis placed on what Christianity may indeed become in the future. Lastly, the participants in this conversation bear a distinct sociological profile, with some exceptions of course. Demographically speaking, the typical participant in the emergent church is in his/her 20s-30s, white, middle to upper class in background (even if current income

---

9. Bebbington, *Evangelicalism in Modern Britain*, 3

is lower), well-educated, and disproportionately male.[10] My research upheld these general trends. However, demographic markers are only a piece of a descriptive portrait of the emergent church. The clearest view of the emergent church is only available through scrutinizing specific settings of the conversation/movement.

Looking at multiple local examples of the emergent church is an effective process for building a general outline of the larger group. To that end, familiarity with several prominent churches around the USA is very helpful. I will also provide a greatly expanded look for the three participating churches in the study. Additionally, I will offer a field note description of my attendance at one service to give an experiential facet to this portrait of the emergent church. Concerning prominent congregations in the emergent church, the following groups are a small, but representative, sample:

- Cedar Ridge Community Church (Spencerville, MD): http://www.crcc.org/
- Church of the Apostles (Seattle, WA): www.apostleschurch.org
- Ecclesia (Houston, TX): http://www.ecclesiahouston.org/
- House for All Sinners and Saints (Denver, CO): http://www.houseforall.org/
- Journey (Dallas, TX): http://www.journeydallas.com/
- Mosaic (Los Angeles, CA): http://mosaic.org/
- Scum of the Earth Church (Denver, CO): www.scumoftheearth.net
- Solomon's Porch (Minneapolis, MN): http://www.solomonsporch.com/
- The Bridge (Phoenix, Tempe, and Scottsdale, AZ): www.thebridgewebsite.com
- Vintage Faith (Santa Cruz, CA): http://www.vintagechurch.org/

In addition to these examples, I visited the following smaller, less influential, groups: Church in the Cliff (Dallas, TX), Emmaus Road Church (Tulsa, OK), and Riverside Community Church (San Antonio, TX). They will figure prominently in the book's discussion beginning in chapter four. From a slightly closer angle, I would like to offer my field note observations of an actual worship experience at Emmaus Road Church in Tulsa, Oklahoma, on June 25, 2011, in order to round out this opening description of the emergent church.

10. Rah and Mach, "Is the Emerging Church for Whites Only?" 16, 20.

Emmaus Road Church met in a repurposed office building that had been converted into a one-room setting with minimal decorations. Concrete floors and exposed wiring were evident. There were many types of seating in the central part of the room, including pews, armchairs, and writing desks. In addition to the central open area, one wing of the main room was a prayer station, and the other wing was an art station. The prayer station was separated from the rest of the worship space by wrought iron votive candle wall dividers that were approximately six feet in height. Along with many candles, there was a desk and chair with prayer cards and a "surrender box" for one's struggles which one would like to give to God. There was also a tissue box, a suggested written "forgiveness prayer," a picture of Jesus with distinctly Palestinian features, a couch, kneeling bench, and an open prayer journal. At any point during the service, participants could get up and head over to the semi-privacy of the prayer station to worship in their own individual fashion. The art station could be visited in a similar manner. Chairs and tables were arranged in no discernible pattern at the art station. Butcher paper, crayons, Play-Doh, markers, and scissors were set up for children. Also, two easels were set up on top of a drop-cloth with blank canvases, along with a variety of paint types and colors, brushes, water, paint thinner, a small wooden mannequin, old *National Geographic* magazines, and artwork completed during previous services. Lamps were provided in this area for additional lighting.

The service began approximately five minutes after the advertised time (6pm on Saturday night) in a relaxed fashion. A prayer reading entitled *An Ancient Prayer in the Celtic Tradition* called the participants to attention. Then, a single musician led congregational singing, accompanied by an acoustic guitar. The songs were simple compositions of the "praise and worship" variety with no written or projected words offered to the gathering as guidance. As the singing progressed, additional participants trickled in, eventually swelling the ranks of those gathered to approximately twenty persons. Most attendees were under thirty, and they adopted a variety of standing and seated postures, seemingly according to personal preference. Some participants sang with closed eyes, some swayed back-and-forth, and some with upraised hands. Children played quietly in the middle of this singing portion of the service. Following singing, community announcements were made, and the children were dismissed for "story time." The sermon followed, and it was entitled "The Sacraments: An Introduction." The speaker lectured on the traditional sacraments in evangelical traditions: baptism and Holy Communion. He then proceeded to introduce the other five sacraments (confirmation, marriage, ordination, confession, and unction) to the gathered participants. In the course of the talk, he connected the celebration of the sacraments to both the theological doctrine of the divinity and humanity of Jesus Christ as well as the Platonic concept of Dualism. Following this explanation, Holy Communion was celebrated by intinction. As the bread was given to each participant, the phrase was repeated, "This is Christ's body, broken for you." As the wine was given to each participant, the phrase was repeated, "This is Christ's blood, shed for you." The service was concluded by another participant reciting the Aaronic blessing of Numbers 6:24-26: "The Lord bless you and keep you; the Lord make his face to shine upon you, and be gracious to you; the Lord lift up his countenance upon you, and give you peace." As the service ended, a rap music video, streaming from the Internet, was projected on the main wall of the meeting space while people casually visited with each other. This video did not appear to have any overt religious content, but it did have Father's Day as its primary theme. After the close of the service, the majority of the attendees headed around the corner to a local restaurant for food and drinks. While this aspect was not an official part of the worship service, multiple participants confirmed that it was a very common informal community ritual. In fact, they touted it as an indispensable piece of their unique church experience.

While each church definitely had its own unique blend for worship services, each church had notable characteristics of experimentation and juxtaposition prominently visible in their community meetings. So, these four pieces of (1) unique worship services, (2) general theological and sociological traits, (3) the combination of a theological school of thought and a social movement, and (4) rejection of traditional church forms all combine to *show* an answer to that difficult question: "What is the emergent church?" Before proceeding to more specific matters, I would like to reiterate that my focus in the following pages is on the process of spiritual borrowing. As enthralling as the emergent church (EC) might be in and of itself, it is really only the jumping-off point for an in-depth sociological investigation into how a group adapts spiritual practices to their own environment and theological beliefs. So, while "What is the emergent church?" is not an easy question to answer, the answer *for this book* is actually, "The emergent church is a fertile environment in which spiritual practices can be transplanted, take root, and bear fruit."

Acknowledgements

I DID NOT INTEND TO write this book; rather, I should say that I did not intend to write *this* book. The germ of the idea for this book goes back—at least—to 2005, and it has changed quite a lot since that first thought. On the way, it served as the basis of my research thesis for my doctorate in theology from the University of Durham between 2008 and 2015. For that stage of the research and writing, I would be remiss if I did not thank my supervisors, Mathew Guest and Mark McIntosh, as well as Gerard Loughlin and Gladys Ganiel who were the readers for my viva. Their comments, both critical and constructive, have gone a long way into bringing this book into a recognizable form beyond the raw data of interviews and field observations.

Necessities of anonymity preclude me from naming all of the interview participants, but I do want to extend my hearty thanks to the people of Riverside Community Church, Emmaus Road Church, and Church in the Cliff. Without your input, there would be no practical and empirical data to ground my theoretical musings. Additionally, I want to thank by name the senior pastors of each of these churches—Scott Heare, Preston Sharpe, and Courtney Pinkerton—for their candor and willingness to answer my endless questions. Further, I extend my gratitude to all those persons who are part of the "conversation" known as the emergent church. I admire intensely your willingness to *try*.

Moving closer to home, I want to thank everyone who read the book or parts of the book in draft form as well as those who got far more than they bargained for whenever they asked me, "So, what are you writing about?" I am grateful beyond words to my parents, Kenn and Linda Wigner, who always encouraged me to search things out for myself. Thanks are also due to Clark, my son, whose birth extended the write-up phase of this project considerably. When the choice is between playing with you and writing, Clark, I will always choose playing with you. Lastly—and most of all—I must thank Leann, my better half, through all these years. You have always been there for reading and editing the manuscript and—most importantly—to argue with me endlessly about the meaning of it all. I love you now and always.

1

Introduction

Since the beginning of the emergent church (EC), participants have demonstrated an interest in the practices of the Christian mystical tradition.[1] However, their interest in spiritual practices is not limited to these practices alone, for the EC "combine[s] ancient forms of worship with the modern, ranging in style from Gregorian chants to Hip Hop, and using icons, candles and incense as aids to worship, plus strobe lights and knee-high clouds."[2] This observation inspires curiosity on several fronts. Significant questions include the following: why are EC Christians interested in practices from the Christian mystical tradition, how are they interested in using these practices in their churches, and how far does this appropriation extend? If emergent churches are employing a wide variety of mystic practices, then how do these practices influence the developing spiritual theology of the EC?[3] They are clearly using these practices, but the question of direct concern in this research project is how deeply they connect to the theological tradition from which these practices arise.

The research created from this line of inquiry will provide insight into cross-tradition appropriation of mystic practices with principal interest in the transferability of mystical theology. I have addressed this research area and its questions in my study through in-depth literary research combined with empirical evidence. In the empirical phase of research, I visited three emergent churches in the southwestern region of the United States of America (USA). Among these churches, I observed multiple services

1. McLaren, *Finding Our Way Again*, 54–55.
2. Gibbs, *ChurchNext*, 128.
3. Bielo includes the following practices: "heightened emphasis on public creedal recitation, public reading of monastic and Catholic prayers, burning incense, replacing fluorescent lighting with candles, setting early Protestant hymns to contemporary music, chanting Eastern Orthodox prayers, using icons, creating prayer labyrinths, following the church calendar for sermons and lectionary readings, using *lectio divina* to read the Bible, and increasing the role of silence." Bielo, *Emerging Evangelicals*, 71.

and meetings, interviewed thirty-eight members or regular attendees, and conducted documentary research on the podcasts and blogposts which composed their archives of sermons and public conversations. My resultant claim is that *the emergent church is appropriating Christian mystical practices by investing these practices with their own theological content.*

In support of this claim, the book will be divided into seven chapters. Following this introduction, the second chapter will focus on the general history of the emergent church as it has developed in the USA along with an introduction to the case study emergent churches. A third chapter will consider the use of Christian mystical practices by the EC according to EC authors. In the fourth chapter, the methodology of empirical data collection and its rationale will be explicated, and the findings of the empirical research process for particular mystic practices will be relayed in the fifth chapter. The sixth chapter will offer analysis of why these practices were appropriated through description of the distinctive theological themes or "anchors" which allow for appropriation and reinterpretation. In the course of conversation, Interviewee 29 provided the term "anchor" as a preferable synonym for a unique theological theme. EC participants did not favor more traditional terms such as *belief, doctrine, dogma, fundamental, tenet,* or *proposition.* Therefore, I found that "anchor" was an appropriate term to use to help define EC theological interpretation. From these findings and their interpretation, a final chapter will offer conclusions by comparing the literature directly with what was observed in the case study churches. Noted areas of contribution for the study and recommendations for further research will round out the final chapter. The remainder of this introductory chapter will treat in greater depth the historical context of the Christian mystical tradition, operating definitions, the current context of the EC, the research claim, the logical reasons and types of evidence set forth for this claim, and the overall conclusions, contributions, and recommendations desired for this book to the academic field of the sociology of religion.

Contexts

The expressed intention of this research study is to examine a particular set of practices within the sociological milieu of the EC. I am not choosing an arbitrary set of practices for research; rather, I am choosing practices which EC leaders themselves locate within the Christian mystical tradition and which they find valuable for appropriation by emergent churches. The purpose of this study is not to focus on the EC itself. An analogy helps to clarify this point. These practices can be likened to "microbes" studied in a particular "solution." In the analogy, the intent is to examine the microbes themselves and how they change depending upon the social context, or solution, in which they are placed. The question to be answered then is: How different are the microbes if they are removed from the original solution and are placed into a new solution? In this analogy, the historical context of the Christian mystical tradition is the original "solution" in which these practices evolved, and the "microbes" are the practices originating in this tradition for the specific purposes of this tradition.[4] The key characteristic of the original social environment is the overall interpretive framework of Christian mystical theology. In fact, since these practices developed specifically as an outflow of Christian mystical theology, one may legitimately question which came first as the practices and the Christian mystical tradition are so interconnected, just as the solution and microbes are so interconnected in the analogy. However, an important disclaimer to note is that the Christian mystical tradition itself does not fit neatly into any single branch or denomination of Christianity. Consequently, difficulties would likely attend any transfer of such practices to a subsection of Christian faith relatively unfamiliar with the mystical tradition. The EC is not particularly distinctive in this regard.[5] The question to be answered, then, is what happens when these practices have been plucked from their original context and placed into an entirely new social context, whatever that context might be. As the practices begin to adapt to this new environment, a researcher can observe whether they take on the characteristics of their new context and/or retain previous environmental traits, just as the microbes may take on characteristics of their new environment or keep characteristics of their previous solution. While this analogy could easily be pushed too far, it serves to accentuate the focus of the study *on these practices* as they are realized in their new context of the EC.

For purposes of clarification, the context of the EC needs some basic introduction in this chapter and a more comprehensive delineation of its development in the second chapter. However, in recognition of the prohibitive scope of studying both the context of the EC and the Christian mystical tradition in sufficient depth, this work will not refer to the original context of the mystic practices comprehensively, but a few introductory comments are absolutely vital to gain a sense of the Christian mystical tradition in order to perceive where these practices originated before proceeding to

---

4. The Christian mystical tradition should not be understood as synonymous with Christianity as a whole, rather, it is a subset within the larger context of Christianity.

5. Gay, *Remixing the Church*, 53. Gay uses examples of transferring traditions in the Gentile churches of the first century AD and the Protestant churches of the sixteenth century.

operating definitions for the study and a more extended look at the EC. To follow the language of the analogy above, a brief comment on the original solution of the Christian mystical tradition offers depth and background for understanding the "microbes" which are the mystic practices. To reiterate, the focus of the study is the mystic practices first and foremost. However, the new "solution" requires an extended discussion due to its nascent status, particularly due to the lack of a formal spiritual theology developed in this context. Conversely, the Christian mystical tradition is well-established and thoroughly researched, so little needs to be said by way of definition. Still, a short introduction to the mystical tradition is helpful for thick description of all the angles which converge as part of the research claim.

Christian Mystical Tradition[6]

Before proceeding to consider the context of the Christian mystical tradition, it is important to note that it is an expansive and multifaceted tradition with centuries of history undergirding it, so the following comments should be viewed as merely introductory. Additionally, the practices considered in this study did not develop within the mystical tradition as independent exercises or disciplines to be utilized singly or in the pursuit of an ecstatic experience; rather, they were developed in the interpretive framework of a total lifestyle which can be succinctly summed up in the goal of the individual mystic: ascent of the soul to God. Mystic practices did not exist as discrete units; rather, they functioned as aspects of the mystical life. This lifestyle was typically divided into three steps[7] or "rungs" on the ladder of ascent: purification, illumination, and union.

The first rung on the mystical ladder is the life of purification, or the purgative life. This step in the mystic journey is typified as a process of separation from worldly priorities and re-orientation to God. Emphasis is strongly laid upon breaking away from the ways and thought patterns of everyday life because an entirely new way of thinking and acting is fundamental for every succeeding stage in the mystic's life. Thus, the way of

---

6. Major works consulted in preparing this introduction included Clément, *Roots of Christian Mysticism*; de Guibert, *Theology of the Spiritual Life*; Garrigou-Lagrange, *Three Ages of the Interior Life*, vols. 1–2; Louth, *Origins of the Christian Mystical Tradition*; McGinn, *Presence of God: A History of Western Christian Mysticism Series*, vols. 1–4; Sheldrake, *Brief History of Spirituality*; Williams, *Christian Spirituality*.

7. While these steps have been separated for purposes of discussion, they are not entirely separate or successive to one another; rather, there is a sense of back-and-forth interpenetrating motion among the steps within the life of an individual mystic.

purification fulfills a critical role within the beginning stages of Christian mysticism as preparation for further endeavor.

A subsequent step in the mystic journey is the way of illumination. In its most basic sense, mystic illumination is a way of knowing in the same way that purgation is a way of preparation. Illumination as a way of knowing builds on the foundation laid by purgation, emphasizing knowledge gained through the intellect *and* practical life-experience. It is also in this stage of the mystic life that one may often have the ecstatic visions and experiences which are popularly associated with mysticism. However, such ecstatic experiences are tangential to the goal of mystical ascent. They are not necessarily detrimental, but they are also not considered indispensable for the mystical life; rather, deepening desire for intimacy with God progresses the individual to the third step of the mystic path.

The final stage in the mystical journey is the way of union. This stage can be interpreted as either the last step of the mystical journey or the objective of all previous endeavors. The way of union carries its own problems of comprehension and elucidation above and beyond the previous stages, only magnified, as it is the doorway into the dominion of the ineffable. Therefore, for the purposes of this brief summary, it will suffice to say that such union is unending fellowship with the divine not in a single moment or experience but as a settled attitude of one's life that is described biblically as prayer "without ceasing."[8]

Consequently, the mystic life conceived as the ascent of the soul to God through the foregoing steps provides the theological and philosophical groundwork and ultimate aim for the development of the particular practices scrutinized within this study. Nevertheless, these theological understandings did not spring forth fully formed all at one time; rather, they matured over a long history through major contributions from particular persons. A short outline of history is necessary to complement this outline of theology in order to locate Christian mystical practices properly in their original historical context.

The Christian mystical tradition has its roots in many precedents of biblical individuals, including Abraham, Moses, St. Paul, and St. John, meeting and communing with God.[9] Belief and practice of such immediacy between worshipper and God was central to the early Christian church, and rigorous practices of self-denial, communal worship, and complete commitment were common traits of the "typical" Christian in the early centuries of Christianity. This ideal was most vibrantly illustrated in the lives of

---

8. 1 Thess 5:17.

9. See Gen 15; Exod 3; Acts 9:1–19; and Rev 1:9–20.

martyrs and the belief that the typical Christian life would end violently as a result of following the example of Jesus Christ. Upon the legalization of Christianity within the Roman Empire, martyrdom, which engendered such sincere devotion, almost completely disappeared. As a result of a new level of acceptance in society, the "ideal" Christian life became less rigorous in practice with less of an expectation of a violent end, and a new ideal emerged that sought ascent of the soul to God through quieter means. Within this new political context, a burgeoning mystical elite looked for a way to separate themselves from what they perceived as the growing compromise and complacency of the church. Consequently, the Christian mystical tradition began to become visible as a separate tradition within the larger umbrella of Christianity.

As the Christian religion become dominant within the Roman world, those who were interested in pursuing the theological goal of union with God separated themselves from the common life of cities, towns, and even other Christians, leading to the rise of monastic forms of mysticism. At first, these dedicated individuals headed to the desert sands of Egypt to live as hermits, as typified in the life of St. Antony, seeking God and fighting sin and Satan in utter (or almost utter) solitude. This first wave of desert hermits attracted the curiosity and growing spiritual interest of fourth century Christians who desired a more arduous faith than what was presented within the main flow of the Christian church. As more and more persons headed to the desert in succeeding generations, it became a practical necessity to group together for life and work into communities of like-minded individuals, and the communal monastery took root. Mystic practices flourished in the focused context of the monastery in which a dedicated mystic could devote the majority of his or her day to the pursuit of God through prayer, silence, liturgy, and so forth. Eventually, these communal settings were exported from the Egyptian desert to other Christian lands, following the example of John Cassian in bringing communal monasticism to the European continent. Monasteries flourished during the European medieval period, and it was this venue that provided the most notable and shaping influence on the Christian mystical tradition for close to a thousand years, yet the mystical tradition was not entirely limited to this specialist context. Nonetheless, Roman Catholic and Eastern Orthodox Christians still primarily locate their mystical elements within the monastic context. Mystical theology and practices have a wider area of operation for these traditions in modern times in more specialized ways, often connected to the use of liturgy and celebration of Holy Communion. On the other hand, close connection, and even identification, with monasticism hampered the spread of the Christian mystical tradition within the nascent Protestant Reformation of the sixteenth century.

By the early 1500s, the Christian mystical tradition and its practices were often viewed as inseparable from the monastic context. Even though many early Protestant reformers, including Martin Luther, were monks themselves or connected to the life of the monastery prior to the Protestant Reformation, Christian mysticism was still often interpreted as relating only to visionary experiences or as part of the obligatory "works" to gain salvation which Protestants sought to reject. As a result, this new Protestant movement which focused on the unmediated relationship between God and humanity did not find a ready ally in the Christian mystical tradition even though the mystical tradition developed for the same purpose as Protestantism, just in an earlier historical period. As a result, Protestants never accessed this tradition in an overarching way.[10] The subsequent movement of Protestant evangelicalism also rejected large-scale incorporation of the Christian mystical tradition, and it is from the context of evangelicalism, which will be outlined more fully in the second chapter, that the EC emerged.[11] So, in brief, the EC emerged from a context that had already been removed from Christian mysticism for centuries. However, before proceeding to a discussion of the context of the EC for analysis of their distinctives, it is necessary to wrestle with a few basic terms utilized in the study that can be defined in various ways.

Operating Definitions

A few terms arising out of the Christian mystical tradition will be used throughout this study. They require precise operating definitions because the terms themselves often take on a variety of meanings. Chief among these terms are the categories of *spirituality* and *mysticism* along with all of their derivative terms such as *spiritual, spiritual practices, mystical, mystical tradition, mystic practices,* and *mystical practices*. It is important to note that the proceeding definitions are my operating definitions. Within the context of lengthy qualitative interviews, EC participants offered their own definitions of these terms. However, as there was little consensus among

---

10. Some sectarian groups within Protestantism, such as Pietism and Quakerism, did eventually access insights from the Christian mystical tradition for central practices in their groups, or, at least, developed their theology along similar lines.

11. While the EC has now spread to mainline Protestantism, it began as a distinctly evangelical movement, cf., Ken Howard, "New Middle Way?," 104; Snider, "Introduction," xvii–xviii.

respondents, their idiosyncratic and divergent definitions are not treated in this text.[12] However, such divergence of definition for these terms does provide a significant clue to the difficulty of integration of these areas among case study churches. So, without any further caveat, discussion can turn to the semantics of *spirituality, mysticism,* and their derivative terms.

Much of the current popularity of the term *spirituality* arises out of its imprecision, and, as a result, it has become a term which is functionally used for any purpose.[13] In recent times, *spirituality* has been interpreted as broadly as *human potential* or as a narrowly as only having semantic value in relation to more obscure terms, such as *the sacred* or *organized religious life*.[14] Prior to offering an operating definition, it is important to note with regard to *spirituality* that the popular distinction of defining *spirituality* as oppositional to *religion* is not intended within this study. Such an opposition only serves to load one term with all the positive connotations that one desires against the other term which is then purported to contain wholly negative elements.[15] While the semantic breadth of this term is noteworthy, a more specific meaning is preferred in this study. The operating definition for this term, which will be used throughout this study, is as follows: *Christian spirituality and its derivative terms refer to the expansive category of every practice that connects the believing individual and/or believing community to the experience of God as Father, Jesus Christ, and Holy Spirit.* This operating definition limits the subject of *spirituality* in three ways with reference to the EC. Most notably, it limits spirituality to the action of connecting human(s) to the divine. Second, it does not seek to investigate how the EC utilizes the spirituality or spiritual practices of other religions, and, second, it asserts that there is no "generic" spirituality which the EC or anyone else can somehow tap.[16] These limiting factors also apply to how *mysticism* is utilized in this book.

For the purposes of this study, *Christian mysticism and its derivative terms refer to the tradition in which an individual proceeds through a series of stages, steps, and practices to the ultimate goal of union with God.* As a consequence, *mysticism* is a narrower term than *spirituality* for the scope of this study, and it can be located within the larger umbrella category of *Christian spirituality*. It is also significant to note that while the definition of

---

12. Definitions of these terms according to EC literary conversation are available in chapter three.
13. Bregman, "Defining Spirituality," 157.
14. Zinnbauer et al., "Religion and Spirituality," 550.
15. Drane, *Do Christians Know How to Be Spiritual?*, 10.
16. Sheldrake, "Introduction," vii.

mysticism does focus on the individual, it is not to the complete exclusion of a communal context. Both *spirituality* and *mysticism* retain individual and communal aspects as considered in this book. Additionally, the term *contemplation* deserves some comment in connection with the operating definition of *mysticism*. Historically, *contemplation* is "[a]n elevation of the mind to God by an intuition of the intellect and a cleaving of the will, both being simple and calm, and no effort being made at reasoning or at stirring up many affections."[17] As is evident from the quoted historical definition, it could easily be used as a synonym for *mysticism* or *mystical*. However, *contemplation* will only refer to a specific mystic practice (i.e., *contemplative prayer*) here in order to avoid confusion.

In summary, while all of these terms have definite points of connection and overlap, *spirituality* is seen as the broadest term, proceeding to more precise definition with *mysticism*, for this latter term is inextricably connected to the particular goal of the soul's ascent to God and the context of Christian history. All terms will appear without the qualifier *Christian* since this study will only deal with other religions' spiritualties and mysticisms when explicitly stated. With these terms clarified, it is now possible to consider the context of the EC before proceeding to the central research problem and its explication.

Emergent Church

To return to the analogy of "solutions" and "microbes" once again, discussion can proceed to investigation of the microbe's new "solution." That is, this research will move to consider for the remainder of the chapter a new context in which these Christian mystical practices have been placed. That context is the EC. A common starting point for background and context of any living social group or movement is to offer a definition of the group; however, the EC defies classification, often intentionally.[18] Such reluctance also extended to interviewed participants, whose definitions had few points of common contact. Additionally, there is considerable speculation whether the EC should be referred to as a movement or not. Leaders often deliberately reject forms of categorization even though broad social dynamics are

---

17. de Guibert, *Theology of the Spiritual Life*, 200.

18. Gibbs, *Churchmorph*, 39–40. Further complicating the matter, the terms *emergent church* and *emerging church* have been used in previous eras without any reference to the present movement. Cf., Metz, *Emergent Church*; Larson and Osborne, *Emerging Church*.

constant within the EC, as noted in sociological research.[19] Conversely, EC leaders and insiders quantify it much more informally as a conversation or "chat."[20] Outsiders, however, tend to prefer the designation of a "movement." The EC also asserts that a complex propositional definition of the conversation/movement is "the wrong place to start," and they greatly prefer descriptive images and stories to shorter definitions.[21] After noting the EC preference for description, it is tempting to conclude that a short operating definition of the EC is not possible. However, an operating definition may be approached through the process of scrutinizing a multi-faceted presentation of characterizations from multiple sources.

First, it is helpful to begin with how the EC wishes to be viewed in a personal and organizational way. Doug Pagitt, pastor of *Solomon's Porch* in Minneapolis, MN, a well-known emergent church, offers such a personal definition by stating, "I am a Christian, but I don't believe in Christianity. At least I don't believe in the versions of Christianity that have prevailed for the last fifteen hundred years, the ones that were perfectly suitable in their time and place but have little connection with this time and place."[22] It is clear already from this statement that the EC thrives on emphasizing contradictions and new ways to consider apparent paradoxes, and this trait is no less prominent when EC proponents describe the larger movement or conversation.[23] Perhaps, the most succinct "definition" of the EC from the inside does not focus on behaviors or beliefs; rather, it presents a vivid image. Following this line of thought, Doug Pagitt uses the specific image of a plumcot to characterize the EC:

> The plumcot suggests that we live in a world of possibility. Somewhere, somehow, someone imagined a new kind of fruit, a new flavor, a new color. Whoever fiddled with the plums and apricots from the face of the earth but to offer something else, an alternative to what was already out there. I think that behind the plumcot is an intuition that life, even if it's just the life of

---

19. Demographic similarity is a significant part of these social dynamics. According to Flory and Miller, "Those that are leaders in innovative churches [the larger category for these researchers within which the EC fits], are college educated, and in many cases graduate school educated, solidly middle class, and successful in their professional lives." Flory and Miller, *Finding Faith*, 37.

20. Kimball, "Emerging Church and Missional Theology," 86. Cf., Byassee, "Emerging from What, Going Where?", 251.

21. Conder, *Church in Transition*, 22.

22. Pagitt, *Christianity Worth Believing*, 2

23. Byassee, "Emerging from What, Going Where?", 251. Cf., Tickle, *Great Emergence*, 153.

produce, is never really settled. There is always room for a new idea, a new thought, a new fruit.[24]

In other words, the EC sees itself as a brand-new entity that has never existed previously, waiting for an interested individual to experience. Additionally, this perspective of EC insiders made quantifiable data on the scale or scope of the conversation very difficult to obtain. As Josh Packard remarks, there is "no central clearing house or anything approximating a denominational structure which keeps tabs on the number of Emerging Church congregations," and emergent churches are "loathe to even keep track of the number of people attending worship services."[25] Due to this issue, numerical estimates will not be offered for the overall size of the EC in the USA. In light of the statements above, an internal definition of the EC is useful in whetting one's appetite to find out more, but it can be very disconcerting if one's purpose is to discover a compact and descriptive definition. However, it is useful to begin a definitional investigation of a living movement with what actual participants say about themselves. For the purpose of finding out what participants say about the EC themselves, interviewees were asked to define "emergent church" in each formal interview. Unsurprisingly, their answers lacked any general consensus, so their responses did not generate a significant source of data to inform a *general* definition of the EC for this study.

Therefore, it is helpful to continue defining the EC by radiating out from its participants to those who once participated but are now critical of the movement. Specifically, a reactionary movement to the EC has developed which has termed itself the *emerging church*, and it muddies the definitional waters because initially *emerging* and *emergent* were used interchangeably to describe the same movement. The current distinction is that the *emergent* church is pursuing innovation in spiritual practice *and theological formation*, but the *emerging* church, as a distinct entity, is concerned with changes in methods of spiritual practice alone (which results in far less appropriation in the area of mystic practices). While there is still considerable overlap between the terminology of the emerging church and the emergent church, the latter group evinces the particular behaviors which inform the direct focus of this study. Additionally, expressions of the EC in non-USA contexts retain usage of both terms. Nonetheless, *emerging* critics of the EC define the EC conversation as "the latest version of

---

24. Pagitt, *Christianity Worth Believing*, xii.
25. Packard, *Emerging Church*, 8–9. Cf., Marti and Ganiel, *Deconstructed Church*, 9–10. Marti and Ganiel also note that the number of EC congregations in the USA have been reported variously as approximately 200 or surpassing 700.

[Protestant theological] liberalism."[26] *Emerging* criticisms of the EC focus on this charge of theological liberalism often without reference to specific doctrines or practices; rather, emphasis is placed on the disparity between the EC and the Protestant evangelical context from which the EC "emerged." In the USA context, this disparity has greater weight due to the strong presence and influence of evangelicals in this country. So, the primary utility of this definition of critique is to bring to the forefront the necessity of defining the EC in distinction from Protestant evangelicalism.

A third and fourth definition arise from critical scrutiny by the academic disciplines of sociology of religion and theology, respectively. From the purview of sociological research, *emergent church* "is a label, created by movement insiders, to mark a dual assumption: that contemporary Evangelicalism is undergoing profound change, and that the Christian Church always has and always will be changing."[27] Similarly, Marti and Ganiel focus on the element of disassociation by defining the EC as "a creative, entrepreneurial religious movement that strives to achieve social legitimacy and spiritual vitality by actively disassociating from its roots in conservative, evangelical Christianity."[28] Sociological categorization of the EC is further buttressed by generational and demographic markers, specifically that the EC "materialized in the mid-1990s, with initial voicings from white, male, middle-class, well-educated, urban, Gen-X pastors, church planters, church consultants, and concerned laity."[29] Conversely, theological researchers approach the EC by concentrating on the movement/conversation as "a groundswell of laypersons, ministers, theologians, and churches who are influenced by, and are responding to, real or perceived worldview shifts from modernity to postmodernity."[30] While these two definitions consider similar areas, they give a slightly different stress either to resistance (sociology) or to adaptation (theology).

While each of these shorter definitions have their merits, the operating definition of the EC for this study combines elements from EC supporter definitions as well as sociological and theological perspectives. First, the EC will be treated primarily as a *conversation* rather than as a broader social movement even though several social markers may be evident among EC

---

26. Driscoll, *Confessions of a Reformission Rev*, 21.
27. Bielo, *Emerging Evangelicals*, 5.
28. Marti and Ganiel, *Deconstructed Church*, ix.
29. Bielo, *Emerging Evangelicals*, 5. Cf., Flory and Miller, *Finding Faith*, 28 (the EC is coupled with the larger category of "innovators" by Flory and Miller). Many of these demographic markers of the EC were corroborated in the empirical research component of this study.
30. Liederbach and Reid, *Convergent Church*, 19–20. Italics original.

adherents. Empirical research at this point supported literary comments because interviewed individuals provided conceptions of the EC so divergent that they augur against categorization as a coherent movement in sociological terms. However, the EC as a *conversation* can be accurately viewed as a *theological* movement since theological movements are primarily delineated according to philosophical and literary discussion, not specific sociological behaviors. In that sense, this book will take seriously that EC Christians are often talking about what *could be*, not what *is*. Second, EC resistance of their previous context, particularly resistance against the pressure to institutionalize in evangelical forms, is a primary characteristic of the EC as a whole. Third, it is vital to note within the operating definition of the EC that adherents uniformly concern themselves with the freshness of their present postmodern context. Fourth, the EC is seeking to adapt Christianity as a whole, both belief and practice, to this new context. Therefore, the operating definition of the EC for this study is as follows: *the emergent church is a loosely organized conversation concerning adaptation of Christianity to postmodernity through substantial change of spiritual practices and theological beliefs inherited from evangelical Christianity*. These foregoing matters of context and definition bring the EC into greater relief in order to create a lens through which the research claim may be glimpsed more clearly.

Research Claim

These contextual and definitional issues articulate necessary background for understanding what the research claim seeks to verify. My specific claim is that *the emergent church is appropriating Christian mystical practices by investing these practices with their own theological content*. The EC is *not* primarily interested with connecting fully to the theology of the mystical tradition; however, they are *mining* this tradition in experimentation to support their own theological and practical emphases. They are utilizing a wide variety of what they term "ancient" Christian practices, but they are chiefly interested in experimentation, using these practices for purposes specific to their context in accordance with their own limiting boundaries for faith and practice. There is little connection with the historical provenance of any particular practice, and any connection is typically due to that person having been raised in a particular tradition or having received prior theological education before becoming involved with the EC. In other words, connection to the historical background of these practices is optional and tangential to the EC process of spiritual borrowing. While emergent leaders often have delved more deeply into the background of particular practices than the average EC attendee, this is not uniformly true, and that background does not become a limiting or boundary influence for EC practice.

I prove my claim concerning this appropriation through research of literature produced by EC proponents and qualitative case studies of three separate emergent churches in the south central region of the United States of America (USA). I interviewed thirty-eight individuals at all levels of participation in these churches, attended multiple services/meetings, analyzed sermons and blog posts, and had various informal conversations with participants in each church. However, before proceeding to specific consideration of research instruments used in gathering data to prove the claim, it is essential to outline the progression of logical reasons which led to the formation of this claim as a hypothesis for testing.

Four logical reasons support the above research claim which became evident through my literary research and qualitative case studies. The first reason why my research claim is logical, as mentioned previously, is that the EC is chiefly interested in innovative ways of being spiritual and "doing" spirituality in what they perceive as an unprecedented context (i.e., postmodernism). This reason is prevalent in the writings of EC leaders, and it is perhaps best encapsulated in the simple statement by Brian McLaren, a noted EC leader: "If you have a new world, you need a new church. You have a new world."[31] While this concern for innovation in a postmodern context has led to the appropriation of many Christian mystical practices that are often eschewed in the Protestant evangelical context from which the EC arose, there is not a uniform reclamation of what they term "ancient" Christian spirituality, a term which the EC uses to refer loosely to the Christian mystical tradition which they never precisely define.[32] My sociological and literary study supported the premise that the Christian mystical tradition is not being applied consistently within the EC. The need to adapt and change Christianity to its new context of postmodernism affects all parts of the EC, not just use of mystic practices. This reason logically supports the research claim in the following manner: a group that is primarily concerned with innovation and contextualization over and against anything else would naturally relegate retaining historical content to a lesser status when using a particular practice.

The second reason why my research claim is logical, which naturally extends from the first reason, is that the EC is not limiting itself to using

---

31. McLaren, *Church on the Other Side*, 11. Cf., Pagitt, *Community in the Inventive Age*, 3.

32. However, a connection with "ancient" Christianity is valued very highly in EC congregations. In fact, one of the interviewees said that the church he founded refers to itself as an "ancient work in modern times" as part of fulfilling this connection.

only ancient practices in their attempt to be relevant to a postmodern context.[33] To clarify, it is apparent from the research findings that practices from disparate origins, not just Christian mystical practices, were open for implementation in these churches. As will be illustrated in later chapters, the use of Jewish, Buddhist, and Hindu practices show the eagerness of the EC to accept and use practices which they deem practical *despite* the theological history of the practice, as long as the ideal of postmodern contextualization is not disregarded in the process. The logical basis for this item of support for the research claim could best be explicated through the subsequent line of reasoning: if the EC is not seeking to reclaim every aspect of what they term "ancient" Christian spirituality, then it would be more likely that they would have a tendency to pick-and-choose from Christian mystical practices according to whatever they would see as a more important purpose (i.e., their primary purpose of postmodern contextualization).

In close relation to this multi-source assimilation, the third reason why my research claim is logical is that the EC is willing to combine disparate spiritual practices in varied configurations, regardless of origin, with a focus on what "works" with their own developing theological distinctives. While the third reason may appear very similar to the second, the logical progression at this point is that the EC is not only *appropriating* practices from any tradition but they are also *combining* those practices which have different origins. It is apparent that they are curious about these practices but only to the extent of how well they work in and mesh with the postmodern context. This postmodern context also helps to provide a boundary for appropriation because an engagement with postmodernity is the purpose for which many practices are integrated into each emergent church. This tendency logically supports the research claim because a group which combines many practices without regard to origin would seem to be primarily interested in the meaning which they can give to practices in a new, postmodern context rather than prior meanings attached to practices.

A fourth major reason supporting the research claim is a natural extension of the previous two reasons: the EC is often not tracing the history of particular spiritual practices or ideas back to original/ historical sources for knowledge of their use. This reason became apparent in even the initial stages of literary research. A notable literary example of this tendency is present in *Velvet Elvis* by Rob Bell, a popular EC author. Following a paragraph concerning Gregory of Nyssa's *Life of Moses* in Bell's book, the passage was footnoted as coming from the ruminations of a personal friend rather than

---

33. Gibbs, *ChurchNext*, 128.

from the work itself.[34] Additionally, within the interviews, multiple participants mentioned Richard Foster and Dallas Willard, who have written popular introductions to the use of Christian mystical practices under the term "spiritual disciplines," as primary influences on their understanding of Christian mystic practices. [35] These introductions focus on the practical application of the practices themselves with very little historical comment. If few EC leaders or participants are reading historical-theological mystical texts, then they are likely unfamiliar with the historical-theological backgrounds to these practices. Therefore, logically they have only their own theological content to place into these practices if they choose to use them at all. These logical reasons are amply supported by the collected and analyzed data, as illustrated through the noted trends within literary and empirical research in later chapters; however, for purposes of introduction, it is useful to provide some brief comments concerning each research instrument and the differing sociological and theological approaches to analysis of the data.

Research Instruments

Two primary research instruments, literary research and qualitative case studies, were utilized in this study on the basis of their ability to gather evidence from differing viewpoints with a particular focus on conceptual and behavioral data. These instruments are valid tools for this study for the following reasons. The range of potential documents for analysis in this type of study is immense, extending from officially published documents all the way to unpublished, ephemeral forms of communication. Literary research, therefore, is a valid method for studying the EC in light of the conversation at the heart of this movement. In fact, since much of the emerging "conversation" happens through various forms of textual communication, literary research is a perfect fit because it is not only possible to collect a significant amount of data but multiple contexts can also be examined through this method. Additionally, literary research is indispensable because it is a common vehicle of theological development, and participants' own theological ideas are the focus of this sociological study. Selection of literary sources will focus primarily on proponents of the EC, and any additional voices will be noted as coming from differing perspectives. The rationale for this selection is essentially circumstantial. Tony Jones explains this situation concisely by

---

34. Bell, *Velvet Elvis*, 34, 182.

35. Foster, *Celebration of Discipline*; and Willard, *Spirit of the Disciplines*. Cf., Webber, *Divine Embrace*, 96. Webber adds the works of Eugene Peterson to this list of influential evangelical proponents of spiritual disciplines.

stating, "The extant literature on the ECM [Emerging Church Movement] is surprisingly thin. Although the movement is relatively young, it has received significant attention in popular media and news media. It has not however, received much attention from scholars."[36] While literary research is appropriate due to the forms of the EC conversation, the living nature of the conversation also recommends the employment of empirical methods of research for data gathering.

While this ongoing nature provides a reason why empirical research is fitting, additional comment is necessary concerning the specific methodology implemented in this study. One of the most basic forms of empirical research is the case study, which has the benefit of wide usage in multiple scholarly disciplines. Therefore, it is broadly understandable in both design and rationale as the prolonged observation of "a single entity, a unit around which there are boundaries. The case then has a finite quality about it in either terms of time (the evolution or history of a particular program), space (the case is located in a particular place), and/or components comprising the case (number of participants, for example)."[37] To show the distinctiveness of a case study, it is important to note that it is distinguished from an ethnography on the basis of its scope. While an ethnography looks at an entire group or culture, a case study concentrates on a particular permutation of a culture/group, such as a specific person, program, or subcommunity.[38] As a result, case study design focuses on the selection of a "bounded system" as the subject for study.[39] For the purpose of this book, an individual emergent church is the appropriate "bounded system" for an in-depth case study. However, three emergent churches from different urban areas of the USA provide the context for the case study portion of this research for the purpose of discovering general theological themes which different emergent churches share as well as noting where individual emergent churches differ significantly. Case studies are also used on the basis of the type of answers which are produced through this methodology. Specifically, case studies answer questions *qualitatively* by providing a "thick" description of a naturally occurring event or series of events.[40] However, they are not limited to a descriptive purpose. They can also provide answers to "discovery-oriented questions" which "are similar to descriptive questions but go one step further—they attempt to discover generalizable

---

36. Jones, *Church is Flat*, 5.
37. Merriam, "Case Study," 178.
38. Leedy and Ormrod, *Practical Research*, 151.
39. Merriam, "Case Study," 179.
40. Dey, *Qualitative Data Analysis*, 31.

principles or models."[41] In other words, case studies lend themselves to theorizing on the basis of the data collected and analyzed, which is an ideal situation for the present project because the research results are intended to identify particular behaviors *and* ascertain theological themes which are used to rationalize these behaviors.

The foremost instrument for empirical data collection which was implemented in these case studies was the interview, expressly the phenomenological interview. The "phenomenological" qualifier for the interviews in this study is used "to understand *people's perceptions, perspectives*, and *understandings* of a particular situation" although the "situation" is the use of mystic practices rather than a single historical event, as is most common with the employment of phenomenological interviews.[42] As a result of exploring a person's perspective in great depth, the interviews were lengthy (averaging one to two hours). While these interviews were loosely structured, they centered upon specific mystical practices that each interview participant identified as being important on an individual or communal basis in his/her church of attendance. This interview type was chosen specifically on the basis of the desired qualitative result: detailed description rather than statistical figures. While the case studies depended on phenomenological interviews, additional methods of data collection were utilized, including observation of corporate worship rituals/services and small group meetings, informal conversation with church members, and evaluation of monological forms of spoken communication (sermons, podcasts, and blogposts).

The resulting data from literary and empirical research necessitated an interpretive frame that could analyze both types of data effectively. In light of the difference in types of data and the research focus on participant perceptions, a grounded theory approach arose as the ideal methodology. While it might seem logical to use a theological frame of analysis, this avenue presented a potential problem. Within theological analysis, the resulting data would be scrutinized in conjunction with a particular proponent of a theological tradition. Such an emphasis on assessment could weight the balance of analysis in the direction of concluding the study with a decision *for* or *against* the EC, at least in comparison with the chosen theological proponent. Sociological models of analysis avoid this type of judgment.[43] This study does not intend to emphasize evaluation; rather, emphasis here is laid upon *description*. Grounded theory is a much more suitable approach than theological analysis since general themes and connections arise through scrutiny of the collected data rather than on *a priori* hypotheses, such as the

41. Moon and Trepper, "Case Study Research," 402.
42. Leedy and Ormrod, *Practical Research*, 153. Emphasis added.
43. Marti and Ganiel, *Deconstructed Church*, 5.

relationship of the EC with a particular theological proponent.[44] While the research claim deals chiefly with how the EC *theologically* understands their experiences and use of practices, a sociological framework is advantageous because it allows participants in both literary and verbal conversations to speak for themselves. With this framework in mind for the interaction of sociology and theology, areas of conclusion, contribution, and recommendation also require some delineation and description at this point.

Conclusions, Contributions, and Recommendations

The essential goal of this study is to ascertain whether or not the emergent church is appropriating Christian mystical practices by investing these practices with their own theological content. However, this overall conclusion arises from investigation of three areas foundational for verifying this claim. First, I examine the relationship in the EC between the individual person and the larger community in the task of theological reflection. I also reach a conclusion with respect to the perceptions of mystic practices within the EC as neutral conceptual containers or as retaining theological baggage from their previous social contexts. Third, I identify the preeminent theological anchor for mystic practice appropriation and reinterpretation and locate it with respect to its centrality to the spiritual borrowing process.

To return to the analogy of "microbes" in a "solution," the primary contributions of this study arise from examining how the different "solutions" affect the "microbes" themselves. In other words, this study examines how the new context of the EC affects the borrowed practices from the Christian mystical tradition. Therefore, this research resulted in the creation of a sociology of EC theological developments. The key contribution of this study is the illustration of the process of moving mystic practices from one tradition to another. Specifically, this book provides an answer to whether mystic practices have an inherent theological content or if they are neutral containers which can be divested or invested with content on the basis of whom is utilizing them. In terms of the microbe analogy, does changing the solution around the microbe change the nature of the microbe itself? Can a mystic practice be removed from its original theological context and still be a mystic practice? If these practices display an inherent theological content, it is a fascinating prospect for the Christian mystical tradition to have an influence through its practices *alone*, apart from its theology, on another tradition which has arisen from a different corner of the Christian mosaic.

---

44. Leedy and Ormrod, *Practical Research*, 154–55.

An additional value of this book is an investigation of the complex relationship of behavior and belief in this process of spiritual borrowing. As noted earlier, this study focuses on how belief influences behavior. However, the results of this research illustrate that belief influencing behavior is only part of the interrelationship of belief and behavior. In fact, this research will show an interweaving process of belief influencing behavior influencing belief. Therefore, the usefulness of dichotomies of belief influencing behavior or behavior influencing belief are called into question. On the basis of belief influencing behavior here, other studies on the subject of spiritual borrowing could be conducted, perhaps beginning from the direction of how behavior influences belief. Recommendations for further research arise as extensions of the different qualitative aspects of the study. Specifically, new studies could be built on the basis of examining spiritual borrowing of mystic practices or on the basis of studying different social aspects of the spirituality of the EC.

Summary of Chapter

In this initial chapter, the aim of the book has been delineated fully as an investigation of spiritual borrowing, particularly as the circumstances of appropriation of mystic practices by the EC. To this end, the specific research claim of the study was identified as *the emergent church is appropriating Christian mystical practices by investing these practices with their own theological content*. The rest of the chapter consisted of providing additional background of the areas under examination and description of the logistics of the study. On the side of offering necessary background, the important contexts of the Christian mystical tradition, operating definitions of the study, and the scope of the EC were discussed. As noted previously, a full consideration of the development of the EC and introduction to specific case study churches will be the subject of the next chapter. On the side of logistics, extended remarks were offered concerning the research claim and the logic supporting it. In addition, research instruments were introduced although they will be considered more fully in chapters three and four. This logistical discussion was then completed by outlining the potential areas of conclusion, contribution, and recommendation that an answer to the particular research claim will provide for the academic study of the sociology of religion. So, from the basis of these introductory matters, discussion can now proceed to a more in-depth look at the emergent church context for appropriation and reinterpretation of mystic practices.

2

The Emergent Church in the United States of America

IN THE "CONTEXTS" SECTION of the last chapter, the focus of this study was clearly designated as an investigation of particular mystic practices. However, an analogy was offered to aid comprehension of how and why this research study is valuable. Specifically, the transplantation of the mystic practices, or "microbes," from the context of the Christian mystical tradition to the EC, or from one "solution" to another is being examined here. While a few comments concerning the context of the original "solution," the Christian mystical tradition, were offered in the introductory chapter, the new context of the EC requires more delineation due to its nascent status. Consequently, the purpose of this chapter will be to provide circumspect discussion of the EC in the United States of America (USA) in general, emphasizing the uniqueness of this context for studying the appropriation of mystic practices. In order to fulfill this purpose, three courses of comment are necessary. First, the history of the development of the EC in the USA will provide essential background for discussion. Second, current developments of the EC will provide the conceptual framework for examining mystic practices within this context. Finally, locating the EC within the larger sociological context of resisting institutionalism and the religious tension between the individual and community will round out a multifaceted portrait of this conversation.

The Legacy of American Evangelicalism

The history of the EC in the USA is inextricably linked to the legacy of American evangelicalism. In fact, it is so linked that when many EC leaders critique Christianity in the USA, they may only be looking at evangelical Protestant Christianity. This mistake is problematic on their part, but it is understandable when one looks at the USA religious milieu. Evangelical Christians compose a significant proportion of the USA religious landscape. In fact, according to a 2008 report by the Pew Forum on Religion and Public Life, 26.3 percent of Americans consider themselves to be evangelical.[1] With a statistic of this magnitude, particularly in light of the fact that almost every permutation of Christianity is present in the USA, it is vital to understand this sizeable group and its uneasy parental status of the EC.

Definitions of evangelicalism differ so strikingly that they tend toward idiosyncrasy. Among the various definitions, there are many representations that are hopelessly broad, which seek to connect present-day evangelicalism to any person throughout history that believed in the *evangelion*, or good news about Jesus Christ.[2] A definition of this scope essentially equates the term *evangelical* with the term *Christian*. Evangelicalism can also be defined in connection with the Protestant Reformation of the sixteenth century, as the term *evangelical* constituted an approximate synonym for *Protestant* at the time.[3] However, the specific history of Protestant evangelicalism is as an English-speaking transdenominational movement which began in eighteenth century Britain with the ministries and writings of John Wesley, Charles Wesley, and George Whitefield.[4] With respect to this initial evangelicalism and its subsequent offspring, there are four characteristics which serve as "family traits" to mark evangelicals: "*conversionism*, the belief that lives need to be changed; *activism*, the expression of the gospel in effort; *Biblicism*, a particular regard for the Bible; and what may be called *crucicentrism*, a stress on the sacrifice of Christ on the cross."[5]

While many within the present-day American movement of evangelicalism may prefer to connect seamlessly with the older evangelicalism of Whitefield and the Wesleys, the most direct link for evangelicals in America is a split among Protestant Fundamentalists over engagement with modern culture in the 1940s and 1950s.[6] This new group was original referred to as "Neo-Evangelicals," but the prefix was soon dropped in common parlance.

1. Pew Forum on Religion and Public Life, *U.S. Religious Landscape Survey*, 5.

2. Webber, *Younger Evangelicals*, 14–15. Webber does not affirm this position, but he notes it as he defines the group that he considers. Cf., Olson, *How to Be Evangelical*, 13.

3. Noll, *American Evangelical Christianity*, 13.

4. Bebbington, *Evangelicalism in Modern Britain*, 1. Cf., Shibley, *Resurgent Evangelicalism in the United States*, 10.

5. Ibid., 3.

6. Webber, *Younger Evangelicals*, 30–32. The Protestant Fundamentalist movement took its name from a series of essays, *Fundamentals* (1919), which were intended to explicate once and for all what the nonnegotiable beliefs of Christianity ought to be.

While the term *evangelical* could be defined more broadly, its more narrow identification with Neo-Evangelicalism and its direct descendants serves three major purposes for this short history. First, Neo-Evangelicals sought to engage the culture in which they lived much as the EC seeks to do. Additionally, it was Neo-Evangelicals which became a noted political demographic in the USA with the election of President James Carter in 1976.[7] They have been conspicuous within the larger USA context ever since, and, finally, it is from this group that the EC has "emerged" most directly. So, when the term *evangelical* is used in proceeding discussion it will refer precisely to Neo-Evangelicalism and its sub-movements, unless specifically noted. Using this operating definition, evangelicalism has had a checkered past on the American religious scene.

While American evangelicalism separated from Fundamentalism in the '40s and '50s, it caught the notice of the larger culture in the 1970s through the presidential election mentioned above *and* in the curious development that evangelical churches were growing swiftly in the USA while Protestant mainline churches were declining in influence and numerical membership.[8] Although evangelical churches allowed for more cultural engagement than traditional Fundamentalism, they retained a reputation for strictness, moral rigidity, and social conservatism.[9] This ensuing infamous reputation has only been heightened in subsequent years, and, as a result, while evangelicals constitute a vast demographic within the mosaic of USA society, they are often viewed with fear and suspicion by many other groups, and they are purported to be theologically judgmental and exclusive even if that reputation is only a result of their enthusiasm for their own theological distinctives.[10] Evangelicals are chiefly known for their theological reputation, but they are also known for their opposition to the philosophical underpinnings of modern culture.

For more than half a century, evangelicals have been engaged in a battle between the "evils" of modernism and the "orthodox" Christian faith.[11] Within a USA context, evangelicals sought to engage and utilize the tools of culture in order to achieve their overarching purpose of "restoring"

---

7. Smith, *Christian America?*, 1.

8. Smith, *American Evangelicalism*, 71. Cf., Kelley, *Why Conservative Churches Are Growing*.

9. Olson, *How to Be Evangelical without Being Conservative*, 17. Cf., Putnam, *Bowling Alone*, 77–78.

10. Noll, "Revolution and the Rise," 129–30.

11. Penning and Smidt, *Evangelicalism*, 167. I use war terminology intentionally within this statement, as it highlights evangelical attitudes on the subject.

America as a Christian nation.[12] The major enemy within this fight was the "demon" of secularization, and its perceived marginalization of God and the Christian faith. Evangelicals might differ on particular points of doctrine, but they agree on this basic worldview. Within the latter part of the twentieth century, this perspective began to erode because the "enemies" changed.[13] The modern milieu which created the "necessity" of the evangelical articulation of the Christian faith had passed.[14] As part of the realization of evangelicalism's need to rearticulate itself in order to be relevant in a different context, many young evangelical leaders began the conversation which became the EC. These overarching features of evangelicalism and its engagement with modernism are more accurately understood as precursors of the EC if delineated further into specific types.

It is erroneous to consider evangelicalism as a monolithic entity, even if one limits the scope of the term *evangelical* to those evangelicals which began as Neo-Evangelicals in the 1940s.[15] Rather, in appropriately examining evangelicalism in the USA, delineation of specific groups is more similar to depicting major emphases in the color and structure of a mosaic than to the simple linear progression of a line drawing.[16] Additionally, evangelicals should not be understood solely through the socio-political stereotype so prevalent in the USA that all are socially conservative, middle-class, Republican individuals that support the status quo.[17] With these factors in mind, there are three broad types to which most evangelicals in the USA have some connection along with a minor strain that is embedded in two of the categories. These three types have been labeled variously by evangelical scholars, but they will be referred to here as Neo-Evangelicals, pragmatic evangelicals, and post-evangelicals.[18] However, prior to description of these types, one cross-strain of evangelicalism is important to note for the history of the evangelicalism in the USA.

---

12. Dorrien, *Remaking of Evangelical Theology*, 193–94.

13. Smith, *American Evangelicalism*, 75.

14. Lyon, *Jesus in Disneyland*, 137. Cf., Wells, *Above All Earthly Pow'rs*, 4.

15. Wells, "On Being Evangelical," 389–90.

16. Noll, *American Evangelical Christianity*, 283–84. Cf., Noll, *Scandal of the Evangelical Mind*, 239.

17. Smith, *Christian America?*, 193.

18. Webber, *Younger Evangelicals*, 30–41. Cf., Driscoll, "Pastoral Perspective on the Emergent Church," 87–88; Carson, *Becoming Conversant with the Emerging Church*, 39–40; Tomlinson, *Post-Evangelical*. Please note that Webber prefers the terminology of traditional, pragmatic, and younger evangelicals. Conversely, Driscoll prefers the terms Church 1.0, 2.0, and 3.0. I chose the specific terminology to avoid any adverse comparisons on the basis of any group being more "original" or any references to relative age.

Since the rise of the neo-charismatic movement in the 1960s, there has been an undercurrent of charismatic influence within evangelicalism.[19] While the original movement of Pentecostalism in the early twentieth century had little influence over the rise of Neo-Evangelicalism, and the two movements have often been in opposition to one another, the newer charismatic movement of the '60s did not stay within a single denominational framework. Rather, it crossed many boundaries, affecting many denominations often associated with Neo-Evangelicalism. In fact, traditional Pentecostalism had gained an air of refinement and respectability by this time, distancing itself from the newer outbreak of charismatic phenomena.[20] What is significant for the EC is that the neo-charismatic movement, "unlike traditional evangelicalism, became increasingly unconcerned about theological issues. It became primarily a relational movement directed toward the emotional and psychological needs of a generation torn by the social upheaval of the sixties and seventies."[21] This relational emphasis allowed the neo-charismatic movement to be better equipped to address the rising tide of postmodernism, and its contribution to the EC is notable in the emergent church's emphasis on relational truth and theology.[22] Therefore, the charismatic strain in evangelicalism has contributed to the rise of the EC primarily through its focus on relationships as well as accentuating "the centrality of the Holy Spirit speaking to believers today through the word of God."[23] This charismatic strain runs through both pragmatic and post-evangelical types, but they cannot be completely defined as charismatic.[24] Conversely, *all* subsequent types of evangelicalism find definition through a progression from the Neo-Evangelical movement.

The rise of Neo-Evangelicalism is in part a reaction to the prior movement of American Protestant Fundamentalism which had gained such notoriety through its opposition to the theory of evolution in the infamous Scopes Trial of 1925.[25] As such, Neo-Evangelicalism can be dated to a variety of organizational establishments, including the National Association of Evangelicals (1942) and Fuller Theological Seminary (1947), as well as to

19. Penning and Smidt, *Evangelicalism*, 169.
20. Creps, "Worldview Therapy," 148.
21. Webber, "Introduction," 13.
22. McLaren and Campolo, *Adventures in Missing the Point*, 257.
23. King, "Emerging Issues for the Emerging Church," 38. Cf., Dorrien, *Remaking of Evangelical Theology*, 205.
24. It has also been noted that the EC mirrors the charismatic movement in its cross-denominational lines of development. Cf., Scott, "Theological Critique of the Emerging, Postmodern Missional Church/Movement," 336.
25. Hart, *Deconstructing Evangelicalism*, 13.

the very visible success of the evangelist Billy Graham and his identification with the Neo-Evangelical movement.[26] In addition to founding new associations, Neo-Evangelicals can be chiefly characterized by their commitment to the same conservative doctrines as Fundamentalists coupled with the belief that "conservative doctrine did not require isolation from American society and institutions."[27] In other words, Neo-Evangelicals sought to engage modern culture for the purpose of communicating conservative Protestant doctrine to a wide audience. As a necessary extension of this purpose, Neo-Evangelicalism was organized structurally and intellectually in opposition to modern patterns of thought while using these patterns to "reason" the truth of Christianity to the modern mind.[28] For '40s and '50s America, this movement provided a counterpoint to major issues of secularization, but the inquisitive spirit of the 1960s created a slightly different cultural climate which led to the development of pragmatic evangelicalism in the 1970s and onward.

Pragmatic evangelicalism does not have as defined a starting point as its predecessor; rather, it consists of a series of developments in reaction to perceived needs. It begins with many expressions of "contemporary" church services in which methods were changed to attract a new generation (in this case, Baby Boomers) while leaving doctrinal issues largely untouched.[29] With this specific generational goal in mind, pragmatic evangelicals moved from a theological emphasis to a practical emphasis on what actually brings people into church buildings. This shift paved the way for relational emphases within the EC. As part of a practical emphasis, churches moved to become "seeker-sensitive" in which the focus of worship and ministries shifted to the needs and wants of the individual person interested in spiritual matters.[30] In connection with a seeker-sensitive emphasis, "megachurches" arose with special focus on creating an entertaining and effective church experience.[31] Additionally, many of the distinctives of church buildings were downplayed, so that a church building might resemble a large office complex, and the simple, logical answers of modern apologetics replaced

---

26. Webber, *Younger Evangelicals*, 30. Cf., Jones, *New Christians*, 12–13.

27. Hart, *Deconstructing Evangelicalism*, 25.

28. Hart, "Church in Evangelical Theologies," 38. Cf., Raschke, *Next Reformation*, 93–94.

29. Kimball, *Emerging Church*, 7.

30. Webber, *Younger Evangelicals*, 41.

31. Ibid., 36. Two of the most successful and well-known megachurches are Willow Creek Community Church, begun outside Chicago by Bill Hybels, and Saddleback Church, founded in California by Rick Warren.

more traditional creeds and confessional statements.[32] In effect, pragmatic evangelicals used many principles from the business and entertainment worlds to create successful, professional, and polished church "shows" that appealed (and continue to appeal) to many Baby Boomers going to church in the USA.[33] Additionally, it is important to note that pragmatic evangelicalism is the most direct link to the USA EC, specifically, and to post-evangelicals in general.

Post-evangelicals, like the EC as a part of them, are currently still in the developmental stage. They are not *post*-evangelicals in the simple sense of being anti-evangelical; rather, they continue on beyond what they see as the furthest end of evangelicalism.[34] They can be most effectively categorized in both positive and negative ways. Positively, post-evangelicals are characterized by their searching attitude.[35] In a negative sense, post-evangelicals react specifically against the developments that created the distinguishing characteristics of pragmatic evangelicalism. As this group began to rise in the late 1980s, both Neo-Evangelicals and pragmatic evangelicals were reeling from several scandals in the evangelical establishment along with the effects of political power posturing.[36] Consequently, post-evangelicals have developed their expressions of church by intentional rejection of the business and political methods adopted by pragmatic evangelicals.[37] Through these traits, it seems difficult to distinguish post-evangelicals from the EC, as they are very closely connected in most respects. However, the EC can be differentiated through action. While all post-evangelicals search for "better" ways than pragmatic evangelicalism, advocates of the EC search through the process of intentional spiritual experimentation. In this sense, the EC is post-evangelicalism "with the guardrails off."[38] Such a spirit of intentional experimentation is evident even in the precursors to the rise of the EC in the USA.

---

32. Wells, *Above All Earthly Pow'rs*, 265. Cf., Smith, *Truth and the New Kind of Christian*, 126.

33. Cole, *Organic Church*, xxv.

34. McKnight, "Five Streams of the Emerging Church," 38. Cf., Tomlinson, *Post-Evangelical*, 28–30.

35. Byassee, "Emerging from What, Going Where?", 250. Cf., Baum, "Emerging from the Water," 195.

36. Penning and Smidt, *Evangelicalism*, 18.

37. Webber, *Younger Evangelicals*, 148. Cf., Kimball, *Emerging Church*, 32–33; Packard, *Emerging Church*, 31, 35.

38. Byassee, "Emerging from What, Going Where?", 257. Cf., Jones, *New Christians*, 230–31.

Specific Precursors to the Emergent Church in the USA

A complete portrait of the EC requires some comments concerning precursors which have given rise to it. For instance, there are general works and contributions by Christian thinkers which have aided the development of the EC in an indirect way.[39] In a more systemic manner, there are three specific precursors which have combined in the USA to allow for the rise of the EC. The first specific precursor is evangelical attempts to reach "Generation X" both through postmodern forms of youth ministry and churches oriented particularly to reach this generation. Another specific cause is the emergence of the understanding of the USA as a mission field, an understanding which has come to be labeled *missional*. A final stimulus is broad, but it is noted by practically every EC leader and author as the primary catalyst for the EC: the rise of postmodern culture in the Western world. With these precursors so delineated, each of them requires explication concerning how they directly influenced the history of the EC in the USA.

Generational Issues

Quite expectedly, ministries that focused on Generation X began as ministries to youth who seemed to be growing increasingly less and less interested in traditional forms of Christian worship.[40] Within the USA context of the 1980s, many youth ministries began to implement early forms of the worship which would eventually typify the EC, as this age range became more and more *absent* from evangelical circles.[41] An important shift toward the EC occurred in this regard as a result of a very practical realization—Generation X was growing up, yet they were not settling down into "contemporary" [i.e., pragmatic evangelical] forms of church.[42] This nascent

---

39. According to Moritz, "Such thinkers who have strongly impacted the emergent church's thought and praxis include the scientist and philosopher Michael Polanyi, philosopher of hermeneutics Hans Georg Gadamer, literary critic and novelist G. K. Chesterton, New Testament historian N. T. Wright, Old Testament scholar Walter Brueggemann, moral and political philosopher Alasdair MacIntyre, missiologist Lesslie Newbigin, philosopher of science and theologian Nancey Murphy, theologians Jurgen Moltmann and Miroslav Volf, ethicist Stanley Hauerwas, post-liberal theologian George Lindbeck, and post-conservative theologian Stanley Grenz." Moritz, "Beyond Strategy, Towards the Kingdom of God," 30.

40. Kimball, *Emerging Church*, 34.

41. Kimball, *They Like Jesus, but Not the Church*, 12.

42. Hübner, "'X' Marks the Spot?", 5.

progression found its first full expression in the establishment of NewSong in Pomona, California by Dieter Zander in 1986.[43] While ministries continued to use emerging worship forms to reach youth, this development heralded the breaking out of the emerging approach for a more general audience. NewSong was eventually followed by other churches such as Mosaic in Los Angeles, CA (1994) and Mars Hill in Seattle, WA (1996).[44] Many of these "Gen-X" churches have been subsequently identified with the EC conversation, and they constitute specific precursors to the conversation. However, the EC can be differentiated from Gen-X churches because it does not seek to limit its reach through generational means (although it still primarily attracts those in Post-Baby Boomer generations).[45] While the development of Gen-X churches is the most tangible aspect of this precursor to the EC, there are also attitudinal features of the Post-Baby Boomer generations that have contributed to the rise of the EC in the USA.

One of the most obvious commonalities among Post-Baby Boomer generations is that they have grown up in the wake of the 1960s counterculture and, often, as children of the Baby Boomers who were involved in it.[46] Subsequently, they imbibed a culture of questioning which has few, if any, established societal mores in comparison with earlier generations. While all of the changes in American life cannot be reduced to the outflow of the '60s, the legacy of the Baby Boomers has profoundly affected how later generations have viewed religion and spirituality.[47] In a general sense, the counterculture deeply widened religious options for the typical American while raising expectations for religious experience.[48] As a result, current generations are seekers, and they are looking for a depth of experience and community which is flavored by the counterculture's taste for "a small-scale,

43. Gibbs and Bolger, *Emerging Churches*, 30. Cf., Rabey, *In Search of Authentic Faith*, 9.

44. Ibid., 30–31.

45. Tony Jones notes, "Thus the emergent conversation has never been about age, but the emergents do tend to skew younger than the average American churchgoer. I [Jones] surveyed eight emergent congregations in May 2006, and the average age was 32.5, whereas the average age of an American in church on any given Sunday is 50." Jones, *New Christians*, 68.

46. Miller and Miller, "Understanding Generation X," 1. However, this circumstance does not make them as cohesive a group as the Baby Boomers who were united by many significant political and cultural events. Cf., Wuthnow, *After the Baby Boomers*, 5.

47. Guder, *Missional Church*, 54–55. Cf., Miller, *Reinventing American Protestantism*, 12; Cf., Wuthnow, *After the Baby Boomers*, 126. Sociologist Robert Wuthnow notes that when younger generations have spiritual questions they are no longer necessarily looking for answers to these questions in an organized religious setting.

48. Tipton, *Getting Saved from the Sixties*, 19–20.

intimate, collegial, and relatively self-supporting commune."[49] Therefore, it comes as no surprise that several manifestations of the EC movement look very similar to communes from the '60s. While these expectations can be interpreted positively in creating the desire for greater commitment, they also have left Generation X and Millennials with profound contradictions between outlook and prospects.[50]

Among the contradictions of Post-Boomer generations, there is a sincere desire for relationship in community coupled with a profound mistrust of traditional, institutional forms of community. As a result, formal religious participation has steadily declined among younger generations.[51] With respect to Christianity, these generations desire personal attention from pastors and other recognized authorities, yet they also may not trust them since they are exponents of the "establishment."[52] Such mistrust is extended to include preconceived opinions of church as agenda-driven, judgmental, oppressive, arrogant, and legalistic.[53] However, mistrust of organized religion is also connected in Post-Boomer generations to an open acceptance of religious pluralism and an expectation that the Christian church should be equally tolerant.[54] The EC differs from its evangelical source in *not* trying to explain matters of propositional belief to Post-Boomers; rather, they emphasize the relational side of the issue. Specifically, despite inconsistent expectations, there is a *hunger* for deep relationships among Post-Boomers, the very kind of relationships that Christianity purports to offer. These relationships are the sort which the EC desires to create.

Another major contradiction within Post-Boomer generations exists between indifference and social conscience. In the tradition of the Baby Boomers, Post-Boomers have a multiplicity of options for seemingly every decision. While it would seem that a multitude of options would create an atmosphere of optimistic anticipation, it is often interpreted by these generations as a "suffocating freedom."[55] As a result of such "paralysis," the siren song of Generation X, which has also been taken up by Millennials, is the now familiar dismissive retort, "Whatever."[56] Permeating apathy is

49. Ibid., 18. Cf., Flory, "Toward a Theory of Generation X Religion," 244.
50. Rabey, *In Search of Authentic Faith*, 27.
51. Putnam notes, "Between the 1970s and the 1990s, church attendance among people under sixty dropped by roughly 10–20 percent." Putnam, *Bowling Alone*, 73.
52. Hendricks, *Exit Interviews*, 127. Cf., Flory and Miller, *Finding Faith*, 9.
53. Kimball, *They Like Jesus but Not the Church*, 69.
54. Beaudoin, *Virtual Faith*, 121. Cf., Piatt and Piatt, *MySpace to Sacred Space*, 34–35; Burke, *No Perfect People Allowed*, 15.
55. Piatt and Piatt, *MySpace to Sacred Space*, 154.
56. Flory and Miller, *Finding Faith*, 10. Cf., Long, *Emerging Hope*, 38.

a distinctive characteristic of these generations due in part to the practical lack of foundation provided by the searching attitudes of Baby Boomers (as well as their emphasis on career over family).[57] However, in opposition to this general mood of apathy, Post Boomers have a social conscience fueled by the need for Western nations to be involved actively in contributing to the needs of others, coupled with a global consciousness.[58] While varying levels of social conscience may be cited for Baby Boomers, it is only with Post-Boomers that generations have arisen with a day-to-day understanding of global matters and of their place in a world where the West does not necessarily deserve a "central" position. As a result, the EC has inherited a social conscience which spurs them on to be involved in social as well as religious issues both in a local and global context.[59] These conscience factors work to engage the second specific precursor of the EC movement: missional consciousness.

Missional Development

The term *missional* has a recent origin, but its origins are connected to the older term *missionary*.[60] The only difference is that *missional* includes domestic as well as international contexts, tapping into recent realizations that Western Europe and North America constitute a large "mission field" in which Christians must learn to operate in a culture that is decidedly post-Christian. For the USA context, the beginning of a missional consciousness stretches back to the international development of an awareness in the UK that Western Europe had become a mission field.[61] Succinctly, the move to being missional necessitates that "the church sees itself as *being* missionaries, rather than having a missions department" which is organized

---

57. Flory, "Toward a Theory of Generation X Religion," 234. Cf., Wuthnow, *After the Baby Boomers*, 20–48.

58. Long, *Emerging Hope*, 47–48. This rise in social conscience may also be coupled with the realization that the EC tends to be composed of those connected with the privileged classes in society. Cf., Smith, "Economics of the Emerging Church," 93–94.

59. Roberts, *Glocalization*, 14. In this work, Roberts coins the term *glocal* to describe "the seamless integration between local and global."

60. Guder, "Church as Missional Community," 114.

61. Gibbs remarks, "The group of scholars who are at the heart of this conversation drew their initial inspiration from the insights of Bishop Lesslie Newbigin, who, on retiring to the United Kingdom following a lifetime of service in India, declared that Western Europe was a mission-field, requiring leaders to develop new skills in exegeting the culture and to restructure the church from a maintenance to a missional mode of operation." Gibbs, "Church Responses to Culture Since 1985," 163.

to facilitate the missionary task in a far-off land.[62] However, this missional perspective represents a greater shift in the church's understanding of itself and its context. Such a shift informs against the use of pre-packaged models of how to function as a church in the USA, and it heightens the impulse to view the Christian mission collectively as a community that seeks to ascertain and embody the meaning of the kingdom of God to a culture that has become unfamiliar with what that means.[63] The EC gains its sense of self and purpose primarily through this precursor—its sense of what the Christian church is supposed to be and do. These missional emphases are applied in two primary ways: the recovery of a holistic view of the church and a new understanding of Western culture.

Missional thinking tends to streamline the role of church in society while heightening the church's place in the life of the individual. Rather than functioning as a social institution which is concerned with certain aspects of an individual's life, missional advocates promote the idea that "[m]ission must take place in and through every aspect of life."[64] The practical outworking of this aim in missional thought is to seek to reunify the Western view of life that has been divided between sacred and secular halves. This impulse has been embodied in the past by pragmatic evangelicals through imitating the secular environment within a sacred atmosphere in order to make sacred contexts seem less alien to those who primarily operate within secularity. However, the EC seeks to be missional in the opposite direction by bringing the sacred *into* the secular, forsaking passive reaction for active engagement with the secular world.[65] Additionally, while this activity may be understood as "evangelism" by pragmatic evangelicals, the EC views the drawing together of sacred and secular as a comprehensive way of unifying the fractured parts of the Western psyche, and they view the early Christian church as a model for this activity. Naturally, in realizing that North America and Western Europe can be considered post-Christian contexts, the EC seeks missional models of what Christians do in a largely alien culture. Nineteenth and twentieth century missionary models are often eschewed for a return to how Christians operated in the first centuries of the church.[66] For the missionally-minded EC, these factors lead to the need to contextualize within the present culture.

62. Kimball, *They Like Jesus but Not the Church*, 20.

63. Conder, *Church in Transition*, 25. Cf., Burke and Pepper, *Making Sense of Church*, 109; Stetzer and Putman, *Breaking the Missional Code*, 2.

64. Hirsch, *Forgotten Ways*, 22.

65. Robinson and Smith, *Invading Secular Space*, 12. Cf., Frost and Hirsch, *Shaping of Things to Come*, 9.

66. Hirsch, *Forgotten Ways*, 22.

The context of the new Western culture is the foundational point for an effective missional response. This understanding begins with the realization that the situation in the West has changed. As Towns and Stetzer put it, "Effective ministry no longer involves drinking afternoon tea with the ladies auxiliary or going out to lunch with board members."[67] According to the EC, Christians should no longer be looking to revitalize the place of the church in the USA; rather, they should have the conceptual framework that Christianity must be established anew.[68] In this perspective, description and definitions of the EC are not entirely complete without some comment on the central role which postmodernism/postmodernity occupies in the collective conversation of the group.

Postmodern Culture

Whether through scrutiny of the literature or direct observation with participants, it does not take long for one to sense the importance of postmodernism for the EC. However, *postmodernism* as a philosophy is not as important to the EC as contextualizing Christianity within the cultural situation they identify as *postmodernity*. This development is a result of the EC claim that it formed as a consequence of encountering postmodernity, or, more precisely, the postmodern individual. In order to appeal to postmodern individuals, the EC began to emphasize a more eclectic approach to Christian faith, to present a *bricolage*.[69] The EC approaches postmodernism from this particular perspective of selective application instead of outright philosophical engagement, and this selectivity determines the level of appropriation and interpretation of postmodernism in the EC. However, while the general postmodern context is crucial to an understanding of the EC as a whole, the differing national postmodernisms within which the EC has arisen help to create multiple strains of the conversation.

One may be aided in understanding the particular variant of the EC in the USA through the realization that postmodernism in the USA has a slightly different pedigree than in other parts of the world. Specifically, postmodernism is not seen as a direct descendant of modernism in the USA;

---

67. Towns and Stetzer, *Perimeters of Light*, 17.

68. Gibbs, *ChurchNext*, 40–41. Cf., Frost and Hirsch, *Shaping of Things to Come*, x. Frost and Hirsch make the same suggestion for an Australasian context.

69. Grenz defines *bricolage* as "the reconfiguration of various traditional objects (typically elements from previous stages in the tradition of the artistic medium) in order to achieve some contemporary purpose or make an ironic statement." Grenz, *Primer on Postmodernism*, 21. Cf., Haselmayer, McLaren, and Sweet, *A is for Abductive*, 101; Wuthnow, *After the Baby Boomers*, 15.

rather, it comes through the lineage of American Romanticism, illustrated philosophically in the works of Ralph Waldo Emerson, Henry David Thoreau, and William James as well as in the literature of Walt Whitman.[70] As a result, postmodernism in the USA has a strong optimistic and pragmatic undercurrent that may not be present in other Western societies. In light of this optimism, the EC spiritual openness is congruent with another vital American trait. As noted by John Drane: "Americans have always been fascinated by the spiritual, partly because many more of them have some living connection to traditional faith communities in churches and synagogues than is now the case in Europe—but also because 'spirituality' in various guises has been a significant influence in establishing the identity of a nation whose origins lay in other countries and cultures."[71] Religious congregational spirituality has played a particularly central role in American public life since religious congregations offer prospects for communal gathering, friendship, mutual support, potential articulation of discontent, and mobilization for social action.[72] This is not to say that the thirst for spirituality does not exist in all forms of the EC, but it is particularly strong in the USA.

The EC does not uniformly imbibe and apply postmodernism in all its aspects. This selective application of postmodernism comes less from an acceptance of postmodernism and more from a rejection of modernism. Postmodernism is seen by the EC as an "antidote" to the modernism of Western civilization.[73] However, this point raises the issue of how the EC understands modernism. Succinctly stated, the EC recognizes modernism as the intersection of three overarching epistemological assumptions: "(1) individualism, which asserts the ultimate autonomy of each person; (2) rationalism, which is characterized by a strong confidence in the power of the mind to investigate and understand reality; and (3) factualism, which insists that the individual, through the use of reason, can arrive at objective truth."[74] In place of these suppositions, the EC builds on two primary postmodern epistemological pillars. First, they view any understanding of reality as *provisionally* rather than objectively true, and, secondly, they deny that anyone has the ability to view reality outside of these provisional constructions.[75] As these assumptions are applied to Christian faith and practice, the EC expresses a sincere doubt that humans have the "ability to know absolute truth

---

70. Grenz and Franke, *Beyond Foundationalism*, 207.
71. Drane, *Do Christians Know How to Be Spiritual?*, 2–3.
72. Ammerman et al., "An Invitation to Congregational Study," 8.
73. McLaren, "Church Emerging," 145.
74. Webber, *Ancient-Future Faith*, 18.
75. Grenz, *Primer on Postmodernism*, 8.

with absolute certainty."[76] This postmodern tendency colors the rejection of traditional church dogma, liturgy, music, and practices.

Nevertheless, for the purposes of this study, it would be tangential to scrutinize minutely the degree to which the EC imbibes or adopts postmodern philosophy or a larger culture of postmodernity even if postmodernism were a defining characteristic of the EC. On the contrary, postmodernism, or at least the context of postmodernity, potentially allows the EC to define and redefine anything in Christianity, including theology and mystic practices, in any way desired under the pretext of cultural contextualization.[77] It is this freedom to contextualize which is a defining mark of the EC. As a result of this freedom to contextualize, each individual EC is shaped in its essence by an inextricable link to its local context, but common developments are also present *among* different emergent churches.

Current Developments of the Emergent Church

While many characteristics could be explicated with regard to individual emergent churches, there are precious few traits which apply to the entire conversation. However, a few notable facets do present themselves upon close scrutiny. Particularly, the attitudinal emphases of questioning, displacement, and community cohere strongly within any permutation of the EC. In addition to attitudinal features, the tension of protest and contextualization describes the active factors characterizing the EC. Lastly, it is vital to make brief mention of how the EC in the USA is situated within the larger international context of the EC. Therefore, a discussion of current developments provides a perspective of the few shared points of contact among emergent churches.

EC Attitudes

First, a distinguishing EC attitude grows out of the common background of questioning which many EC followers share. Questions by EC members often form concerning the inconsistencies of Christian faith and practice, particularly those inconsistencies present within evangelicalism. For instance, an EC participant might question the consistency of the "need to have singular and firm opinions on the protection of the unborn, but not

---

76. Bielo, *Emerging Evangelicals*, 8.
77. Erdman, "Digging Up the Past," 241.

about how to help poor people and how to avoid killing people labeled enemies who are already born?"[78] As another avenue, EC Christians often begin questioning through more directly personal circumstances, such as a result of "experience and encounters that challenged [them] to look and listen beyond the limits and boundaries of [their] own traditions."[79] These queries may also be framed as doubts, which have a definite negative connotation within many branches of the Christian church, but not within the EC.[80] Doubts are seen as positive tools which help the EC move away from quick and easy answers. Proliferation of questions *without* answers among those within the EC conversation often leads to feelings of dislocation as a second characteristic attitude.

A growing sensation of displacement based on the aforementioned questioning is what led many in the EC to leave their previous Christian tradition(s). EC Christians relate a feeling of tension between what they have experienced in Christianity previously and their present questions.[81] However, while these questions dislocated them from their previous tradition(s), in the EC, this inquisitive spirit gave birth to self-awareness and a level of disquietude, which they often enjoy. This tension between past and present is not only attributed to previous faith experiences of individual EC participants but also to developments in the larger culture of the USA or other respective Western countries, namely postmodernity. In other words, those within the EC movement "are conscious that *they grew up in a postmodern world*,"[82] becoming the children of rather unlikely parents: "the historical Christian Church" and "the post-modern cultural milieu."[83] A final attitude of strong stress on community should be considered in light of the foregoing overarching qualities of questioning and cultural dislocation.

Perhaps, the best way to begin a discussion of EC emphasis on community is through the eyes of outside observers. For instance, sociologists Flory and Miller state the following: "These groups, whether emerging or more established churches, organize their approach . . . so as to focus on *building community* within the religious group and to engage in various ways with the larger culture."[84] This focus on community cannot be overemphasized, but it

---

78. McLaren, *Everything Must Change*, 3.

79. Gay, *Remixing the Church*, 1–2.

80. McLaren, *New Kind of Christian*, xiii–xv.

81. Burke, "Emerging Church and Incarnational Theology," 51.

82. Webber, *Younger Evangelicals*, 47. Webber notes this characteristic toward a group that he denotes as "Younger Evangelicals," which encompasses more than just the EC, but he locates the EC within this larger movement.

83. Jamieson, "Post-Church Groups," 66.

84. Flory and Miller, *Finding Faith*, 14. Emphasis added. Also, as noted in ch. 1,

can be misunderstood. Even as the EC seeks to engage and is composed of members of younger generations, it is significant to recognize that there is a generational gap between younger and older generations with respect to community ties. According to sociologist Robert Putnam, younger generations find community in family, friends, and ties with co-workers in much the same way as older generations, but they "felt less connection to civic communities—residential, religious, organizational—without any apparent offsetting focus of belongingness."[85] Attempts by these younger individuals to engage in the wider culture, therefore, are often not through established civic organizations but through innovative associations birthed out of their immediate context. As part of this task, an initial perceived obstacle for the EC is to dispel stereotypes of Christians, particularly as judgmental and as hypocritical.[86] An important part of this process in the purview of the EC is to move beyond common evangelistic tactics and methods which seek to "target" specific people groups rather than create an appealing community which individuals would desire to engage.[87] In addition to dispelling negative stereotypes, advocates of the EC also recognize the change in perception of communal need within the Western context.

With regard to community, three USA cultural developments, though not necessarily limited to the USA, and one international development attract the notice of the EC. In a broad sense, the initial development is a change from the family as the standard of community to the optional associations among friends.[88] Consequently, as noted by sociologists, a second development manifests in which the expression of community is interpreted less through familial bonds and more through shared experiences.[89] While these two developments can be easily linked, a third development is problematic for the others. Namely, the proliferation and prevalence of electronic means of communication have created a substantial outlet for pseudo-community in which the isolated individual entirely controls his or her experience with and perception by others.[90] This development heightens the sense of necessity for face-to-face community, but it also raises expectations for the level

---

Flory and Miller locate the EC as part of a larger sociological category of "innovators" in church life in the USA.

85. Putnam, *Bowling Alone*, 275.
86. Piatt and Piatt, *MySpace to Sacred Space*, 43.
87. Sweet, *FaithQuakes*, 90. Cf., Piatt and Piatt, *MySpace to Sacred Space*, 146.
88. Long, *Emerging Hope*, 51–52.
89. Flory and Miller, *Finding Faith*, 20.
90. Brasher, *Give Me that Online Religion*, 102–7.

of perfection in how community will suit the individual's needs and wants.[91] Therefore, the EC often seeks others who have shared similar experiences as them, but they are often over-idealizing the perfect sense of community which they seek through these new-found friends. Another issue that is not directly related to these developments, but impacts them nonetheless, is the rise of a global consciousness in which community cannot simply extend to one's immediate associations.[92] Rather, global social issues compete for attention, and, as a result, the EC has moved not only from considering community as opposed to isolated individualism but also from considering community in a primarily local context to a global one. In light of the attitudes of questioning, dislocation, and community, the EC within the USA engages in the activities of protest and contextualization.

EC Activities

The attitudes of questioning, dislocation, and community first appear for the EC in the activity of protest, specifically protest of their previous religious tradition, evangelicalism.[93] Major proponents of the EC seek to mitigate this negative feature through broadening its reach in order to see protest as a trait of the larger postmodern culture[94] or as a reasonable reaction to the perceived lack of evangelical Christianity delivering on its promises of hope for a better world.[95] The EC also strives to reinterpret activities of protest to be more positive. This reinterpretation begins through the reminder that toleration and acceptance are functional "protests" of the exclusivity of evangelical Protestantism.[96] Additionally, protest is portrayed not in terms of deconstruction but as "creative and collaborative construction of the *future* church."[97] Paradigmatically, the EC only purports to use protest as a means to break down barriers to authenticity and contextualization in present-day culture.[98]

---

91. Guder, *Missional Church*, 43–44.

92. Engel, "Search for Christian Authenticity," 121–22.

93. Unsurprisingly, the characteristic of protest within the EC can scarcely avoid a negative connotation, particularly since the movement's entire scope has "a flavor of protest," according to its critics. Cf., Carson, *Becoming Conversant with the Emerging Church*, 14.

94. Sweet, *FaithQuakes*, 183–84.

95. McLaren, *Everything Must Change*, 34.

96. Burke and Pepper, *Making Sense of Church*, 19, 127.

97. Conder, *Church in Transition*, 14. Emphasis added.

98. Burke, "From the Third Floor to the Garage," 35.

Another hallmark of the EC is the drive to contextualize as a non-negotiable activity in order to communicate the Christian gospel in a postmodern context.[99] While admitting that the very concept of postmodernism is interpreted amorphously and eclectically, the EC sees the promise of a good fit between the Christian faith and this worldview if Christianity can be properly contextualized into postmodern terms.[100] In this activity, the EC views the primary task of Christianity as reframing the message of Christ "into the flesh and blood and sweat and dirt of the setting."[101] However, the issue which arises given this aim is how *far* should contextualization go? There is a consensus among leaders in the EC that methods of relaying the Christian message can be freely exchanged and reinterpreted, but disagreement over how much the message itself should be reinterpreted led to the division between the emerging and emergent church.[102]

Whether stated in terms of fear or hope, the heart of the EC is embodied in the expression, "If you have a new world, you need a new church. You have a new world."[103] As noted previously, they view contextualization as an essential, not optional, activity. For EC adherents, McLaren's statement is not sensational; rather, it is a practical declaration of the reality that increasingly few people find any purpose or answers in the Christian church, even those already within it. Perhaps, this reality would be most easily grasped through the story of an EC participant coming into contact with the thoroughly postmodern person with whom the EC hopes to engage:

> When she sat down next to me in first class on the flight to New York, I knew that she was the kind of person who regularly traveled there, up front. I was bumped up from coach by the airline, but I suspected that she paid for her seat. To be honest, I was intimidated by this woman, who was probably around my age. She wore torn jeans—the kind that are *really* expensive and come pretorn—complemented by a shabby chic wool sweater. And she was pregnant. I never spoke to her, just observed. As we were taking off, she was editing a very hip-looking graphic novel with the blue pencil of a savvy New York editor. I, meanwhile, was attempting to hide the fact that I was reading a Bible—how uncouth! And once we reached cruising altitude, she pulled a

---

99. McManus, "Global Intersection," 239.

100. McLaren and Campolo, *Adventures in Missing the Point*, 249. Cf., Haselmayer, McLaren, and Sweet, *A is for Abductive*, 23.

101. McLaren, *New Kind of Christian*, 106.

102. Carson, *Becoming Conversant with the Emerging Church*, 27–28. Cf., Hansen, "Pastor Provocateur," 46.

103. McLaren, *Church on the Other Side*, 11. Cf., McLaren, *Secret Message of Jesus*, 4.

> sleek MacBook Pro out of her bag. I hesitatingly opened my Dell dinosaur and began typing up a Bible study. I was outmatched. A very vanilla suburbanite Christian pastor from Minnesota next to the hippest of New York editors, "I write books," I wanted to say. But I dared not, for a New York editor is like a unicorn—if you talk to her, she'll disappear. Or she'll stab you in the heart with her horn. But then, about halfway through the flight, she closed her Mac and tilted her seat back. What happened next has stuck with me ever since. She took a rosary out of her pocket, draped the prayer beads over her pregnant belly, and spent the next hour surreptitiously praying with her eyes closed. Neurons in my brain began to misfire. "Does . . . not . . . compute": a New York editor of graphic novels praying the most traditional of Roman Catholic rituals. I thought she was an enlightened, liberal member of the "East Coast elite." But instead she was praying to the Blessed Virgin. I would have been less surprised had she tried to blow up her shoe.[104]

As so vividly depicted above, this movement seeks to reimagine Christian faith in just such a new context, yet the scope of this reimagination remains ill-defined and shadowy. Therefore, it is beneficial to portray the EC as a reimagination in progress. Part of this reimagining, or "remixing" as termed by Doug Gay, is that EC participants are seeking to supplement their existing spirituality with practices from different traditions and religions.[105] The appropriation and reinterpretation of mystic practices fits conceptually within this impulse to reimagine, remix, and contextualize. A drive to appropriate also fits within the broader sociological context of the EC, as will be delineated below. However, before proceeding to the social context of the EC in the USA, it is also important to consider the international presence of the EC and how international developments directly affect the EC in the USA.

International Influences

Many peculiarities of the USA context have been cited in the development of the EC, yet this movement has grown as well in other contexts, particularly in the United Kingdom (UK) and Australasia, without any of the factors listed above.[106] Two major contextual differences are noteworthy with par-

---

104. Jones, *New Christians*, 1–2.
105. Gay, *Remixing the Church*, 73, 92.
106. Important Australasian voices include Michael Frost, Alan Hirsch, and Steve

ticular focus on the culture of the UK. First, as a major contrast to American culture, the UK consists largely of urban centers.[107] This aspect is particularly noteworthy due to the almost exclusively urban context of the EC in both countries. For instance, the EC has flourished in the "club culture" which is present to a greater extent within the UK than within the USA.[108] Second, the EC is also linked contextually to evangelical and Pentecostal Christianity, both of which have a much stronger presence within the USA.[109] Additional ecclesiastical factors differ between the USA and the UK.

Foremost among the differences between these national contexts is the widespread secularization of the UK and Europe which has been in motion since the end of World War I and which has only reached the USA in full-scale with the aftermath of the social upheavals of the 1960s.[110] Along with the chronological extension of this process, secularization within the UK has been less socially and economically stratified than in the USA. While the European working classes have become as secular as their intellectual elite, "[a]mong working and lower-middle class Americans, however, religion seems to be thriving."[111] As a result of these variations, American attempts to reach the "unchurched" prior to the EC concentrated on reaching out to those who were not part of a church *at present*, but, within the UK and other European countries, the "unchurched" may have had no practical Christian faith experience for multiple generations.[112] Therefore, the EC represents one of the first attempts in the USA to address an overtly secularized context, which is quite a familiar situation for the UK. Still, in order to not offend those who have had personal negative church experiences, American expressions of the EC are often separated from established churches and denominations. This is often not the case within the UK where emergent churches may be a separate "congregation" within a larger church community, and emergent groups not associated with an established church are much less likely to be labeled a "church" in the UK.[113] With these

---

Taylor.

107. Gibbs and Bolger, *Emerging Churches*, 24.
108. Ibid., 25.
109. Berger, Davie, and Fokas, *Religious America, Secular Europe?*, 11–12.
110. Gibbs, *ChurchNext*, 13–14.
111. Hatch, *Democratization of American Christianity*, 211.
112. Gibbs and Bolger, *Emerging Churches*, 19.
113. Ibid., 41. Cf. Jamieson, *Churchless Faith*, 16; Sine, *New Conspirators*, 33, 36; Guest, *Evangelical Identity and Contemporary Culture*, 134–67. Guest considers the specific example of the emergent group *Visions* as located within the more established church body St. Michael-le-Belfrey in York, UK.

differences noted, the direct influence of the UK on the EC movement in the USA may be considered.

Discussion of influence cannot simply be left at the point of which country "came up" with the EC initially. In fact, it is difficult to tell where the EC first emerged. Conversations concerning the role of culture, individual disillusionment with easy answers, and the desire for a third alternative out of many faith dilemmas occupied many within both countries, particularly in the late 1980s and early 1990s. Two major works, *Quantum Spirituality* (1991) by Leonard Sweet and *The Post-Evangelical* (1995) by David Tomlinson, at this time brought these discussions to a larger audience in their respective countries although neither of these works specifically outlines a movement or uses EC terminology in a definitive way.[114] Frost, Hirsch, and Taylor hold respective positions in the Australasian permutation of the EC conversation.[115] So, it is unfair to uncritically gloss over the interrelations among international EC variants, such as saying that "Post-evangelicalism is a sort of British cousin to the Emerging Church" or that Sweet is simply the American Tomlinson, as EC critics often do.[116] While Tomlinson's work has been influential in the USA and Australasia, especially more so than Sweet has been internationally, it is not the most seminal international influence on the USA EC.

It is necessary to note that one development which would seem to influence the EC in the USA is actually a misleading clue. An early precursor of the EC within the UK was the development of "alternative worship" or "alt.worship" which began to address the issue of cultural context within the scope of worship.[117] While this movement eventually reached the USA, only rarely do EC leaders cite it as a shaping factor.[118] Rather, the single greatest decisive international influence on the EC in the USA comes in the writings of missiologist Lesslie Newbigin. In short, his experience is as follows:

---

114. Sweet, *Quantum Spirituality*; Tomlinson, *Post-Evangelical*.

115. Cf., Frost and Hirsch, *Shaping of Things to Come*; Frost, *Exiles*; Frost and Hirsch, *ReJesus*; Taylor, *Out of Bounds Church*.

116. Pettegrew, "Evangelicalism, Paradigms, and the Emerging Church," 159. Cf., Carson, *Becoming Conversant with the Emerging Church*, 25.

117. Gay remarks, "Within the UK, the term 'alternative worship' was coined in the early 1990s as a descriptor for a number of innovative new 'services' inspired by the pioneering and innovative work of a group called the Nine O'Clock Service (NOS), based in the city of Sheffield in the north of England. NOS was based in an evangelical Anglican congregation, which had been strongly influenced by the Charismatic Renewal and, at that point, by the ministry of the late John Wimber." Gay, *Remixing the Church*, 7.

118. Cleaveland, "Presbymergent," 124.

> Lesslie Newbigin was born and raised in England when it was a "Christian nation." In 1936 he went to India as a missionary, and for over thirty-five years he labored to share Jesus in a primarily Hindu country. In 1974, at the age of sixty-five, he returned to England and was quite surprised to discover that the Christian nation he had left behind had now become a mission field itself.[119]

His writings articulate the missional impulse which EC proponents in the USA only considered in a vague sense beforehand.[120]

While the starting point of the EC conversation may be difficult to pinpoint geographically, cross-pollination among contexts proceeds with great enthusiasm on all sides. Within the USA context, Brian McLaren terms this development as "open source spirituality," and he opens it up to historical and denominational contexts along with geographic ones.[121] This mentality allows for the sharing of content and its adaption. As an extended example, "Fresh Expressions" is an EC "offshoot" which is currently enjoying great success in the UK.[122] In line with the historical considerations of this chapter, Fresh Expressions might be best understood as a UK analog to the Young Leader's Network (YLN) in the USA. The narrative of Fresh Expressions as a discrete entity begins with the Church of England report, *Mission Shaped Church* (2004), which articulated the need for the Church of England to extend their understanding of church in the following way.

> A fresh expression is a form of church for our changing culture established primarily for the benefit of people who are not yet members of any church. It will come into being through principles of listening, service, incarnational mission and making disciples. It will have the potential to become a mature expression of church shaped by the gospel and the enduring marks of the church and for its cultural context.[123]

Fresh Expressions serves in the UK as an organizational body associated with organic and amorphous socio-theological developments in much the same way that YLN, which eventually became Emergent Village, has in the USA. However, even in this analog position, UK distinctives are easy to glimpse in Fresh Expressions.

---

119. Kimball, *Emerging Church*, 68.
120. As a representative example, see Newbigin, *Proper Confidence*.
121. McLaren, *Finding Our Way Again*, 57–58, 65.
122. Packard, *Emerging Church*, 9.
123. Quoted in Marti and Ganiel, *Deconstructed Church*, 137.

In contrast to the USA context, Fresh Expressions displays the UK tendency for the EC conversation to show up in more established forms of religious life.[124] From the outset of the project, the Church of England partnered with the Methodist Church. The Congregational Federation and United Reformed Church quickly became participants in the program as well.[125] Official EC associations within established denominations have been far less successful in the USA. Moynagh and Harrold note that Brian McLaren has expressed admiration "that an ancient institutional church should experiment with new styles of church alongside of existing expressions."[126] As an additional difference from the USA context, and perhaps as a result of such established sponsorship, Fresh Expressions has quite a significant numerical impact in the UK with over 750 churches listed in their online directory by 2009.[127] As a contrasting demographic, James Bielo estimates fewer than 750 emergent communities of any type exist in the USA.[128] While there are distinctive characteristics in the UK context for aspects of the EC conversation, the example of Fresh Expressions in the UK, and its esteem from the USA side of the conversation, shows the influence of the EC conversation beyond national boundaries. So, international influences join EC attitudes and activities to serve as general developments of the EC conversation. However, the only way to glimpse the full scope of the EC is to view it through the larger sociological context in which it can be situated.

Sociological Context of the Emergent Church

While academic treatment of the EC is surprisingly thin, especially from a social scientific perspective, there are a few seminal studies in this developing subject area. Specifically, *Emerging Evangelicals* by James Bielo, *The Emerging Church* by Josh Packard, and *The Deconstructed Church* by Gerardo Marti and Gladys Ganiel provide critical engagement with the EC conversation. Marti and Ganiel introduce the appropriate lens for this subject by characterizing, "the ECM [Emerging Church Movement] as an *institutionalizing structure* made up of a package of beliefs, practices, and identities which are continually deconstructed and reframed by the *religious*

---

124. Ibid., 21

125. Moynagh and Harrold, *Church for Every Context*, 59.

126. Ibid., 51.

127. Ibid., 59. Packard notes that such a high number needs to be verified by an independent source before being given full social scientific credence. Packard, *Emerging Church*, 9.

128. Bielo, *Emerging Evangelicals*, 26.

institutional entrepreneurs who drive the movement."[129] In other words, the EC conversation fits in the larger sociological framework of resistance to the institutionalizing process.[130] This aspect of resistance connects to protest, contextualization, and community, as delineated above. EC conversationalists consistently characterize themselves as resistant to institutions as well as resistant to the impulse for institutionalization of their own conversation. In fact, they argue for a reduction of institutionalism within every aspect of Christianity.[131] However, what is most interesting is how they proceed to resist. A consideration of the sub-themes of authenticity, uniqueness, and disruption explains the EC opposition to formal organizations which in turn will help to locate the EC in the overarching sociological interaction of the believing individual and the religious community.

An important piece of EC resistance to institutionalization grows out of a sustained critique within the conversation of institutions as inherently artificial. In this line of thinking, an institutional religious organization is created through top-down pressures in order to sustain an association for the purpose of either manipulation or coercion, typically in terms of homogeneity of belief. EC participants reflect this critique at the larger Christian church as well as postmodern society as a whole. As Bielo notes, "Authenticity provides an entry into that analysis."[132] The EC conversation presents their critique of institutional artificiality and their desire for authenticity within their verbal and textual communication, but this critique/desire also characterizes the stylization of EC worship and the distinctive nature of the spaces which they inhabit. Marti and Ganiel consider the aspect of authenticity directly through comment on the perspectives of their research subjects: "Those who participate in pub churches see them as an escape from church atmospheres and a refuge for open discussion centered on an unpretentious, egalitarian, and spiritually neutral space."[133] In a word, these participants crave *authenticity*, and they interpret authenticity in terms of being unpretentious, egalitarian, and spiritually neutral. This desire for authenticity, while not wholly unique to the EC conversation, is the gateway to what is most singular about the EC as an institutionalizing structure which seeks, as an apparent paradox, to resist institutionalization.

In the sense of sociological context, the EC presents its uniqueness through a resistance to institutionalization, but the full extent of that

129. Marti and Ganiel, *Deconstructed Church*, 8.
130. Packard, *Emerging Church*, 1.
131. Marti and Ganiel, *Deconstructed Church*, 26.
132. Bielo, *Emerging Evangelicals*, 17.
133. Marti and Ganiel, *Deconstructed Church*, 13.

uniqueness can only be glimpsed by unpacking just what participants are resisting and how they are seeking to resist. The first clue to what participants are resisting is present in just who the EC perceives as their "target demographic," although they would strongly object to usage of that term. EC practitioners seek to engage the "dechurched" rather than the "unchurched," meaning that "[r]ather than trying to attract people who have never been to church, the unchurched, the Emerging Church often appeals to people who have had negative experiences with institutional religion."[134] So, the EC conversation appeals to those who have prior reasons or experiences to predispose them against religious institutionalization. While this development often makes EC participants intentionally wary of recreating the worst aspects of institutionalism from their previous religious tradition, they still face the "threat" of isomorphic pressures. Josh Packard concisely defines *isomorphism* as "the process whereby organizations adopt similar practices and structures over time resulting in a dominant organizational form both within and across fields."[135] In order to resist these pressures to conform as the conversation grows larger and more visible, EC adherents strongly reject any organizational procedure across the breadth of the conversation "whether dominant or alternative, bureaucratic or hierarchical or democratic or consensual."[136] However, the question remains, "How exactly are they resisting institutionalization?"

The uniqueness of the EC conversation is not only limited to the vehemence of its stated resistance but is also present in the strategies which they employ to fit within this sociological environment of resistance. Marti and Ganiel insightfully list general resistance strategies employed across the scope of the EC conversation:

> Such strategies include deliberately limiting the power and influence of professional clergy; expecting laypeople to take initiative within congregations; limiting flows of information between professional clergy and laypeople to a need-to-know basis (since laypeople are not expected to "report back" on all their activities); allowing congregational activities to end before they become institutionalized; deliberately disrupting normally taken-for-granted religious ideas, routines, and rituals; emphasizing inclusivity rather than religious boundaries; and stressing the independence of local religious communities.[137]

---

134. Packard, *Emerging Church*, 8.
135. Ibid., 4.
136. Ibid., 13.
137. Marti and Ganiel, *Deconstructed Church*, 28. Cf., Packard, *Emerging Church*, 150.

While each of these strategies plays a role in the broader context of resisting institutionalization, one specific strategy has great bearing on the research subject of mystic practices: "deliberately disrupting normally taken-for-granted religious ideas, routines, and rituals." Sociologically speaking, the *appropriation* of mystic practices proceeds on this basis. Packard helps to explain this fit in his comments on institutional patterns: "Indeed, an organization which truly resists institutionalization is not one which seeks to create its own patterns, but one which seeks to make the patterns themselves subject to constant *criticism and interrogation*."[138] In other words, the EC appropriates and reinterprets mystic practices as a piece of the larger sociological process of revaluating their entire religious tradition. This ongoing process of criticism and interrogation emphasizes the "inherent heterogeneity" of Christian faith by borrowing from *"multiple approaches to spirituality."*[139] While this process locates the utility for the appropriation and reinterpretation of mystic practices collectively, sociological observations of the conversation also shed light on how specific practices are selected and implemented in emergent churches.

EC Christians appropriate and reinterpret discrete mystic practices on the basis of individual spirituality and the worth of each person as theologian. The proceeding chapters will fully show this basis in literary conversations and empirical research. However, this connection can be traced sociologically from two different angles. First, a focus on the individual and what he or she brings to the spiritual "table" is in line with the broader sociological strategy of disruption as noted above. Packard makes this relationship clear by linking disruption of routine "to a particular individual rather than a set of procedures."[140] Tying mystic practice appropriation to an individual rather than a faceless institution also meets the desire for authenticity as considered previously. Second, this basis connects to the EC heritage of evangelicalism, particularly as present in the USA context. Marti and Ganiel question the completeness of the EC break from evangelicalism. For Marti and Ganiel, the EC strongly identifies with the margins of accepted Christian religiosity, "[y]et, despite their orientation of being marginalized, all share a deep sense of mission . . . regarding the future of Christianity."[141] This deep sense of mission lines up with the characteristic impulse of activism among evangelical Christians. Additionally, Marti and Ganiel rightly locate the reactionary roots in the larger narrative of Christian critique

---

138. Packard, *Emerging Church*, 147. Emphasis added.
139. Marti and Ganiel, *Deconstructed Church*, 30. Emphasis in original.
140. Packard, *Emerging Church*, 150.
141. Marti and Ganiel, *Deconstructed Church*, 16.

of modern society, and they note that the EC, as a result, "is sometimes considered to be merely a reinvented evangelicalism."[142] In addition to this link to evangelicalism, a focus on individualist spirituality is a sociological characteristic of American religion as a whole, which can be traced at least as far back as Emerson, Whitman, James, and the Transcendentalists.[143] While this characteristic is not necessarily absent in an international context, it is particularly influential in the USA. So, while the EC conversation can be sociologically located through its feature of critique and resistance to religious institutionalism, the direct focus of EC spiritual borrowing of mystic practices also fits within the broad social relationship between the individual and the community.

The most prominent social and theological theme in the EC conversation is community, but the ultimate question is what exactly is meant by *community* and how does the individual fit within it? Comments from EC authors on this social issue will be considered at length in the next chapter, and the development of that anchor will be discussed empirically in later chapters. At this point, however, the best entry point into such a broad discussion is through the specific studies of Packard and Marti/Ganiel before proceeding to a more general sociological discussion. It is helpful to start with what EC Christians mean by *community* and *individual* as well as how they see these two terms interacting. Once again, a useful entry point is to begin by referring to what EC participants are resisting. While they are generally resisting institutionalization, they are specifically resisting institutionalization that follows the pragmatic evangelical model of a church community. Packard outlines that model succinctly in stating, "This highly rationalized system has been adopted and imposed, sometimes wholesale, from the business world, frequently making large churches indistinguishable from large corporations (Thumma 1996). Indeed, it is not uncommon to hear pastors openly admit to viewing themselves as the CEO of the church."[144] EC participants are strongly resisting such an institutional idea of community. They are rather opting for ideas of community "based on difference and tension rather than agreement and dogma."[145] While this situation makes it increasingly difficult to speak of generalizations in EC theology, this very circumstance provides an entry into a sociological description of what type of community and individual the EC expects.

---

142. Ibid., 23.
143. Flory and Miller, *Finding Faith*, 11–12.
144. Packard, *Emerging Church*, 13.
145. Ibid., 145.

Social constraints of conformity are very few within the EC, but a corresponding increase in the level of expectation of involvement balances out any lack of boundary. As will be discussed at length in following chapters, emergent churches are generally welcoming to a fault, and inclusivity is a feature impressed on many participants as well as outside observers. So, it is "easy" to get into an emergent church, but the real question is what is expected of an individual once he or she has become part of this open, welcoming community. Essentially, the focus on "difference and tension," as noted by Packard, results in increased expectations for the individual. One cannot attend a meeting of the EC and simply expect a tidy, pre-formed theology or devotional "thought for the day," for "[t]here is no standardized product to consume. Indeed, the only real way to extract anything as stable as a theological framework . . . would be to engage in the conversation and decide for oneself what made the most sense."[146] In other words, the flip side of freedom in the community is the responsibility of the individual to think for himself or herself, to be an autonomous self-directing entity in terms of religious belief and subsequent action. The individual therefore becomes the basic unit of theology for the EC. In this way, a strong focus on community results in great variety and individual expression in theology and spirituality, not as contradictory results, but as a direct line of sociological processes.[147] This very development explains how each emergent church can look so different from another and yet still be recognizable as an emergent church. Such individualism is not incompatible with community *if* that community is fundamentally a community of inclusivity and responsibility. Literary and empirical research throughout this study confirmed this insight with respect to the context of the EC, but supplementary factors from the larger sociological context also impacted the research results.

An additional sociological factor impacting EC views of individuality is a generational emphasis. While the EC cannot be simply limited to a generational movement, a strong generational component is clearly evident in the conversation. Along with this generational location, some particular facets to the interaction of individual and community may be glimpsed. Post-Boomer generations have grown up in an environment that required self-direction, and they have brought that skill to the EC. However, along with that skill, they have brought a corresponding desire which flavors their ideal conceptions of community. Flory and Miller describe this relationship by observing, "This generation grew up with parents who were seldom home. These kids had to raise themselves, and often in chaotic

---

146. Ibid., 159.
147. Marti and Ganiel, *Deconstructed Church*, 191.

circumstances. Today they don't want to be stimulated so much as loved."[148] In other words, the coin flips both ways. Many participants in the EC are very skilled at self-determination in spirituality and religion, so individual expectations are not viewed so much as responsibility as they are viewed as "business as usual." The real expectation then is to bring those skills to bear in creating the inclusive community which they crave. In other words, the expectation of the individual and community for the EC could be summed up, as Flory and Miller do, as the creation of a place "where one can be both personally fulfilled, and where one can serve others."[149] This factor can be tied to the present research subject through the high social value placed on individual customization. Christian Smith's broad-based sociological study of young adults in the USA, *Souls in Transition*, supports such a link. As noted above, mystic practices collectively can be appropriated on the basis of disruption of patterns, but on the level of each mystic practice singly, and each individual singly, mystic practices are appropriated and reinterpreted through "the subjective personal sense of 'what seems right' to them, what fits their experience, what makes sense to them given their viewpoint."[150] So, the generational connection functions, especially with respect to mystic practices, to reinforce and emphasize that "the absolute authority for every person's beliefs or actions is his or her own sovereign self."[151] While such a strong individualistic impulse would seem to tip the balance of religious determination to the side of the individual, another factor offers a check for unmitigated individualism.

The emergent church's view of the community is greatly impacted by the increasing influence of globalism. In much the same way that the EC conversation is affected by the presence of so many Post-Boomer voices, the conversation also takes into account the reality of an ever-shrinking world. In fact, to tie the two factors together, Flory and Miller note that "Post-Boomers grew up being exposed to multiple worldviews through media, schools, and in their own neighborhoods."[152] The practical effect of this exposure was to make these generations constantly aware of varying perspectives. The religious aspect of globalism is religious pluralism which implicitly mitigates the appeal of monolithic organizations and religious tendencies to exclusivity, yet globalism also provides a check on the absolute sovereignty of the individual. Specifically, the greatest check on the "abso-

---

148. Flory and Miller, *Finding Faith*, viii.
149. Ibid., 185.
150. Smith and Snell, *Souls in Transition*, 156.
151. Ibid., 49.
152. Flory and Miller, *Finding Faith*, 8.

lute" sovereignty of the individual in the EC is the sovereignty of all other individuals. In other words, what one chooses religiously has to remain in a competing spiritual marketplace and cannot be set up as absolute for others. So, globalism buttresses the EC sense of community even as generational developments buttress the EC sense of individuality in order to arrive at the "difference and tension" which Packard perceives. To recap, sociological studies of the EC locate the conversation firmly in their resistance to institutionalization which in turn can be located in the broader socio-religious discussion of the individual and community. Interestingly, the USA context of the EC as considered here emphasizes this tension as well.

Finally, the broad sociological context in which the EC fits is the tension between the individual and the community, but the USA environment provides one last insight before discussion can proceed past matters of theoretical sociological argument. While the discipline of the sociology of religion "emphasizes religious groups and social expressions of religion," the specific avenues of the social scientific study of spirituality in the USA have developed a little differently.[153] Specifically, as Flory and Miller concisely delineate, "the dominant theme within the sociological study of spirituality in the United States has been the individual in pursuit of her or his own often idiosyncratic, spiritual journey, especially as epitomized by 'Sheilaism.'"[154] This research focus represents a greater emphasis in American life on the primacy of the individual for self-determination in all aspects of life. While social groups and communities definitely impact the creation of meaning for an individual, the individual him/herself is viewed as essentially autonomous. Sociological research on spirituality in the USA is more individual-centric as a result, and the EC in the USA has to contend with this social environment. It is for this reason that EC discussions of this larger socio-theological issue occur under categories of "community" alone. The individual is not excluded from these conversations; rather, the status of the individual is so firmly established in American life and thought that EC participants feel no need to discuss the matter directly.

As a result, the specific sociological studies of the EC discussed in this chapter do not speak at length to the type of individualism being rejected. So, to take a step back and speak in more general sociological terms, the EC interacts with two competing views of individualism without naming either one. First, the EC conversation itself is a manifestation of the rejection of the "Protestant ethic" in which individuals legitimate themselves

---

153. McGuire, *Religion*, 43.
154. Flory and Miller, *Finding Faith*, 11. Cf., Bellah et al., *Habits of the Heart*, 221.

by their own actions in both religious and secular enterprises.[155] Second, emergent churches implicitly accept a privatized individualism in which the individual constructs a private system of meanings, choosing from a wide assortment of religious representations (which include traditional religious representations). Such individual religiosity receives not significant support from the primary public institutions (e.g., the spheres of work, education, law, politics); it is virtually totally "privatized"—supported by and relevant to relations in private life such as the family, social clubs, and leisure-time activities.[156]

The unique design of many emergent churches illustrates this implicit acceptance of privatized individualism in that their worship spaces are redesigned to resemble private life with family, clubs, etc. Also, coming full circle to the concept of institutional resistance, the informality of relationships in the community is an aspect of privatization, which would be lost, or at least muted, by institutionalization. However, the tension of the individual and community in the EC actually serves to mitigate the major difficulty present in privatized individualism. Specifically, "individual autonomy has been redefined to mean the absence of external restraints and traditional limitations in the private search for identity."[157] Within the EC, the competing autonomous selves provide a boundary, fuzzy though it may be, through dialogue, and it is to discussion of that dialogue in EC literature that this study now turns.

Summary of Chapter

Within the course of this chapter, the general context of the EC has been thoroughly discussed. While the principal purpose of the study is to examine the appropriation of mystic practices, it is also essential to understand the particular milieu in which that appropriation occurs. In other words, to refer to the major analogy of the study, the purpose of this chapter has been to clarify the "composition" of the new "solution," or context, to which the "microbes," or mystic practices, have been transplanted. This clarification has followed three paths: history, current developments, and sociological context. Speaking generally, the differentiation of the EC from its evangelical roots can be considered attitudinally, actively, and internationally. The EC sets itself apart from other Christian traditions in its attitude of

---

155. McGuire, *Religion*, 192–93. First articulated by Max Weber in *The Protestant Ethic and the Spirit of Capitalism*.

156. Ibid., 228. First articulated by Thomas Luckmann in *The Invisible Religion*.

157. Ibid.

questioning, displacement, and community. Additionally, the EC is distinct from other groups by their focus on the actions of protest of their former context and contextualization to their new cultural setting. These characteristics were filled out through the provision of some historical background illustrating the reasons why the EC developed in the USA in the way that it did in distinction from international expressions of the EC conversation. Then, comments locating the conversation in the broader developments of resisting institutionalization and the religious interaction between the community and the individual situated the placement of the EC within current social scientific research. Now that the context of the EC has been fully described, it is possible to proceed to the focus of the study: appropriation of mystic practices. With this focus in mind, discussion will begin by investigating what EC literary conversations say about this type of spiritual borrowing in chapter three.

3

Literary Evidence of Emergent Church Use of Mystic Practices

THE HEART OF THE EC is a conversation, and much of this conversation has been taking place through various means of textual communication. Whether it is through innovative venues such as blogs and online discussion forums or more traditional print media, the EC is talking. They are talking about a seemingly boundless range of subjects, and no issue, position, or doctrine is "off the table" for discussion or re-imagining. Spiritual issues are some of the most popular topics in this conversation, and the introduction/inclusion of mystic practices is conversed over readily. Notable EC literary proponents, both in USA and international contexts, who often approach these subjects include Brian McLaren, Todd Hunter, Rob Bell, Michael Frost, Spencer Burke, Leonard Sweet, Peter Rollins, Doug Pagitt, and, especially, Tony Jones.[1] While it may be difficult to glimpse general themes within the conversation due to the multiplicity of voices and viewpoints, the EC definitely displays a tendency to view mystic practices pragmatically. In other words, these practices are of interest because of *how* they can be used, which according to Brian McLaren, one of the leading lights of the EC, is to "help us become someone weighty, someone worthy of a name and reputation, someone who makes survival worthwhile by turning life's manure into fertilizer."[2] Additionally, these practices are of interest because of *why* they are being used by the EC; that is, what meanings are attached to the practices by the EC.

This bifurcated perspective of *how* and *why* offers an interpretive framework for the EC conversation with regard to the integration of mystic practices. It is best, therefore, to approach the literary side of this subject by

---

1. Jones's book *The Sacred Way* is the most comprehensive treatment yet available of EC assimilation of mystic practices.
2. McLaren, *Finding Our Way Again*, 14.

scrutinizing some pragmatic areas of comment where EC proponents write about the use of mystic practices. First, it is practical to begin by inquiring exactly what the EC means by *spirituality*, *mysticism*, and the *mystical tradition*. Next, attention will be given to outlining the rise of interest in mystic practices by the EC. Third, after delineating lines of interest, investigation of particular practices can begin through scrutiny of *how* emergent churches are using mystic practices according to EC literature. Finally, this information will be drawn together into a conceptual framework of theological distinctives, or anchors, which serve as reasons *why* the EC uses mystic practices. Consideration of each of these four areas serves to clarify the appropriation of mystic practices by the EC through answers to the questions of *how* and *why* within literary sources.

Meanings

A fitting place to begin examination of EC literature is in asking, "What does the EC mean by *spirituality* and *mysticism*?" As noted in the first chapter, there are some terms at the heart of this study which require careful definition and explanation. Particularly, the terms *spirituality* and *mysticism* along with their derivatives can be defined in multiple ways. While operating definitions for the purposes of this study have been offered, it is advantageous at this point to emphasize differences among these operating definitions and the terms as discussed by EC authors. Additionally, EC literary understandings of the term *mystical tradition* require some brief discussion, for this term is occasionally distinct from the general term *mysticism* for EC proponents. So, with this purpose in mind, it is helpful to consider definitions from EC literature of *spirituality*, *mysticism*, and the *mystical tradition*.

Spirituality

At first blush, EC definitions of *spirituality* and its attendant derivatives do not look that different from the operating definition for this study. For instance, EC proponents characterize spirituality as "everything that goes into being in a relationship with God"[3] and that the goal of spirituality is "to be enlivened by God's Spirit."[4] However, upon closer inspection, these definitions are shaded with some very important undertones. First, an EC understanding of spirituality begins with realization of an apparent crisis

---

3. Haselmayer, McLaren, and Sweet, *A is for Abductive*, 268.
4. Jones, *Sacred Way*, 26. Italics original.

situation surrounding present-day intense hunger for all things spiritual.[5] Next, this undertone of crisis is aided by the constant appeal to *spirituality* by postmoderns to the point that EC leaders claim that the terms *postmodern* and *spiritual* are as inextricably linked as the terms *modern* and *skeptic*.[6] A third undertone revisits the pragmatic emphasis for EC permutations of spirituality. In simplest terms, the EC hungers for a spirituality that leaves room for the unknown—that embraces mystery rather than challenging it.[7] While this desire would logically seem to circumvent a practical stress, EC writers do not view it that way; rather, they root their practicality in personal experiences. They begin their spirituality with a recognition of spiritual experiences that cannot be explained or understood through scientific or rational means, and they want a spirituality that fits these experiences into an overall framework for day-to-day living.[8] These undertones combine to lead the EC in a search for *spirituality* that means a "fusion of everyday sacredness" over and against the realm of "religious fundamentalism."[9] As a result, these slight nuances deepen the EC meaning of *spirituality*, and they also serve to create a very negative connotation for the term *religion* in opposition to *spirituality*.

Unlike the operating definition of *spirituality* for this study, the EC definitely views *spirituality* and *religion* antithetically. In their own words, "Religion, it seems, is often about what makes us different and separates us, while spirituality seems to be more about what we can hold in common and what might connect us."[10] While this semantic separation by the EC may seem overly simplistic, they argue that there has been a general semantic shift within Western culture in preference for the term *spirituality* over *religion*. Rob Bell, a prominent EC pastor, anecdotally illustrates this shift by relating,

> Last year some friends asked me to be the pastor for their wedding ceremony. They had been together for a while and decided to make it official and throw a huge weekend party, and they invited me to be a part of it. They said they didn't want any Jesus or God or Bible or religion to be talked about. But they did want me to make it really spiritual. The bride said it in her own great

---

5. Keel, *Intuitive Leadership*, 179–80.
6. Sweet, *Quantum Spirituality*, 74.
7. Frost, *Exiles*, 100–101.
8. Bell, *Velvet Elvis*, 74.
9. McLaren, *Finding Our Way Again*, 5.
10. Burke and Taylor, *Heretic's Guide to Eternity*, 37.

way, "Rob, do that thing you do. Make it really profound and deep and spiritual!"[11]

As an outflow of this perceived cultural shift, the EC and their postmodern constituency assert that *spirituality* and *religion* have become polar opposites. Spirituality is egalitarian, but religion is chauvinist. Spirituality is countercultural, but religion is establishment. Spirituality is experiential, but religion is absolutist. Spirituality is transformational, but religion is propositional. Spirituality is *practical*, but religion is *theoretical*. The list could continue on indefinitely.[12] It is vital to highlight this antithetical relationship because it raises a significant issue for EC utilization of mystic practices in connection with mystical theology. Principally, the disconnection of *spirituality* and *religion* also represents sundering *practices* from established theological *beliefs*,[13] so the EC logically can utilize practices without equivocation concerning their theological provenance. This issue of disconnection between practice and belief becomes more foundational for an EC understanding of *mysticism*.

Mysticism

According to EC authors, knowledge of and interest in *mysticism* does not begin at the point of history or belief but at the point of practical experience. In short, "Mysticism begins in experience; it ends in theology."[14] As a result, the EC literature directs focus to mystical experiences, and these experiences are interpreted theologically through the lens of postmodern culture. EC leaders assert that their interest is born out of the winds of cultural change, for "The disenchanted world is seeking radical reenchantment," and mystical practices can bring about such change.[15] With such a focus on mystical experiences as a source of cultural capital, the EC defines *mysticism* in a general sense, emphasizing the connection between mysticism and wonder.[16] In other words, *mysticism* is synonymous with *mystical experience*, and *mystical theology* is synonymous with *awe*. In the EC, this awe replaces a more developed mystical theology, and it has a pragmatic weight placed

11. Bell, *Velvet Elvis*, 75–76. Cf., Henderson and Casper, *Jim & Casper Go to Church*, 103. This passage contains a more comprehensive treatment of the general cultural shift mentioned above.
12. Burke and Taylor, *Heretic's Guide to Eternity*, 58–60.
13. Ibid., 79. Cf., Frost and Hirsch, *ReJesus*, 12.
14. Sweet, *Quantum Spirituality*, 76.
15. Haselmayer, McLaren, and Sweet, *A is for Abductive*, 201.
16. Ibid., 307.

on the utility of mystical practices and experiences for the awakening of an individual to what, in their words, is "truly important: the spiritual life and our walking of that path."[17]

What does "walking of that path" actually look like in the EC? It has two notable and interpenetrating outcomes. First, walking that path enhances an EC perception of the world all around them as speaking of the "reality of God."[18] Second, this mystical sense motivates the individual EC conversationalist as well as the larger group to take an active role in remaking the world, with an emphasis on the present world as the appropriate context for Christian hope and anticipation.[19] While it would not be surprising if this generalized sense of *mysticism* might lead the EC away from a consideration of the historical Christian mystical tradition, this divergence has not been comprehensive because the EC expresses an interest and connection to this tradition, but a few words are necessary to clarify exactly what they mean when considering this tradition.

Mystical Tradition

In short, the *mystical tradition* is understood inconsistently in the EC. To clarify, the EC is somewhat aware of the mystical tradition, as that tradition which developed in Christian history around the three-step process of mystical ascent. However, such historical knowledge is not viewed as essential for appropriation of practices, so EC participants are perfectly willing to put their own spin on what they assimilate from this tradition.[20] The EC describes the purpose of the mystical tradition in their own terms, specifically that they can "*experience* the living God in this life in ways that range from gentle and subtle to dramatic, ravishing, and electrifying."[21] With this experiential purpose serving as a selective device, the EC mines the mystical tradition for individual practices and exemplary persons "who were not only theologically astute and renowned contemplative pray-ers, but who were also servants."[22] Suffice it to say, EC proponents refer to the *mystical tradition* as a whole and to specific permutations, but they stress an experiential and experimental meaning for this tradition rather than a meaning which perceives the *mystical tradition* in a historically faithful way. Mystic

17. Seay and Garrett, *Gospel Reloaded*, 92.
18. Scandrette, "Week in the Life," 137.
19. Bell, *Velvet Elvis*, 150.
20. McLaren, *Finding Our Way Again*, 147–48.
21. Ibid., 92.
22. Jones, *Sacred Way*, 191–92.

practices, stories of mystics, and anecdotes of experiences are selectively considered on the basis of personal interest. This highly individualized view of the *mystical tradition* on the part of the EC flows out of their rise of interest in mystic practices.

Rise of Interest in Mystic Practices

The foregoing section illustrates that the trend of EC interest for mysticism lies in personal preferences that EC participants have and then use as a basis for appropriating mystical practices. An additional piece of the puzzle concerning EC interest in mystic practices is located within a historical delineation of this rise of interest. This rise can best be understood as a three-step process: evangelical interest in *spiritual disciplines*, the EC desire for connection to "ancient" Christianity, and the ideals and individuals from the mystical tradition which the EC most aspires to emulate.

Evangelical Interest

The beginning of EC interest in mystic practices is within the evangelical interest in spiritual disciplines. This starting point becomes clear when one recalls that the EC most directly emerged out of evangelicalism. As a result, most EC participants, and definitely EC leaders, have a common heritage in the subculture of evangelicalism. A small piece of this common heritage is a basic introduction to mystic practices under the pseudonym of *spiritual disciplines*. In this vein, Tim Keel relates a personal journey which is common for EC Christians.

> Like many, I discovered Richard Foster and his book *Celebration of Discipline*, and it had a profound impact on me. In the 1980s evangelical writing on spiritual practice was that book. Period. Fortunately he wrote more. From there, I moved to his *Devotional Classics*, a book sampling the writings of Christians throughout time and from different traditions. A whole world opened up before me and sent me on a quest and into a heritage that I did not know I possessed.[23]

Along with Foster, other EC leaders note the influence of Dallas Willard and Eugene Peterson who published books on similar topics in the wake of nascent evangelical interest in spiritual disciplines.[24] An understanding of

---

23. Keel, *Intuitive Leadership*, 114.
24. Hunter, *Giving Church Another Chance*, 17. Cf., McLaren, *Finding Our Way*

the entry of mystic practices into EC thought under the guise of spiritual disciplines is vital to grasping how the EC utilizes these practices. By way of a commonplace metaphor, Tony Jones notes the EC understanding of the *purpose* of spiritual disciplines: "While athletic practice makes us stronger, physically and mentally, so we're more present during a competition, spiritual discipline means making less of ourselves so we can be more aware of what God is up to."[25] Scrutinizing this metaphor allows one to glimpse how the EC views mystic practices. While the overall aim of exercise usually falls into a limited number of purposes, such as keeping in shape, preparing for a competition, or rehabilitation, specific exercises can be used for almost any purpose that an individual can dream up.[26] Following this line of reasoning, even as various physical exercises can be suited to individualistic purposes so mystic practices can also be customized. As a metaphorical illustration, it may be observed that one does not need to question the historical provenance of push-ups in order to utilize them effectively. Would it not follow logically that use of mystic practices, if they are analogous to physical exercises, also would not require historical sensitivity? While the EC follows this line of reasoning, they paradoxically still assert a desire for connection to what they term "ancient" Christianity, and mystic practices are typically included as means, or at least partial means, of engendering such a connection.

Connecting to the Ancients

The EC is about the future; however, they do not envision ushering in a future that is completely new and unknown. Rather, EC proponents connect their visions of future spirituality to the past, particularly the ancient past. While EC leaders readily converse about a coming spiritual "revolution," Peter Rollins clarifies EC expectations of this revolution with the disclaimer, "It is not then a revolution that is in the process of creating something new but rather one that is returning to something very old."[27] Stress on this connection is frequent in EC writings, yet it is coupled with a caveat. The EC desires to revive the "ancient" practices, but they freely admit that such revival is partial and incomplete for two reasons. First, the EC aspires to keep one foot planted in the mystical Christian past and keep one foot in the quick-paced,

---

Again, vii.

25. Jones, *Sacred Way*, 32.

26. McLaren, *Why Did Jesus, Moses, the Buddha, and Mohammed Cross the Road?*, 169.

27. Rollins, *How (Not) to Speak of God*, xv.

innovative present. This specific circumstance engenders a fascination with the past coupled with a desire not to be bound too closely to it, for the EC does not wish to smother creativity with a restrictive tradition.[28] As a result, other Christian traditions, such as the Catholic, Orthodox, or Anglican traditions, are respected and borrowed from, but they are never asserted to be "the final resting place—they have limitations of their own."[29] This first reason for a partial assimilation of ancient Christianity flavors the EC by an eclectic grasp of the past, and the second reason is characterized by emergent churches reaching out to the postmodern future.

A strong postmodern tendency is to turn nostalgically to the "ancient" as that which is better, purer, and cleaner than modernism. While this turn affects many aspects of the EC conversation, it is very easy to glimpse it in their desire to incorporate mystical practices. Almost wistfully, EC leader Tony Jones imagines that "[h]aving not experienced the cynicism of our postmodern age, the ancient saints pursued Jesus with a relentlessness we can hardly imagine."[30] This viewpoint is not limited to the EC postmodern imagination; in fact, evangelical theologian Jeff Keuss notes this trend toward an interest in "premodern religions" within the larger evangelical fold as well.[31] However, the EC focuses this general trend through an intense curiosity with Christian mystic practices with seemingly little rumination on the historical situation of each practice other than its age. For instance, Tony Jones notes the increase of interest in mystic practices with the noncommittal wondering, "[m]aybe it's that there's something mystical and mysterious about these ancient rites, like we're tapping into some pretechnological, preindustrial treasury of the Spirit."[32] In this statement, Jones unintentionally stresses the postmodern perspective that the ancient and premodern are categorically better than the modern, coupled with an outlook on mystic practices as appealing to the EC experience through their "weirdness."

It is this "weirdness" which is the key to unlocking the mystery of EC appropriation of mystic practices uncoupled from mystic theology. Patrick Malloy incisively cuts to the heart of this disconnection, as noted in EC literary output:

28. Sweet, *Quantum Spirituality*, 182.
29. Pagitt, *Christianity Worth Believing*, 142.
30. Jones, *Sacred Way*, 18. Cf., Tickle, *Emergence Christianity*, 174–76.
31. Keuss, "Emergent Church and Neo-Correlational Theology," 461.
32. Jones, *Sacred Way*, 17–18. Cf., Bielo, *Emerging Evangelicals*, 100. Bielo notes this turn particularly toward ancient, not present-day, monasticism from a sociological perspective.

> Yet, while emergent Christians have begun to import the ancient patterns they have seen in the Anglican, Roman, and Eastern traditions, they have not embraced the theologies embedded in the practices. Instead, emergent Christians have unreflectively retained (speaking generally, as one must of everything in emergence) the dominant theology of the tradition from which most of them are emerging. The ancient symbols are reappropriated, but the patristic conviction that the symbols and symbolic actions constitute an objective, efficacious encounter with the Holy is not. These symbols are used because they make an impression.[33]

Malloy hits on the lynchpin of EC utilization of mystic practices, as noted in their literature and as will be illustrated in the empirical research results in chapters five and six. Specifically, the EC utilizes mystic practices, but they are experimenting with them on the basis of an essentially evangelical theological perspective in which these practices "make an impression," but they do not have a connection to a larger sacramental viewpoint as is true in Catholic, Orthodox, and Anglican traditions. Without additional theological boundaries, the EC evinces a noted freedom in roving about the mystic tradition, finding many ideals and examples from all corners of Christian mystical history that are only connected through the themes for which the EC finds them inspiring and valuable.

Ideals and Individuals

The EC gateway to interest in mystic practices begins in the soil of evangelical spirituality which focuses on "personal Bible study and devotion, free-form prayer, and personal conversion to a relationship with Jesus Christ."[34] However, it is the restrictive limitations of such a spirituality which EC adherents seek to sever. General dissatisfaction with the boundaries of traditional evangelical spirituality and enchantment with spiritual disciplines nurtures a hunger noted poignantly by EC leader Rob Bell:

> I am learning that I come from a tradition that has wrestled with the deepest questions of human existence for thousands of years. I am learning that my tradition includes the rabbis and reformers and revolutionaries and monks and nuns and pastors

---

33. Malloy, "Rick Warren Meets Gregory Dix," 449.
34. Jones, *Sacred Way*, 29.

and writers and philosophers and artists and every person everywhere who has asked big questions of a big God.[35]

While this hunger has chiefly been exemplified in an EC willingness to try many different mystic practices, it has also manifested through an attentiveness to particular Christian mystics as exemplars in one way or another.

For instance, emergent churches look to Meister Eckhart as a mystical proponent in agreement with them concerning their views on propositional statements in theology. These views can perhaps be best characterized by the slightly satirical comment by Peter Rollins that "To believe is human; to doubt, divine."[36] Eckhart is not appropriated by the EC in a total way; rather, he is hinted at through particular emphases which the EC enlists his aid to support. When asserting that right belief is subservient to a sense of invitation for God to enter the individual, Eckhart is a ready "ally" although the EC still reveals an evangelical theological interpretation by emphasizing conversionism through this assertion, which would be foreign to Eckhart.[37] Spencer Burke and Barry Taylor go a bit further in seeking to unbalance stress on "traditional" religious statements through reference to Meister Eckhart's cryptic challenge that "Only those who dare to let go can dare to reenter."[38] This progression of thematic emphasis climaxes in Peter Rollins' bold statement that Meister Eckhart "balked at the presumption of those who would seek to colonize the name 'God' with concepts."[39] So, in Meister Eckhart, the EC finds a notable mystic that will "join" them in rejection of what they see as modern and evangelical. However, EC utilization of mystics as ideals does not stop with negative emphases, for EC leaders assert that EC Christians have learned and implemented many positive traits from mystics.

Brother Lawrence provides a glimpse of how a particular mystic practice is assimilated through reference to an exemplary individual. With reference to daily action, multiple EC leaders note the model of Brother Lawrence and his practice of constant perception of God, that is "Practicing the Presence of God."[40] This practice is interpreted quite widely within the EC and is regularly encouraged for implementation, but EC proponents do not feel any necessity to adhere faithfully to the source of this practice. Notably, Michael Frost utilizes the practice of the presence of

---

35. Bell, *Velvet Elvis*, 14.
36. Rollins, *Insurrection*, 19.
37. Rollins, *How (Not) to Speak of God*, 71.
38. Burke and Taylor, *Heretic's Guide to Eternity*, 55.
39. Rollins, *How (Not) to Speak of God*, xii.
40. Frost, *Exiles*, 64. Cf., McLaren, *Finding Our Way Again*, 63.

God only as a jumping off point to motivate EC participants to practice hospitality, generosity, (social) justice, environmental stewardship, and mission; however, the points of connection among these practices are never considered.[41] So, while the EC displays a vague interest in Brother Lawrence's idea of practicing the presence of God, it is an interest born out of an eagerness to fit a practice to an EC purpose, regardless of whether a logical connection among the constituent pieces exists or not. This eclectic blend of role models, mystic practices, and EC emphases finds its fullest flower with regard to the issue of social action.

Multiple mystics serve illustratively for the EC in matters of social justice. One of the most notable characteristics of the EC conversation is a particular concern for social justice issues concerning poverty, famine, justice, governmental control, and war. These emphases are even more striking when one remembers that the EC conversation primarily arose out of Protestant evangelicalism which in the past has often left social issues to their Protestant mainline counterparts, at least in the USA context. As EC leaders have begun to stress social involvement, they have looked around the entire scope of Christian history for advocates of social concern and change. A paradigmatic illustration of the use and understanding of mystics in this regard is readily available in Brian McLaren's comments on Françoiș Fenelon:

> Seventeenth-century French bishop and mystic Françoiș Fenelon seemed to grasp this [the nature of war] when he said, "All wars are civil wars, because all men are brothers. Each one owes infinitely more to the human race than to the particular country in which he was born." Wars play out a framing story of *us versus them* that seeks to take precedence over the deeper and higher framing story of God's global family table, where *us* and *them* are equally invited, equally wanted, in the biggest "us" of all. No less striking than his family imagery, though less often appreciated, is Jesus' sensitivity to ecology—evident in his many parables about farming and fishing and weather. He knows the natural world intimately and makes hillside and seashore his preferred classrooms. One imagines him being interrupted by an incoming flock of crows, who then appear in his next parable, or one imagines children gathering flowers while their parents listen to Jesus speak, and then those flowers appear in the next part of his sermon.[42]

---

41. Ibid., 69–70.
42. McLaren, *Everything Must Change*, 126.

While Fenelon's comments on war are particularly applicable to McLaren's point, the level of adaptation of a mystic for the EC conversation is more telling in McLaren's interpretive comments following the direct quote, asking for the reader to utilize his/her imagination to move from Fenelon's comments to a wistful portrait of Jesus as a nature-loving mystic standing against the horrors of war and ecological misuse. The implication is that Fenelon supports McLaren's interpretation of the character and actions of Jesus.

Other mystics similarly utilized by EC leaders include the desert fathers and mothers, St. Benedict of Nursia, and, especially, St. Francis of Assisi.[43] More recent examples, such as Bl. Theresa of Calcutta and Dorothy Day, are considered with respect to the balance of contemplation and action. Illustratively, Day is singled out by Todd Hunter as masterfully combining active work among the poor with "common church practices like early morning, daytime and evening prayer; celebrating Mass; silent retreats; and the advice of a spiritual director."[44] Evidently, the EC is interested in mystics as examples, particularly when they overlap with EC concerns, but this interest raises curiosity with regard to the level of interaction between the EC and the role models they point out, especially in light of the disjointed nature between mystic practices and evangelical theology as previously noted.

Essentially, emergent churches are *interested* in spiritual disciplines, in connecting to the ancients, in individual mystics as ideals; but how far does this interest extend? While this entire study is focused on this line of questioning, it is advantageous at this point to focus such a query through the lens of EC literary output. While mention of particular mystics is a telling mark of EC literary interest, citation of these examples provides some clarity concerning the depth of interest. As a representative case, Rob Bell, a leading author in the EC conversation, writes the following:

> The Eastern church father Gregory of Nyssa talked about Moses' journey up Mount Sinai in Exodus 19. When Moses enters the darkness toward the top of the mountain, he has moved beyond knowledge to awe and to love and to the mystery of God. Gregory insists that Moses has not arrived when he enters the darkness of the mountaintop. His journey and exploration have only really begun.[45]

While this quote appears appropriately within Bell's discussion, the citation with which Bell references his example is not Gregory's *Life of Moses*; rather,

---

43. Jones, *Sacred Way*, 191–92. Cf., McLaren, *Finding Our Way Again*, 191; Scandrette, "Week in the Life of a Missional Community," 142.

44. Hunter, *Giving Church Another Chance*, 153.

45. Bell, *Velvet Elvis*, 34.

his citation simply mentions that a friend told him this story.[46] Similarly, Timothy Stoner relates his thoughts concerning St. Teresa of Avila with the opening comments identifying her as part of "a story I heard" rather than connecting his consideration of the mystic on any further level of interaction or research.[47] While these citation issues appear minor, they are illustrative of a larger situation, precisely that the EC is not always engaging the mystical tradition on the level of interaction with primary sources. They are interested in each mystic and the practices supporting his/her pattern of life in a pragmatic and experimental way as far as the mystic's purpose coincides with theirs.[48] EC literary comments display this bearing even more clearly as scrutiny turns specifically to the appropriation and reinterpretation of mystic practices.

Appropriation and Reinterpretation of Mystic Practices

The rise of interest in mystic practices within the EC is complex as is evident from the foregoing comments. Consideration of specific appropriation and reinterpretation of mystic practices within emergent churches from a literary perspective also requires complex description on several fronts. First, exploration breeds eclecticism, at least in the case of the EC, and eclectic aspects of EC application of mystic practices deserves significant explication. Next, the connections between EC use of mystic practices and EC focus on mystical experiences necessitates some comment. Finally, from these bases, discussion can lead into full attention on individual mystic practices as considered from the literary side of the EC conversation.

Eclectic Application

Emergent churches center on change. While debate could be greatly extended concerning whether emergent churches desire change or simply seek to react to it, the fact of the matter is that an EC spirituality focuses on options rather than requirements.[49] Additionally, these multitudinous options are often paradoxically presented as points of entry into a unified holistic

---

46. Ibid., 182.
47. Stoner, *God Who Smokes*, 66–67.
48. Sweet, *I Am a Follower*, 131–34.
49. McLaren, *Finding Our Way Again*, 5.

spirituality.⁵⁰ However, literary portraits of the resulting bricolage of spiritual and mystic practices do not present an image of a holistic spirituality, but the EC moves in that direction at least to the point of seeking a spiritual fusion which is observed by both EC insiders and outside observers. From an insider perspective, Brian McLaren refers to this fusion in metaphorical terms: "It's new, but it's old. It's working with the same ingredients and the same practices, but combining them in fresh—and some would say tasty and nourishing ways."⁵¹ Outside observers Shayne Lee and Phillip Sinitiere note this eclecticism in more descriptive terms as crossing "historical, geographical, and denominational borders to offer an eclectic mix of evangelical, Roman Catholic, and Eastern Orthodox practices to enhance spiritual experience and fortify spiritual formation."⁵² So, emergent churches by their own admission and by outside observation are eclectic in their inculcation and application of mystic practices, but what does this eclecticism look like on an individual and corporate level?

On an individual level, EC eclectic utilization of mystic practices embodies freedom and practicality. Stress is not laid on correctness of a particular action or practice but on immediacy and activity. As a result, all sorts of combinations of practices are possible, and EC leaders are quick to interject that the boundaries of historically Christian practice are permeable at this point. For instance, Tony Jones, a noted EC advocate and former coordinator of *Emergent Village*, freely states the value he finds in combining the Christian practice of centering prayer with the Hindu body positions of yoga.⁵³ He also advocates creating a personal monastic-type Rule for one's life, and, in the example he provides, Roman Catholic, Eastern Orthodox, and Jewish practices all make an appearance.⁵⁴ Jones' suggestion of the creation of a personal Rule is notable in its integration of practices from various faith traditions, but it is just as innovative that he encourages a "do-it-yourself" approach to creating a monastic-type Rule. For the EC, customization follows experimentation, and both are birthed out of eclecticism on an individual level. However, this eclectic trend is not confined to the personal level, for even more visible examples of eclecticism appear in communal configurations of the EC.

From an early point in the EC conversation, literary participants displayed their aspirations for eclecticism and integration in corporate

50. Pagitt, *Christianity Worth Believing*, 85.
51. McLaren, *Finding Our Way Again*, 56.
52. Lee and Sinitiere, "New Kind of Christian," 85.
53. Jones, *Sacred Way*, 126.
54. Ibid., 198.

worship gatherings. In fact, these gatherings intended to foster "experiences that emphasize congregational involvement with multiple opportunities for group interaction."[55] This assertion concerning experiences serves to raise the question of what these "experiences" and "opportunities" actually look like. This question is answered, at least in one specific permutation, by the sociological observations of James Bielo, who chronicles the happenings of an "Artwalk" by an EC group in a local art museum. Within this context, Bielo notes that the group engages in a corporate experience of *lectio divina* followed by what he describes as "the Artwalk process: we would 'find a corner,' read a chosen text of scripture, spend an hour walking the museum alone, journal our thoughts ('there is no right or wrong way, just journal'), then meet for lunch and 'share what the Holy Spirit taught us.'"[56] It is a distinguishing characteristic that this EC worship gathering bears little resemblance to a typical evangelical worship service. In fact, this particular EC group, according to Bielo, focuses on three recurring worship events: "a biweekly 'Artwalk,' a weekly journaling group, and a monthly 'Maproom.'"[57] The exploratory and eclectic nature of EC worship is not bound together through a common tradition; rather, EC literary advocates assert that these innovative worship events are grounded in a common goal of "experiencing God,"[58] and it is this experience of God which serves to carve out a niche for mystic practices on the corporate and personal levels of the EC literary conversation.

Mystical Experiences

Mystic practices are attractive to the EC through the lens of mystical experiences. In fact, EC interest in mystic practices arises on a personal and anecdotal level specifically from experiences which EC participants are at a loss to describe. These moments are simply "holy," according to EC participant description, and EC Christians have had great difficulty in fitting them into the theological interpretive framework bequeathed to them from their evangelical forebears.[59] Understanding of these experiences and their place with respect to EC interest in mystic practices begins for the EC with

---

55. Frost, *Exiles*, 291.

56. Bielo, *Emerging Evangelicals*, 77.

57. Ibid., 76. "Maprooms" consisted of various prayer/worship stations, which changed content based on that month's topical focus. A participant could visit these various stations to foster spiritual experiences or look at spiritual ideas from new angles.

58. Ibid.

59. Bell, *Velvet Elvis*, 40.

hunger—a hunger for immanence and a sense of God as subject rather than object.[60] Doug Pagitt captures this line of reasoning with respect to experiencing God by saying, "A God who is distant and removed is not better than a God who is engaged and caring. A God who is immovable is not better than a God who is participating. A God who is up and out can never outdo a God who is down and in."[61] Mystical experiences then form a common basis for interest through a shared hunger rather than through shared experience. This development is quite notable because the EC bears the marks of postmodern disconnection from institutional support, particularly at this point. In other words, the locus of mystical experience shifts away in the EC viewpoint from shared experiences, such as the celebration of Holy Communion, to give greater emphasis to mystical experiences of a highly individualized variety, and shared experiences are interpreted in individualistic ways.[62] A highly individualized approach to mystical experience colors the EC utilization of mystic practices and also informs exactly what the EC means by the term *mystical experience*.

As noted in the previous definition section, the EC defines *mystical experience* in a profoundly general sense. Leonard Sweet, a noted EC leader, describes this type of experience, which he terms *threshold experience*, as "that step, that sight, beyond which chronology fades and synchrony enters, where life begins to take on new colors, words mean different things, and emotions speak different messages."[63] Whether in definitional or descriptive terms, EC conversationalists can be frustratingly vague in delineation of a concept which is so foundational for their spirituality, yet they prefer to shine light on these experiences metaphorically with particular focus on artistic connections. As a paradigmatic example of this trend, Brian McLaren treats mystical experience through the following image:

> Imagine a great violinist who gives two hundred concerts a year. Let's say that three of her concerts were disastrous—she had the flu, or her bridge broke in the middle of the evening, or a fire alarm buzzed five minutes into her first song. Let's say that 190 of her concerts were good—some stronger than others, but the crowds were satisfied. And what were the remaining seven concerts? They were exceptional, the reviewers might say: inspired, transcendent, ecstatic. They might even use the term *magical*,

---

60. Rollins, *How (Not) to Speak of God*, 23.
61. Pagitt, *Christianity Worth Believing*, 109.
62. Drane, *After McDonaldization*, 34. Cf., Mann, *Atonement for a "Sinless" Society*, 159.
63. Sweet, *Quantum Spirituality*, 227.

but of course they don't mean it in a literal sense. They mean that some inexplicable things converged that night, and the music somehow unleashed latent power that was unknown the other 193 nights. The violinist herself can't explain this. She feels on those nights that she has been taken up to a higher level, that on those seven nights, a glorious mystery has filled her and the audience and the sound waves that connect them. She may not even want to speak of it, because doing so somehow cheapens the experience.[64]

These metaphors serve to illustrate the individualistic, ecstatic, and highly eclectic nature of mystical experience for the EC, and, by extension, these images open a literary window into what the EC expects from mystic practices and how they expect to implement them. Now the next logical step from the groundwork of definition, rise of interest, eclecticism, and mystical experience is to consider the individual practices which the EC seeks to appropriate.

Individual Mystic Practices

On the basis of the foregoing background issues, the actual mystical practices which the EC uses can be approached from a literary perspective. However, the first issue which arises in individual consideration of these mystic practices is *which* practices should be considered. For the purposes of empirical research, such a list of twenty-one discrete, but possibly overlapping, practices was devised. Unfortunately, no single "official" list of these practices appears in one literary location; rather, I compared lists from several proponents and outside researchers and compiled a single list from these various sources.[65] The resulting list included centering prayer, the Eucharist, confession, contemplative prayer, the Daily Office/fixed-hour prayer, fasting, icons, the Jesus Prayer, *lectio divina*, the liturgical calendar/church year, liturgical prayer, meditation, pilgrimage, practicing the presence of God, prayer labyrinths, the rosary, making the sign of the cross, silence, solitude, spiritual direction/spiritual friendship, and the stations of the cross. Discussion of the appropriation of these practices will follow two paths within this

64. McLaren, *Finding Our Way Again*, 93–94. Cf., Perriman, *Otherways*, 162. Perriman notes a similar example utilizing film rather than musical composition.

65. McLaren, *Finding Our Way Again*, 21. Cf., McLaren, *Secret Message of Jesus*, 222–23; Bielo, *Emerging Evangelicals*, 71; Malloy, "Rick Warren Meets Gregory Dix," 446–47; Jones, *Sacred Way*, 33–194. Jones, *Sacred Way* and McLaren's *Finding Our Way Again* had the most comprehensive lists and treatment of specific mystic practices among EC literature.

chapter. This section will consider *how* mystic practices are implemented in the EC, according to literary comments. The following section will outline *why* these practices are utilized in terms of the specific theological anchors which allow for EC appropriation and reinterpretation. So, in view of this division, investigation can proceed to a literary understanding of *how* mystic practices can be assimilated into an EC context.

The EC utilizes mystic practices, but they are quick to note that these practices "should be seen as options available to us, not as requirements imposed on us."[66] In this light, EC authors do not give equal consideration to all practices noted, and they often do not offer extended comment on all practices that appear on their literary lists. In view of this circumstance, the proceeding literary consideration of each practice may *seem* incomplete because EC leaders often mentioned a practice without offering any further comment. Additionally, these practices are often subsumed into larger categories of religious practices, such as "ancient-future" practices or kingdom practices, which also contain further practices that do not solely find their origin in the mystical tradition.[67] In all of these various categories of practice, the EC retains focus through a conceptual framework of particular theological anchors which map to individual practices. While the next section will introduce these anchors, beginning with comments on the practical integration of practices will aid in clarifying the process of appropriation. In this context, the following consideration of individual practices is arranged alphabetically because differing sources valued practices quite variously.

One mystic practice often advocated by EC leaders is centering prayer. From literary sources, this practice is advocated in essentially the same form as that which is presented by its creators Thomas Keating and M. Basil Pennington, and EC writers, such as Tony Jones, note this connection.[68] Centering prayer is historically connected to the contemplative prayer methods first articulated in John Cassian's *Conferences*, and EC proponents occasionally note this historical origin along with the permutations of this mystic practice as it moves historically forward through other prominent sources such as *The Cloud of Unknowing*, St. Teresa of Avila, and St. John of the Cross.[69] The interesting twist that enters the EC discussion concerning this practice is the explicit rejection of an inherent purpose for the practice, and their willingness to combine it with disparate spiritual practices. For

66. McLaren, *Finding Our Way Again*, 97.
67. Whitesel, *Inside the Organic Church*, 145. Cf., Hunter, *Giving Church Another Chance*, 111.
68. Jones, *Sacred Way*, 74.
69. Ibid., 72.

instance, as mentioned above, Tony Jones related a personal experience of combining centering prayer with meditative yoga; however, this story is told after he referenced the fact that centering prayer was originally distilled as a method in order to provide a Christian alternative for Eastern religious practices that had been introduced to the West, including yoga.[70] This circumstance highlights two important observations that recur in EC discussion concerning many particular mystic practices. First, literary sources often obliquely mention historical tradition in explaining a particular practice, but, second, they often present anecdotes or prescriptions for implementation that hint at a highly personalized interpretation of the practice. Centering prayer aptly illustrates this development although this pattern is not absolutely uniform for all practices. For instance, a practice which diverges from this pattern is the celebration of the Eucharist or Holy Communion among emergent churches.

Another practice that EC adherents are embracing is the celebration of the Eucharist or Holy Communion. While this practice is generally one of the few which EC participants did enact within their previous evangelical context, they are approaching this mystic ritual in a different way according to EC proponents and outside observers. An outsider perspective, such as the one provided by Patrick Malloy, is quick to note that the most easily distinguishable characteristic of EC Eucharistic worship is its frequency.[71] Emergent churches tend to celebrate Holy Communion every week. Insider perspectives, conversely, focus on an increased liturgical and sacramental apparatus surrounding the celebration of this mystic practice. Todd Hunter, an EC literary proponent, zeroes in on this increased sacramental viewpoint by stating, "Life is imparted *at* or *during* the Eucharist ... Thus in Communion we not only give thanks and receive the power of Christ, we then live as he lived (as if he were in our place), which in turn leads *others* to give thanks for our lives."[72] This sacramental aspect is buttressed by an EC understanding that Holy Communion becomes less an act of symbolic remembrance of a past sacrifice and more a "rite of identification" into a specific community with particular focus on the connection between *members* of the community rather than connection with the divine.[73] Connection with the divine becomes located in other mystic practices for the EC, such as the use of icons.

70. Ibid., 72, 134.

71. Malloy, "Rick Warren Meets Gregory Dix," 447.

72. Hunter, *Giving Church Another Chance*, 139. Italics in original.

73. Mann, *Atonement for a "Sinless" Society*, 159. Cf., McLaren, *Why Did Jesus, Moses, the Buddha, and Mohammed Cross the Road?*, 211.

EC authors advocate the utilization of icons in prayer with a fascinating juxtaposition of focus on the reclamation of an ancient art form and gateway to mystical experience alongside a focus on postmodern interpretations of symbolism. EC Christians compare icons to other art forms in the following way:

> A Western painting—which is undeniably going to be more accomplished in terms of realism, perspective, lighting, anatomy, and so forth—moves us in our imaginations and our emotions. We engage with it like we do a movie or a story. An icon hits us in a different way, though. In comparison, it is very still. It is silent. We find ourselves coming to silence as we stand before it. An icon somehow takes command of the space around it. It re-sets the baseline of our awareness.[74]

In this sense, icons are interpreted by the EC in an overtly worshipful manner. EC leader Tony Jones continues this line of thought in comparing the purpose of an icon in prayer with the purpose of the Bible as a means through which God can speak to the worshipper, using an analogy that would strike a chord with any evangelical.[75] However, this practice is not lifted strictly from older traditions; rather, additional connotations are attached to it, reinterpreting the value and import of the practice for implementation. For example, Sweet, McLaren, and Haselmayer do not directly connect the use of icons to worship; instead, they view icons through the lens of postmodern recovery of symbol. According to these authors, the true value of an icon lies within its symbolic power, for "[s]ymbols are thick texts that mediate our understanding and experience of the world."[76] They also extend this symbolic sense of icon to shift the locus of meaning from mystic ascent to God to an outward communitarian look with the prescriptions, "Go outside to find icons: Look for Christ in the faces of the poor and needy; find the image of God in other people."[77] A similar progression from historical introduction to free reinterpretation is also noticeable in the practice of *lectio divina*.

Multiple literary sources written by EC leaders advocate *lectio divina*, or simply *lectio*, to one extent or another. In most texts which talk about *lectio*, a brief definition of the practice is offered in a similar spirit to the one provided by Michael Frost and Alan Hirsch: "*Lectio divina* is a traditional way of combining prayer and reading the Scriptures so that the Word of

---

74. Jones, *Sacred Way*, 98.
75. Ibid., 102. Cf., Whitesel, *Inside the Organic Church*, 23–24.
76. Haselmayer, McLaren, and Sweet, *A is for Abductive*, 151.
77. Ibid., 152.

God [Jesus Christ] may penetrate our hearts so that we may grow in an intimate relationship with the Lord."[78] Such a simple definition is often combined with an expressed purpose for implementation that focuses on the necessity to "overcome the distance between written text and dynamic Word,"[79] but there are hints in EC literature of different purposes. First, EC authors passionately personalize the practice of *lectio*.[80] Personalizing interpretations through *lectio* turn the focus of scripture passages decidedly inward, so that the participant is primarily concerned with his or her "inner self" and the benefits which God can offer to an individual through the practice.[81] Interestingly, EC writers couple with this personal focus a willingness and dedication to utilize *lectio* in the context of corporate worship, often in combination with music.[82] These literary observations offer practical possibilities for integration of *lectio*; however, the true malleability of this practice and its utility to the EC is as an open container for meaning as illustrated in the writings of Leonard Sweet. He moves in the space of three sentences from an introduction of *lectio* to relating its various steps as "the Christian's 'Om.'"[83] While the locus of meaning attached to *lectio* in the EC shifts back and forth from the personal to the communal and from the traditional to the eccentric, the use of liturgical prayer and the liturgical calendar has a more unifying communal purpose and implementation, according to EC literary discussion.

In a broad sense, the EC is implementing liturgy, or liturgical prayer, and the liturgical calendar in a way that is familiar to many Christian traditions, although not evangelical ones. Liturgy is connected to a specific, set form of public worship, often centered around the celebration of Holy Communion. While the EC stresses, in a particularly evangelical tone, that this public worship extends far beyond the bounds of corporate worship, they are decidedly considering liturgy only with respect to public, communal worship.[84] However, emergent churches feel free to experiment with what can be combined with liturgy in the context of public worship.[85] Similarly,

78. Frost and Hirsch, *ReJesus*, 148.
79. Ibid.
80. Jones, *Sacred Way*, 48.
81. Ibid., 53.
82. Whitesel, *Inside the Organic Church*, 113.
83. Sweet, *Cup of Coffee at the Soul Café*, 64.
84. Hunter, *Giving Church Another Chance*, 114. However, they often connect the meaning behind this liturgy to remaking Christian community and identity. Cf., Clark, "Renewal of Liturgy in the Emerging Church," 76.
85. Snider and Bowen, *Toward a Hopeful Future*, 197–266. Snider and Bowen include a lengthy appendix in which they propose an order of worship combining

use of the liturgical calendar is advocated by EC leaders, such as Brian McLaren, on the basis of the utility to mark the days and seasons in order "to tell our children the stories of our faith community's past so that this past will have a future, and so that our ancient way and its practices will be rediscovered and renewed every year."[86] Nevertheless, the EC also attaches to these typical liturgical understandings their own twist.

In a practical sense, it is quite noticeable that the EC is using liturgical prayer in an innovative way since they approach liturgy and the liturgical calendar with the same spirit of experimentation as other practices. Certain days and seasons are celebrated while others fade into the background. Liturgical prayers can vary from Sunday to Sunday, or they may even be originally composed by members of that particular emerging congregation. This engagement with liturgy coupled with a willingness to tweak liturgy is born out of an impulse toward participation, according to EC literature, and this participation is often presented in terms of creating a more embodied spirituality,[87] a concept which will be considered more fully in the next section on theological anchors. This internal EC drive is coupled with an external focus as well. Specifically, the EC seeks to utilize liturgy as a tool to communicate with their postmodern target audience which craves stories, and liturgy presents the story of Jesus "through symbolic enactment, allow[ing] the whole of the sensual self to close the space/time gap and know intimately that same moment of intent, betrayal and public display of selfless sacrifice and narrative coherence."[88] As a result, liturgical prayer for the EC, as for many other Christian traditions, has a decidedly corporate focus. A contrasting mystic practice which the EC also explores is the spiritual use of meditation.

In many EC sources, meditation varies in definition and utilization, which is not a surprise, since this mystic practice is employed in other Christian traditions with similar levels of variance. However, EC leader Tony Jones, in his work on mystic practices *The Sacred Way*, presents some concise distinctions concerning various historical types of meditation. With respect to discursive, or imaginative, meditation, Jones presents the guided and corporate nature of this practice by referring to its use by Ignatius of Loyola.[89] Jones also presents nondiscursive, or apophatic, meditation as an

---

lectionary readings from the Revised Common Lectionary with interactive prayer stations.

86. McLaren, *Finding Our Way Again*, 27–28.
87. Haselmayer, McLaren, and Sweet, *A is for Abductive*, 235.
88. Mann, *Atonement for a "Sinless" Society*, 150–51.
89. Jones, *Sacred Way*, 80–81.

individualistic process of emptying in which "no images or words are used, resulting in a total emptying."[90] While these distinctions are not unique to the EC, the ways in which each type of meditation is approached in EC literature indicate the experimental, embodied, and eclectic nuances which this conversation passes on to meditation.

When approaching group discursive meditation, Jones is quick to add that participants should be offered an opportunity to engage their senses whether through journaling, drawing, or some other form of *artistic* expression.[91] On the other hand, discussion of nondiscursive meditation allows for some interesting connections with the practice of centering prayer as well as Hindu and Buddhist mystic practices. This exploratory experimentation is vibrantly displayed through an off-hand comment by Tony Jones: "[I]t's linked with the recent popularity in the West of Eastern religions, resulting in books with such titles as *Christian Zen* and *Christian Yoga*. While this makes some Christians nervous, others revel in the fact that God is revealed in all truth, no matter the religion of origin."[92] The entrenched implication at this point is that the "nervous" Christians represent the evangelical seedbed from which the EC emerged, and the "reveling" Christians are those connected to emergent churches. This specific example illustrates the larger trend in EC spirituality not only to experiment but to experiment enthusiastically. Experimental and embodied impulses find an additional outlet in the EC use of the mystic practice of pilgrimage.

Notably less EC literary output is devoted to the practice of pilgrimage than to other mystic practices, but it is still enjoined as a practice for potential exploration and implementation by the EC, particularly with respect to the embodied nature of this practice. Definitionally, pilgrimage is connected both to a sense of "wandering and distance."[93] Affixed to this understanding of the practice as necessitating wandering and distance is an EC conversational engagement with the concept of sacred space—the idea that some locations are more blessed or holier than others. The tangibility of spirituality that is evoked by such a viewpoint is particularly attractive to EC proponents.[94] Additionally, EC literary discussion situates pilgrimage in connection to meditation. For instance, Jones reflects on such a connection:

> [While on a pilgrimage,] [w]ithout the benefit of a Discman or an mp3 player, there was little to do but talk to your copilgrims,

90. Ibid., 80.
91. Ibid., 83.
92. Ibid., 80.
93. Ibid., 151.
94. Ibid., 153.

think, or pray. This "peripatetic meditation" had a purifying effect on the pilgrim, and the pilgrims returned to their home villages changed. Not only could they tell stories of adventures and ornate cathedrals, they had been reflecting on the state of their lives for weeks on end.[95]

So, pilgrimage connects to the physicality of spirituality through the engagement of physical action, notably walking, and EC conversationalists also advocate personal investigation of the usefulness of prayer labyrinths on this basis.

In contrast to only passing EC mention of pilgrimage, many EC writers consider and support the use of mystic practice associated with walking labyrinths. According to leading EC author Michael Frost, "Labyrinths are an ancient Christian spiritual practice, and following the path into and out of the labyrinth becomes a walking meditation and a metaphor for our spiritual journey as individuals and within community."[96] These labyrinths hold great attraction for EC practitioners because they offer an active spiritual practice which engages the entire body in prayer.[97] While the EC seeks to engage the historical tradition of the labyrinth, they do not feel bound by conventional forms of the physical apparatus used in praying this way. In fact, EC authors note a particularly wide and creative range of permutations of labyrinths in EC personal and communal practice. For instance, many emergent churches have experimented with multimedia labyrinths which combine traditional elements with "ambient spaces filled with projected visual wallpaper, dance music, and chill-out zones."[98] While multimedia labyrinths illustrate the characteristic EC favoritism for eclectic and novel combinations of spiritual practice, their creativity extends to the point of composing labyrinths which one can print off of a website and "walk" with his/her fingers.[99]

In the midst of all of this creative ferment, Tony Jones succinctly explains the focus of labyrinths for the EC:

> We enter and follow a path, not knowing where it will take us, but knowing we will eventually arrive at the center. Sometimes the path leads inward toward the ultimate goal, only to lead back outwards again. We meet others along the path—some we meet face-to-face stepping aside to let them pass; some catch up to us

---

95. Ibid., 154.
96. Frost, *Exiles*, 297.
97. Jones, *Sacred Way*, 128.
98. Frost, *Exiles*, 297.
99. Jones, *Sacred Way*, 132.

from behind and pass us; others we pass along the way. At the center we rest, watch others, pray.[100]

Although theological anchors for reinterpretation of practices will be the subject of the next section, it is vitally significant to note what the EC participant does when he or she reaches the center of the labyrinth: rest, watch others, and pray. These activities offer an insight in microcosm into the purpose of mystic practices for the EC as a whole.[101] First, these practices are advocated as a means to help the busy, harried postmodern to slow down and rest, so he or she can focus before proceeding on to any further practice or purpose. Next, focus turns outward to the persons surrounding this individual in community, and it is this simple change in attention which manifests the EC social concern and how it permeates all of their practices, whether borrowed from the mystical tradition or not. Finally, the EC participant shifts viewpoint once again in the mystic practice to an experience of or a communing with God. This progression is quite notable as it flips the typical emphases of the mystical tradition in which communing with God is the chief aim and other emphases are regarded as an outflow of this primary emphasis. The practice of silence follows a similar progression of emphasis on self, others, and then the divine.

Silence is a difficult mystic practice to consider discretely, for it serves as a context for many other mystic practices both in the EC and other Christian traditions. EC literary output recognizes this difficulty, and, as a result, they praise its use but give little comment concerning practical implementation. In lieu of particular suggestions for practice, EC leaders often focus on purposive facets of silence. In connection with the progression noted above (self, others, the divine), the EC first considers silence through the lens of self. Tony Jones notes that this starting place is a necessity rather than a preferential position because "many of us avoid silence and solitude—because our self-identities are bound up in busy-ness."[102] Therefore, EC literary conversations about silence start by questioning the issue of action as the locus of identity. The perspective of the EC shines through in the next step of this progression, particularly through the question, "Where then will we find identity?"[103] Their reasoning then proceeds to turn outward to look at others after focusing on self, and then looking upward to God. This progression as noted in silence, labyrinths, and other practices is one which may be enacted by an

---

100. Ibid., 131.

101. Tony Jones also notes the extension of these foci to other mystic practices, such as his brief consideration of rosaries and Eastern Orthodox prayer ropes. Cf., Ibid., 65.

102. Ibid., 42.

103. Ibid.

individual EC participant, but participants can also engage with others in this process by utilizing the mystic practice of spiritual direction.

Emergent appropriation of spiritual direction offers a picture of how the EC tends to transform a historical mystic practice by its own emphases. First, there is a general, vague recognition of the antiquity of the practice. In the case of spiritual direction, EC conversationalists connect the practice with a disciple sitting at the feet of Jesus, or at least one of the desert fathers or mothers.[104] On the basis of this image, the unfamiliar pieces of the practice are then described. For instance, EC leader Tony Scandrette defines the task of a spiritual director as helping "a person to listen to the voice of God speaking through the events and circumstances of life, connecting the realities of Scripture to the particularities of daily life."[105] Then, the practice can be reinterpreted to appeal to present or potential EC participants. With spiritual direction, focus is placed on the spiritual directee as a "self-selected seeker" who desires a "personalized approach to spiritual formation."[106]

For the practice of spiritual direction, the hierarchical model that is prevalent in Roman Catholic and Eastern Orthodox Christianity is eschewed, and a new model is substituted that is more in keeping with postmodern tastes. In promotion of such a model, Tony Jones describes it in the following manner:

> [T]he spiritual director isn't necessarily older or more experienced than the directee. Instead, the director is seen primarily as a companion on the spiritual journey—one who is committed to taking time to listen to the spiritual goings-on of the directee. The underlying belief is that God communicates directly with us. Thus, the director is not an expert who speaks for God, but one who helps others notice God's communication with them.[107]

The resulting shape of spiritual direction is informed by the ancient practice, but it is freely reinterpreted for a postmodern context. Typically, this interpretation of a mystic practice within the EC is made without any reference to present-day utilization of this practice in other traditions. For example, present-day models of Roman Catholic or Eastern Orthodox spiritual direction are hardly consulted at all in the literary definition and development of the practice for the EC. Use of the final practice considered, the stations of the cross, follows this pattern as well.

---

104. Ibid., 110.
105. Scandrette, "Week in the Life of a Missional Community," 140.
106. Ibid.
107. Jones, *Sacred Way*, 112.

Emergent churches often interpret the stations of the cross very creatively. As an illustration, the stations may be utilized outside of their usual liturgical context of the celebration of Holy Week. Additionally, the form of multiple stations in the context of worship may be divorced from the specific content of the stations of the cross as part of a remembrance of the Crucifixion. Sociological researcher James Bielo notes such a situation in an emergent church where a monthly "Maproom" invited participants to walk and meditate upon various stations connected with the topical interest of that particular month.[108] Even when utilization of the stations of the cross is limited to the traditional fourteen stations, the meaning attached to this practice is interpreted primarily in a personal and communitarian sense rather than in a connection with the divine. Tony Jones highlights this emphasis by saying, "the beauty of the Stations [is] that the suffering of Jesus unites me with all others—past, present, and future—who have endeavored to follow him all the way to the Cross. And it also unites me with me, with every time I've made the Stations, when I've been flying high and when I've been in the depths of despair."[109] It is truly this matter of conceptual emphasis which marks EC implementation of mystic practices so strikingly. While EC adherents often appropriate mystic practices in innovative ways, the theological beliefs through which the EC reinterprets these practices display the greatest distinction.

Theological Anchors

As the previous sections have displayed that the EC is appropriating mystic practices without a significant concern for strict loyalty to their provenance, literary research also indicates the theological content with which EC conversationalists wish to imbue them. However, prior to description of theological content, consideration of the issue of *doing* theology is necessary. Specifically, how conscious are EC participants of engaging in a theological task? On the surface, EC authors such as Tony Jones assert: "What's really intriguing about emergent Christianity? The theology."[110] Should this assertion about the role of theology be taken at face value? Sociological observations reveal that much of the theology of the EC falls under the category of "epistemological critique" of evangelical theology.[111] In light of the culture of

---

108. Bielo, *Emerging Evangelicals*, 76. Cf., note 226 for additional description of this practice.

109. Jones, *Sacred Way*, 136.

110. Jones, *New Christians*, 96.

111. Bielo, *Emerging Evangelicals*, 10.

resistance within the EC, many participants may view themselves as reacting against particular theological views rather than engaging in theological formation of their own. However, literary and empirical research reveals that the EC is doing theology, but in a surprising way. As noted by Marti and Ganiel, EC participants "are expected to be involved in shaping and choosing congregational practices," and this process of shaping and choosing *is* the theological task as EC practitioners conceive it.[112] The insights of sociologists Flory and Miller clarify this relationship significantly:

> [T]heology matters to these churches, but not as a splitting of fine points of doctrine, or a continual chorus of "it's rational" or that "we need to be relevant," but in the sense that their beliefs —their theology—includes *doing* something about issues both local and global, such as poverty, AIDS, education, hunger, homelessness, and other similar problems.[113]

In other words, EC participants and authors see themselves as doing a practical type of theology in line with the vocation of "organic theologian" as one who "unlike the stuffy and authority-laden academic theologian . . . understands the importance and role of popular culture in the shaping of ideas and the communication of values."[114] So, for the EC, the theological task is primarily *active* rather than *reflective*, and the anchors[115] which they invested into their appropriation of mystic practices affirms this emphasis.

Trends reveal five major theological anchors invested into the practices and which work together as a conceptual framework to *allow* for appropriation and reinterpretation of the practices themselves.[116] The first, and most prominent, anchor for emergent churches' unique use of mystic practices is the concept of *community*. Another conceptual anchor for the appropriation of mystic practices by the EC is a common desire for applicability to the postmodern context through the value which they place on *relevance*. A third theological anchor for mystic appropriation is a noted characteristic of the EC as a whole. Many EC authors display

---

112. Marti and Ganiel, *The Deconstructed Church*, 29.

113. Flory and Miller, *Finding Faith*, 183.

114. Ibid., 190.

115. It is helpful to remember at this point, as first said on page 2, that the term *anchor* was discovered in the course of empirical research as preferred substitute for more traditional language, such as *doctrine* or *belief*. So, it also affirms an active perspective.

116. While theological analysis is primary in this book, the delineation of this conceptual framework could also be likened to the socio-analytic practice of grounded theory in which categories arise naturally through the course of research. In a socio-analytic context, grounded theory is an alternative to assigning data to preexisting categories developed by the researcher prior to examination of gathered data.

a significant preference for questioning previous categories and systems, and they are not necessarily looking for answers; rather, they are vitally interested in stressing the necessity and beauty of *mystery*. Additionally, the EC roots their appropriation of mystic practices in a desire to combine *contemplation with action*, particularly social action, stressing a parallel active pathway to complement the contemplative pathway presented by the mystical tradition. A final theological anchor for these churches is a focus on *embodied spirituality*, or the physicality of spirituality, which allows EC participants to express an outward bodily aspect in spiritual practices in order to connect with their overall concept of community. Ensuing investigation of each of these stated anchors will reveal how the EC adapts mystic practices to their own theology.

Community

Even a cursory examination of literary sources reveals that the EC places a high value on community. An in-depth examination of EC literature, however, reveals that community is the primary focus of the EC in general. Many EC authors seek to extend this communal focus to be central for the appropriation of mystic practices as well. It is within the context of community and relationships among individuals that the EC understands God. To illustrate, EC leader Tony Jones considers the process of appropriation within the EC in terms of the Eastern Orthodox theological concept of *perichoresis*, or interrelationship of all members of the Trinity with each other, and it is through this lens that "emergent Christians are convinced of the priority of relationship for understanding [themselves]."[117] Within this framework, questions of faith and practice are chiefly considered in relation to other persons in community rather than in relation to God or propositional teachings about God.[118] While there is a distinct theological connection at this point, the EC is also quick to note the postmodern influence in their stress on community, for "emergent Christians consider the individualism of the modern era a blight that eventually led to holocausts and pogroms."[119] As a result, this twin influence of relationship and postmodernism undergirds the EC emphasis on community. This divided focus is particularly notable, for it pulls the EC away from exact alignment with postmodern thought on spirituality, which is still functionally individualist, as it stresses the elasticity

---

117. Jones, *New Christians*, 166.

118. Burke, "Emerging Church and Incarnational Theology," 47. Cf., Nash, *An 8-Track Church in a CD World*, 120–21.

119. Ibid.

of spirituality to adapt to an individual's needs and desires, as observed by sociologist Kieran Flanagan.[120] Essentially then, the EC focus on community can be delineated as a simple progression of linked assumptions. Brian McLaren articulates this progression clearly by stating, "I'm assuming that this whole thing is not all about me. I'm assuming that the community of faith doesn't exist for me. I'm assuming that my own contemplative practices aren't ultimately about me. I'm assuming that maturity as a spiritual human being isn't complete unless it sends me out of myself into the faith community."[121] Therefore, it is apparent that EC literary sources emphasize the importance of community in EC theology, and this stress is also displayed in the implementation of specific mystic practices.

EC appropriation of mystic practices includes significant literary comment on and recommendation of practices which flourish in a community context. This emphasis is even apparent in the application of particular practices that would typically seem to be individualistic or those not solely arising from the mystical tradition. For instance, at Solomon's Porch, a prominent emergent church, hospitality is an intentional practice for the entire community, and the meaning connected to this practice is quite explicitly spiritual, for, in their own words, "[t]he real point of this brand of hospitality is the spiritual formation that takes place when we share the rhythm of regular life with one another."[122] In other words, the simple act of including others in daily tasks which typically occur privately within postmodern culture is viewed by the EC as a spiritual act. EC emphasis on community also leads them to employ mystic practices which would have been specifically taboo within their previous evangelical context. A notable literary example of this assimilation and application is in EC experimentation with the *Spiritual Exercises* of St. Ignatius of Loyola, which require a community context for practice.[123] An even more central literary example is present in EC appropriation of liturgical prayer and use of the liturgical calendar, for EC writers explicitly link implementation of liturgy to the literal meaning of *liturgy* as "the work of the people."[124] Engagement with liturgy also connects to the rhythm emphasis mentioned above in connection to hospitality. Additionally, EC authors are making specific communitarian connections in the liturgy surrounding Holy Communion in which, in their own words, "we [EC participants] are reminded of the reality that

120. Flanagan, "Visual Spirituality," 231–32.
121. McLaren, *Finding Our Way Again*, 114.
122. Kenney, "Mark 3," 50.
123. Jones, *Sacred Way*, 91.
124. McLaren, *Finding Our Way Again*, 101.

ideal intent must be acted out in the realm of the physical, for the body is the link between the self and *the public world*."[125] In these ways, EC leaders adapt various mystic practices to a stated theology which is focused on community, and this pattern of adaptation to EC theological anchors continues in how EC literature privileges the issue of relevance over tradition with concern to mystic practices.

Relevance over Tradition

One of the larger theological areas of EC literary conversation is the subject of relevance, and EC writers hold the appropriation of mystic practices in *tension* between this anchor of relevance and the mystical tradition from which the practices originate. To begin to illustrate this tension, it is necessary to encapsulate what EC writers mean by the value of relevance. Such an example is readily available through an anecdote provided by leading EC writer Doug Pagitt:

> Until Shelley's [Pagitt's wife] illness came along, I had never been one to question my doctors. I went in when something was wrong with my body, they told me what to do about it, and I got better. It wasn't a formula that needed changing. Until, of course, it did. In our pursuit of answers about Shelley's health, we found ourselves asking new questions, questions the members of the established medical community didn't answer. It wasn't that they couldn't or wouldn't tell us what was going on. The problem was that the whole mentality of Western medicine is based on a set of assumptions and expectations and ideas that take the conversation about health care in a certain direction. We wanted to have a *different* conversation, one that involved a different set of assumptions and expectations and ideas than the illness management conversation. Expressing our interest in more integrated, holistic options was like speaking a foreign language. The fact that our conversation diverged from that of our regular doctors wasn't their fault. It wasn't our fault. It wasn't anyone's fault any more than it's my fault that I speak English and my friends in Guatemala speak Spanish. The issue wasn't that the doctors were just being old-fashioned or close-minded. It's that we began asking questions they simply weren't equipped

---

125. Mann, *Atonement for a "Sinless" Society*, 151. Emphasis added. Cf., Pagitt, *Community in the Inventive Age*, 68–70.

to answer. But the more we dug into natural health alternatives, the more we felt like we'd arrived at the motherland.[126]

This story exemplifies a larger theological approach that is common among EC participants. Specifically, in matters of spirituality, as well as health, EC proponents feel the necessity for a new conversation which is different from previous spiritual conversations to such an extent that there is no touchstone with their previous ways of talking theologically (i.e., evangelical theology). As a result, emergent churches strive to see things in a new way and try new practices with little focus other than experimentation and the desire for relevance of these new ways to their conversation. In this way, relevance drives their selection and assimilation process in regard to specific mystic practices and spirituality in general.

In the context of relevance, EC participants draw from their own experiences and other traditions in order to provide an aggregate of practices which suit their needs. From the side of their own experiences, EC writers often note a type of "deconversion narrative," so-termed in sociological language, in which their former evangelical tradition became stifling.[127] While this observation is notable, it is important also to point out that this deconversion does not result in complete disbelief in Christianity but in a lateral move to another Christian tradition. However, this common experience does not end at the point of switching denominational allegiances; rather, it may continue through multiple changes to the point of a different type of conversion "to a different way of holding traditions in general."[128] While this process affects an EC participant's entire theological outlook, particularly with respect to his/her spirituality, it has the specific effect of creating a new vantage point to view potential spiritual practices. Brian McLaren refers to this new primacy of the utility of practices over their tradition of origination as "open source spirituality," which he defines as the progression of events in which "[o]ld sectarian turf wars are giving way to a sharing of resources—heroes, practices, flavors, and styles of practice. And this, in a way, is itself a new practice, namely, the sharing of previously proprietary practices."[129] This realization on the part of McLaren is the crux of how the EC literary conversationalists ground the borrowing of mystic practices. On this basis, EC Christians feel free to appropriate practices that even seem to be deeply tied to a specific Christian tradition, such as the use of icons, the Jesus Prayer, the rosary, the sign of the cross, and the stations of the cross. In short, these practices are

126. Pagitt, *Christianity Worth Believing*, 70–71.
127. Bielo, *Emerging Evangelicals*, 81. Cf., McLaren, *Finding Our Way Again*, 58.
128. McLaren, *Finding Our Way Again*, 58.
129. Ibid.

epistemologically grounded for the EC not in the original tradition of each practice but in the new perspective developed by the EC of sharing practices based on relevance and pragmatic usefulness.

The anchor of relevance affects all EC theological borrowing, but it is particularly essential for emergent churches to lift a particular mystical practice out of its original context. While this anchor was not considered to be the central anchor by EC writers, it was definitely an essential theological piece for their process of spiritual borrowing. This matter of relevance *allows* for EC appropriation, and the quality of relevance is invested theologically into the process of appropriation to guide reinterpretation and adaptation for use in a postmodern context. While this anchor explains how and why the EC appropriates mystic practices, it does not fully explain why they experiment with them with such great alacrity. For an anchor that approaches appropriation from this angle, an investigation of the role of mystery in EC literary output is necessary.

Mystery

EC dealings with mystery as a theological anchor illustrate just how deeply the appellation of *conversation* is indicative of emergent churches. Essentially, the value of mystery for the EC is based on the value of questioning. This line of questioning roots itself in an observation articulated by many EC leaders, but most succinctly by Spencer Burke and Barry Taylor in saying, "Still, in spite of our best efforts, there are always things that arise outside the system—realities of life that don't fit neatly into the religious boxes we have made."[130] Burke and Taylor raise the issue that mystery is a feature of life no matter how detailed one's theology may be, and EC conversationalists pick up and extend this observation from an inevitable reality to a celebrated outcome of Christian faith. Rob Bell, another prominent EC figure, exemplifies this progression by noting that "[t]rue mystery, the kind of mystery rooted in the infinite nature of God, gives us answers that actually plunge us into even more . . . questions."[131] With such a high value placed on questioning within the EC conversation, the theological anchor of mystery spreads to every aspect of EC life including spirituality.[132] This progression explains the theological value which EC participants place on mystery; however, it does not adequately explain how mystery connects to the appropriation of mystic practices. For this further part of the conversa-

130. Burke and Taylor, *Heretic's Guide to Eternity*, 28.
131. Bell, *Velvet Elvis*, 32.
132. Sweet, *Learn to Dance the Soul Salsa*, 107.

tion, it is necessary to reflect on how a high value on mystery works out practically in EC thought and practice.

On a practical level, EC conversationalists value mystery by embracing paradox within their lives. Leonard Sweet approaches such an embrace with a neologism. Specifically, Sweet encourages EC adherents to think of themselves as *mysterians*, which he defines as one who "believes in the paradox that the more we know about life, the more we know we don't know."[133] As a result, incongruities, even those with respect to theological belief and spiritual practice, are not to be feared; rather, they are to be welcomed.[134] Emergent churches and those individuals who find them inviting actively seek out mystery by juxtaposition and contradiction often without any rhyme or reason undergirding the resulting aggregate of beliefs and practices. Leonard Sweet, Brian McLaren, and Jerry Haselmayer note this quality pithily in a series of statements attributed to EC leader Tony Brigstock: "I'm a total mystic and a total rationalist. I'm a complete truth nut yet embrace confusion. I'm radical but totally balanced. I'm humbly human and boldly spiritual. I'm a Jesus person but hate Christianity."[135] It is in this spirit of *proud*, not apologetic, theological paradox that EC leaders advocate appropriation and reinterpretation of mystic practices. Simply put, EC participants are encouraged to revel in the new-found freedom of juxtaposing disparate practices without any necessity to be historically faithful to a particular tradition. However, this celebration of paradox does not mean that EC writers see no points of contact between their value of mystery and the value of mystery for the mystical tradition.

While EC conversationalists anchor their spiritual eclecticism in a theology of mystery, they glimpse potential points of contact with apophaticism in the mystical tradition. Emphasis on this possible connection illustrates that EC writers are indeed engaging with historical mystical sources on some level, even if the EC conversation is by no means bound to these sources. To be precise, EC authors tend to view apophatic elements of the mystical tradition in a general sense of developing the theological insight that "God is found profoundly in the darkness." They then relate their own interpretations and connections only to this general theological reflection. Most notably, EC leaders equate mystical apophaticism to postmodern deconstructionism since both of these areas raise the issue of the limits of human ability to know. It is in this unstable area of the unknown that emergent churches joyfully locate the anchor of mystery and embrace

---

133. Ibid., 67.
134. Jones, *New Christians*, 168. Cf., Rollins, *How (Not) to Speak of God*, 34–35.
135. Haselmayer, McLaren, and Sweet, *A is for Abductive*, 101.

mystic practices as ways of meeting God in the darkness. As part of this perspective, EC literary discussion finds a place for mystic practices like contemplative prayer, meditation, practicing the presence of God, silence, and solitude that center on the inability of the human to comprehend God fully. While many mystic practices find a theological home in the concept of mystery for the EC, a tension arises from the reflective, contemplative nature of many of these practices in opposition to the high value placed on action by many EC conversationalists.

Contemplation with Action

The theological anchor of contemplation with action is the way the EC understands the necessity to incorporate both "active" and "passive" practices. This integration of contemplative and active practices is first glimpsed in EC literary output in their strong rejection of the separation of contemplation and action which they claim is a notable feature of evangelical spirituality.[136] Integration of practices becomes more noticeable when EC writers stress an active way to complement the contemplative practices which they borrow from the mystical tradition. This active way is the subject of much comment within the EC conversation because it does not map exactly to the mystical tradition's designation of *active*. Tony Jones argues that "practices in which you engage your body, whether it be by depriving it of food (e.g., fasting) or walking (e.g., Stations of the Cross)" simply aren't active enough for the EC.[137] While these active practices from the mystical tradition are not discouraged, the EC connotation of action also involves strong encouragement of social action. For instance, Brian McLaren lists spiritually active practices such as "showing hospitality to strangers—or 'the other' . . . associating with the lowly . . . practicing neighborliness, including toward enemies . . . preferring the poor rather than showing favoritism to the rich."[138] As a result of this active focus, many seemingly individualistic mystic practices are implemented in emergent churches for expressed social reasons. For instance, confession, fixed-hour prayer, pilgrimage, and prayer labyrinths are appropriated with strong social justice interpretations. Additionally, the EC includes involvement in a spiritual community as an essential part of the relationship be-

---

136. Hunter, *Giving Church Another Chance*, 116.

137. Jones, *Sacred Way*, 20.

138. McLaren, *Finding Our Way Again*, 119. Cf., Wilson-Hartgrove, "Mark 12," 164–65. Please note that Wilson-Hartgrove primarily considers this impulse as it affects neo-monasticism rather than the EC, but it applies to the broader EC movement as well.

tween contemplation and action. Indeed, this aspect is almost a third way connecting contemplation with action, for, as McLaren points out, "the way of community is about the inward journey, not the journey into *me* but the journey into *we*."[139] Therefore, the anchor of contemplation and action allows for *amalgamation* of mystic practices into the *aggregate* spirituality of the EC, yet this assimilation is not a smooth, easy process.

Within EC literary output, the theological anchor of contemplation and action is often coupled with the injunction for balance. This necessity for balance is not unique to the EC; rather, it is a common trait in the utilization of mystic practices.[140] Interestingly, this balancing issue is one of the few common characteristics between mystic practices utilized in the mystical tradition and these practices as implemented in the EC. Participants are urged to find a tenuous balance between contemplation and action through what Burke and Taylor term "mystical responsibility," which shifts the theological focus from adhering to specific beliefs, as is stressed in evangelicalism, to "*living* in faith."[141] With this new emphasis, EC authors urge the reinterpretation of mystic practices according to a sense of responsibility which "seeks to recover all of life for God."[142] Exactly how a sense of mystical responsibility accomplishes this task may be difficult to understand when considered solely on an abstract level; therefore, an anecdotal example is useful. EC leader Tony Jones relates the following story of how a mystic practice urged an EC participant, Frank, toward acceptance of those who are on the margins of society:

> Later, at the bar, I asked Frank about this. He said that he'd been meditating on that passage just a few days before, engaging in an ancient Benedictine practice called *lectio divina*, or "holy reading." Considering how he'd been on the receiving end of a few excommunications himself, the passage had a special poignancy. As he prayed, he thought about the "publican and the heathen," harking back to the King James language of his youth. The final line of that passage in the King James reads, "If he neglect to hear the church, let him be unto thee as a heathen man and a publican." The ban on publicans and heathens meted out by the Pharisees, Frank thought, but Jesus did just the opposite:

---

139. Ibid., 99–100. This focus on community can often lead to unexpected ways in which a mystic practice may be employed for the good of the community. For instance, art is often a focal point of mystic practices in emergent churches. Cf., Whitesel, *Inside the Organic Church*, 62.

140. Ibid., 72–73.

141. Burke and Taylor, *Heretic's Guide to Eternity*, 216.

142. Ibid., 212.

he opened up the kingdom to those who were shunned. Jesus was turning the Pharisees' own practice of shunning publicans and heathens on its head![143]

This anecdote demonstrates how an EC adherent employs a mystic practice in order to obtain a socially active result. So, the anchor of mystery *allows* for the appropriation of mystic practices, the anchor of contemplation with action *integrates* mystic practices to other EC spiritual practices, especially practices connected to social action, and the final anchor to be considered, the anchor of embodied spirituality, illustrates how the appropriation and reinterpretation of mystic practices *fits* into the overall framework of EC spirituality.

Embodied Spirituality

The greatest theological anchor for appropriation and reinterpretation of mystic practices by the EC literary conversation is the desire for an *embodied spirituality*. To begin, it is important to note the provenance of this term. Sociologists Richard Flory and Donald Miller coined this term specifically to describe EC spirituality in the following way:

> The radical thing to us was that they [EC conversationalists] could make that switch given the different conceptions of theology, including such strange—at least to Protestants—practices of venerating the saints, praying to Mary, or kissing the garments of the priest. When we started asking questions of these young adults, we found that they were much more interested in what we have come to call the "embodied spirituality" inherent in these traditions, where, as one person told us, participating in the different elements of the liturgy is like "being in the orchestra instead of watching a performance."[144]

However, the EC has attached two understandings to this term which follow two distinct paths.[145] It is notable that mystic practices find a place of utilization and location in both paths. The first path for embodied spirituality in the EC takes the qualifier *embodied* in a literal sense. In other words, EC writers take the human body into account in their spirituality. They see the human body through a holistic sensibility viewing each human being

---

143. Jones, *New Christians*, 91.

144. Flory and Miller, *Finding Faith*, vii.

145. Nevertheless, community is the most important anchor for an *overall* EC spirituality, according to the literature.

as "an interconnected whole" of mind, body, and spirit.[146] A holistic view of the body within EC spirituality attracts the postmodern individual who comes from an emerging postmodern culture which is "body fixated."[147] As a result of this holistic perspective, emergent churches employ mystic practices which engage the senses as a means of communicating the value of the Christian message to the postmodern individual. Communicating through the senses uses the language with which the EC is most familiar, the language of experience. These individuals find engagement with God through bodily actions such as prayer in particular postures, making the sign of the cross, walking the stations of the cross, praying with icons, and fasting.[148] For these postmodern individuals, including EC participants as well as those they seek to convert, embodied action provides engagement of creativity and energy where matters of theological argument and assent to certain beliefs only provides boredom. Therefore, a literal sense of *embodied* spirituality does open a specific niche for mystic practices within the EC, yet the second path of interpretation of embodied spirituality provides a place for mystic practices that might be even more central to EC spirituality.

For the EC, an embodied spirituality is also a spirituality that is not bound to traditional religious margins. EC authors stress that participants not retreat from an ever more secular world; rather, they emphasize the necessity of responding to secularity positively by seeking out secular spaces and actively sacralizing them.[149] In other words, EC conversationalists write about claiming ordinary actions and objects as potential opportunities for spirituality concentrated on the present world, rather than on an after-life, along with more intentional forms of social action and social justice. This tendency has also been noted by sociological researchers, such as James Bielo, in that emergent churches actively reject "distinctions between the public and private, sacred and profane."[150] As part of this sacralizing impulse, EC participants can theologically locate their spirituality in many actions,

---

146. Pagitt, *Christianity Worth Believing*, 74.

147. Haselmayer, McLaren, and Sweet, *A is for Abductive*, 47.

148. Jones, *Sacred Way*, 163, 170, 174. Cf., Haselmayer, McLaren, and Sweet, *A is for Abductive*, 47. It is important to note that these practices may be principally located within an individual's body, but the EC still views the impact of the practices in communal terms. For instance, fasting is connected to the observance of the liturgical calendar by EC proponents. Cf., Clark, "Renewal of Liturgy in the Emerging Church," 82.

149. Sweet, *Learn to Dance the Soul Salsa*, 19. Cf., Jenkins, "Postmodern Evangelicalism," 187. Jenkins provides an acknowledgment of the need for such engagement from an evangelical perspective, displaying that this type of engagement is not necessarily representative of an EC rejection of evangelicalism.

150. Bielo, *Emerging Evangelicals*, 95. Cf., Bell, *Love Wins*, 32–35. Bell provides a perspective of this development from an EC proponent standpoint.

ordinary and ritualistic, including practices that are pulled from other religious traditions or no religious tradition at all. With respect to individual mystic practices, this process is often connected to EC literary discussions of practicing the presence of God contextually and then, through practicing the presence of God, to all other practices. Engagement with social action issues also falls under the expansive umbrella of embodied spirituality.[151] This trend would seem to inform against the incorporation of mystic practices on the basis that they seem to be even more removed from "ordinary" life than most religious practices, but EC writers assert that these practices find an entirely new niche within this form of embodied spirituality.

Mystic practices are anchored in EC theology through both perspectives of total embodiment. Todd Hunter demonstrates this perspective by relating his attitudinal focus when experiencing corporate worship, "So when sitting quietly in a sanctuary, thinking and praying while beautiful music plays, I know I have only ascended the diving board. Once the benediction has been pronounced, I walk out the door ready to splash into the realities of life."[152] From this vantage point, Hunter is grounding spiritual practices in an embodied spirituality that is primarily concerned with present, everyday life. Mystic practices are particularly shifted in their purpose and goal through the application of this perspective. Within the mystical tradition, these practices are part of a total life focused on the ascent of the soul to God, so they retain a framework of *preparation* for life after death, and they are useful for everyday living in a secondary way. In the purview of the EC, these purposes are flipped so that preparation for everyday life becomes the primary aim of each practice. EC authors, such as Doug Pagitt, offer examples of this shift of focus through particular practices. For instance, with respect to the purpose of *lectio divina*, Pagitt proclaims, "The living Bible invites us to step into the stories, not as observers, but as participants in the faith that is alive and well and *still being created*."[153] Therefore, the EC anchor of embodied spirituality is a focus on a continually growing spirituality that is changing and developing by the moment, and, in this new theological framework, it is quite clear to see not only how the EC appropriates mystical practices but also how they experiment with them so freely.

---

151. Gibbs, *Churchmorph*, 50.

152. Hunter, *Giving Church Another Chance*, 68.

153. Pagitt, *Christianity Worth Believing*, 67. Emphasis added. Cf., Hunter, *Giving Church Another Chance*, 96; Bielo, *Emerging Evangelicals*, 82. Bielo presents a sociological perspective of how this type of *lectio divina* is practiced by an entire group of EC participants.

Summary of Chapter

In retrospect, it appears that all of this information only serves to draw to a fairly obvious point, which EC leaders note themselves—the EC shifts the purpose of mystic practices away from the aim of making one "more religious" to making one "more alive."[154] However, it was necessary to proceed through the foregoing discussion because it can be quite difficult to understand exactly what EC writers intend by such a nebulous phrase as "more alive." In light of this difficulty, exact definitions given by EC authors for the terms *spirituality, mysticism,* and *mystical tradition* provided a solid basis for further discussion. Moving on from semantic issues, a historical note added important depth concerning the rise of interest in mystic practices first among evangelicals and then as inherited unevenly by their EC offspring on the basis of personal curiosity. Issues of initial interest in mystic practices connected to a specific consideration of the practices themselves through EC authors' emphasis on eclecticism in spirituality and the primacy of mystical experiences. Lengthy comment on issues of motivation leading to interest proceeded to a particular discussion on the appropriation of specific mystic practices, as noted in EC literary conversations.

The EC is experimenting with mystic practices from all corners of the Christian faith often with absolute freedom to interpret and combine practices, investing them with novel concepts in seemingly no discernible theological or sociological pattern; however, five theological anchors provide a pattern for appropriation and reinterpretation of mystic practices into EC spirituality. First, an emphasis on community and participating in community *disconnects* EC spirituality from the highly personalized and individualized spiritual practices of evangelicalism. As a result, emergent churches are often seeking to fill this void in regard to spiritual practice. In their search, EC literary proponents are aided by a second anchor, the primacy of relevance over tradition. In other words, emergent churches and the individuals they support feel quite free to *borrow* aspects from any tradition as these elements may be relevant to their own needs. This particular anchor echoes the pragmatic impulse noted at the outset of this chapter. Third, as the EC begins to *combine* practices and ideas gleaned from disparate areas, the theological anchor of mystery allows them to create an aggregate spirituality that is not bound by a highly specified system of doctrine. This high value on mystery allows for EC writers and participants to coexist comfortably with paradox and contradiction among issues of belief and practice.

---

154. McLaren, *Finding Our Way Again*, 182. These terms also fit with the pragmatic purpose as described by McLaren at the outset of the chapter as "help[ing] us become someone weighty." McLaren, *Finding Our Way Again*, 14.

Fourth, through this new aggregate spirituality, EC authors *reinterpret* the contemplative attitude created by mystic practices by constant injunctions to combine contemplation with action, bodily and socially. Finally, the EC conversation theologically *fits* the subject of borrowed mystic practices within their larger aggregate spirituality which they refer to as an embodied spirituality. Embodied spirituality may be interpreted by EC authors as a holistic spirituality that includes the body along with mind and spirit or as a spirituality which supports a continuing creative, life-giving impulse shaping and creating new theology in the ordinary activities of everyday life as well as overt social action. In both understandings, mystic practices find utility and a specific niche. So, the aforementioned theological anchors work together to move the EC from the social context of evangelicalism to a new sociotheological niche in which mystic practices are permissible spiritual options. These anchors work together progressively to *disconnect* the EC from the strictures of evangelical spirituality, to *borrow* spiritual practices from other traditions, to *combine* practices in new, eclectic configurations, to *reinterpret* any theological baggage of borrowed practices, and to *fit* these practices in the total embodiment of their own spirituality.

Therefore, as scrutinized in EC literature, appropriation of mystic practices makes perfect sense along with the freedom to reinterpret them, combine them with paradoxical practices, and invest them with new meaning. However, it still remains to be seen whether this abstract and sophisticated process is precisely enacted within local expressions of the EC, and it is in line with this issue that comment will turn to empirical research. Empirical research will begin in chapter four with an explanation of research methodology and introduction to case study churches, continue in chapter five with a detailed report of findings and in chapter six with an analysis of empirical findings in comparison to the theological anchors introduced here. Finally, literary and empirical findings will be evaluated in conjunction with each other within the final chapter of the book, leading to the conclusions, contributions, and recommendations of the study.

4

Empirical Methodology

THE COMPLEX PROCESS OF EC spiritual borrowing observed in EC literature raises the issue of verification. In order to deal with this question, particularly in light of the EC as a *current* conversation, empirical methods of research can be combined with literary modes of examination to tender a more complete picture of EC spiritual borrowing of mystic practices. While the structure of the third chapter was determined by the progression of semantic, historical, and theological interest on the part of EC mystic practices, issues of empirical study can be delineated in a simpler progression. Specifically, empirical methodology can be amply illustrated by answering the questions of *what*, *why*, and *who*. With regard to *what*, the first section of this chapter will consider structure of the methodology employed for the empirical study. To this end, the epistemology of method in qualitative research will be briefly outlined along with its implementation through case studies. Within these case studies, data has been collected through the research instruments of phenomenological interviews and ethnographic participant observation. Basic introduction to these methods will form the foundation for looking at how empirical research was conducted within this particular study prior to answering the more focused question of *why*.

The question of *why* in more familiar terms is the consideration of the *rationale* for empirical research as utilized in this study. In other words, justification will be offered concerning the reasons for choosing qualitative methods over quantitative ones as well as explanation concerning the suitability and implementation of case studies, utilizing interviews as the primary data collection instrument. Also, rationalization will be provided concerning weighting a phenomenological approach over an ethnographic one while still including multiple methods within the empirical portion of the study. Consequently, consideration of methodology (*what*) and rationale (*why*) will present the necessary background for analysis and interpretation of empirical data of individual mystic practices in specific emergent churches as delineated in the proceeding chapters. Profiles of each case study church will round out this chapter to answer descriptively the question of *who*.

Explanation of Empirical Methodology

The first step in explicating the specific blend of methodologies implemented within this study is to describe generally the various pieces and instruments of empirical research. In light of this purpose a brief description of empirical research is necessary with central focus on its qualitative form. Following this general depiction of empirical research, more specific explanations of case study design and the various instruments employed will be presented. Notably, surveys, phenomenological interviews, and limited ethnography through participant observation were utilized within the overall framework of three case studies within the empirical research component of this study. These descriptions of data gathering tools will be followed by a short introduction to grounded theory as the mode of analysis for the study. Comments in this section will focus on each methodological component in its *general definition*, and specific application to the present study will be fully considered within the following rationale.

Empirical Research: Qualitative and Quantitative

For an explanation of the empirical methodology employed in this study, it is best to begin briefly with a consideration of empirical research as a branch of knowledge-gathering, focusing on its qualitative and quantitative forms. In its simplest form, empirical research is predicated on the active process of a researcher who "would go into the field and collect 'data': comments, observations, answers to questionnaires, interviews, tapes of rituals or whatever. This data was then brought home to the university and analysed as 'facts.'"[1] It is this foundational process that characterizes empirical research in both qualitative and quantitative forms. These types of empirical research begin to distinguish themselves on the basis of the kind of "data" which they retrieve. Succinctly stated, "Qualitative data deals with meanings, whereas quantitative data deals with numbers."[2] The difference in data gathered extends to a difference in conceptual logic with regard to analyzing that data. Specifically, quantitative data lends itself to deductive reasoning in which a researcher

---

1. Stringer, *On the Perception of Worship*, 86.
2. Dey, *Qualitative Data Analysis*, 3.

begins with a hypothesis then either proves or disproves it on the basis of the specific data collected. Qualitative research and analysis approaches data from an inductive perspective, allowing inferences to rise out of many detailed observations.[3] As a result of this difference in data collecting and analyzing procedures, different types of interpretations arise.

Qualitative research is the empirical methodological framework chosen for this study on the basis of its process of analysis, intended goal, and applicability to the case study model. First, qualitative research encourages the development of categories *from* examination of data collected rather than developing categories *prior to* examination of collected data. As a consequence, analysis of data results in very specific interpretation that is bound to its unique context.[4] While the bounded nature of such interpretation might seem to be a detriment to this type of research, it can actually function as a unique strength, depending on the overall goal of the researcher. Qualitative methods of research are not intended to return a conclusion that is demonstrable, repeatable, and generalizable; rather, their aim is to produce "thick description" for the purpose of allowing outsiders to comprehend a "culture from the inside in the terms that the participants themselves [use] to describe what is going on."[5] Therefore, qualitative research focuses on describing a particular group with the purpose of *understanding meanings* within that group not *reproducing results* from that group. In this overall qualitative framework, specific methodologies are well-suited to gather the type of data that is most applicable for this purpose. Notably, the case study model provides the essential boundaries through which thick description can be realistically produced of a specific subject. However, in addition to the goal of thick description, the case study model itself requires more in-depth discussion.

Case Study

While the term *case study* might be a familiar one, some definitional and clarifying comments are still useful for full explanation of the methodology for this study. One of the most basic forms of qualitative research is the case study, and this methodology has the benefit of wide usage in multiple scholarly disciplines. Therefore, it is broadly understandable in design, but, to specify for the research project presented here, a case study is the prolonged observation of "a single entity, a unit around which there are boundaries. The

---

3. Leedy and Ormrod, *Practical Research*, 102–3.
4. Ibid., 102.
5. Robson, *Real World Research*, 186.

case then has a finite quality about it in either terms of time (the evolution or history of a particular program), space (the case is located in a particular place), and/or components comprising the case (number of participants, for example)."[6] It is important to note that a case study is distinguished from an ethnography on the basis of its scope. While an ethnography looks at an entire group or culture, a case study concentrates on a single permutation of a culture/group, such as a specific person, program, or sub-community.[7] As a result, case study design focuses on the selection of a "bounded system" as the subject for study.[8]

Case study design is characterized by the bounded nature of the research subject and by the types of questions which can be answered through this methodology. For the purpose of this research, an individual EC is the appropriate "bounded system" for an in-depth case study. However, three emergent churches from different urban areas of the USA provide the context for the case study portion of the research for the purpose of investigating cross-case theological anchors which different emergent churches share. These specificities will be more fully explicated within the proceeding rationale section of this chapter and in the practical details of implementation of research method described in chapter five. Case studies are also distinctive on the basis of the type of questions which are answered through this methodology. Case studies answer descriptive questions by providing a "thick" description of a naturally occurring event or series of events.[9] However, they are not limited to a descriptive purpose. They can also provide answers to "discovery-oriented questions" which "are similar to descriptive questions but go one step further—they attempt to discover generalizable principles or models."[10] In other words, case studies lend themselves to theorizing on the basis of the data collected and analyzed; however, they remain firmly on the descriptive, qualitative side of empirical research because resulting theories are only applicable in so much as different cases resemble the case studied. Case studies are also valuable through the range of data collection instruments that are applicable in this context including surveys, interviews, and participant observation.

---

6. Merriam, "Case Study," 178.
7. Leedy and Ormrod, *Practical Research*, 151.
8. Merriam, "Case Study," 179.
9. Dey, *Qualitative Data Analysis*, 31.
10. Moon and Trepper, "Case Study Research," 402.

Data Collection Instruments

The present study utilized three principal methods for data collection: surveys/questionnaires, phenomenological interviews, and participant observation. Each of these methods requires brief definition in order to comprehend its general applicability for gathering data in a qualitative case study context. While other data collection instruments also lend themselves to case study design, the reasons that these tools were chosen will be fully explicated in the rationale section below. At this juncture, primary emphasis is laid simply on defining and describing each of these methods in a general sense. However, even at the outset, it should be noted that these instruments were not employed equally within the study; instead, phenomenological interviews were the primary data collection instrument. Surveys chiefly served the purpose of assisting in selection of interview participants and lending some structure to the resulting interview. Participant observation provided additional background to buttress insights provided through the interviews themselves. Nonetheless, the relative utility of each data collection instrument for the study rests on its basic structure; therefore, the instruments of questionnaires, phenomenological interviews, and participant observation each require some description before proceeding to any discussion of rationale for empirical methodology as a whole.

While questionnaires or surveys are typically data collecting instruments in quantitative research, they also have applicability for qualitative methods of gathering information. From a quantitative perspective, the survey is "a method of collecting data from or about a group of people, asking questions in some fashion about things of interest to the researcher for the purpose of generalizing to a population represented by the group or sample."[11] While qualitative research can utilize surveys for collecting data about a group in a similar fashion, the purpose for the gathered data changes slightly. Surveys in qualitative research create a "sampling frame," which is "a resource from which you can select a smaller sample."[12] In other words, a survey's *primary* purpose within a qualitative study is to aid in the selection of a research sample rather than to gather data on a previously delineated sample. This aim is ideally suited to the case study context when the selection of a representative sample is not necessarily possible, such as when one depends on voluntary participation in interviews. In this context, a survey is an ideal tool for selecting a relevant range for the research sample

---

11. Nelson, "Survey Research in Marriage and Family Therapy," 447.
12. Mason, *Qualitative Researching*, 102.

rather than a representative sample.[13] Additionally, surveys within a case study may function as a means to help structure and guide the interview process once they assist in the selection of interviewees, and questionnaires did operate in this manner within the present study.

The foremost instrument for data collection which was implemented in these case studies was the interview, expressly the qualitative phenomenological interview. The terms *interview, qualitative,* and *phenomenological* all deserve a few explanatory comments. While the interview is a very common research tool that is used widely across multiple disciplines, it can be structured in different ways according to the intended type of data to be gathered. *Qualitative* interviews are structured with fewer questions which are phrased to elicit very detailed responses, and they are generally conducted with fewer participants in a research sample due to the intended depth of information to be gathered.[14] The *phenomenological* qualifier which is appended to the data collection instrument used in this study refers to interviews which have the specific purpose of attempting "to understand people's perceptions, perspectives, and understandings of a particular situation."[15] In other words, phenomenological interviews are centered on gathering data with regard to *meaning* given by participants rather than simply *behavior* which can be interpreted by a researcher. So, phenomenological interviews are ideal for a study, like this one, in which the researcher(s) intends to focus on the meanings and interpretations which the study *participants* attach to certain experiences rather than through a researcher's direct observation.

In distinction from phenomenological methods of gathering data, ethnographic methods of data collection focus on the immersion of a researcher in a culture or group which is unfamiliar to him or her for the purpose of interpreting a group's behaviors.[16] This immersion is typically achieved through primary reliance on the method of participant observation. Participant observation requires researcher immersion for an extended period of time in order to observe systematically "dimensions of that setting, interactions, relationships, actions, events and so on, within it."[17] Through this lengthy time of immersion, the researcher amasses a substantial amount of data which is interpreted through his/her sense of understanding and meaning as not only an observer but also a participant.

13. Ibid., 92.
14. Weiss, *Learning from Strangers*, 1, 3.
15. Leedy and Ormrod, *Practical Research*, 153. It should be noted that the "particular situation" in this context is the implementation of various mystic practices within the EC spiritual context.
16. Pearson, "Foreword: Talking a Good Fight," viii.
17. Mason, *Qualitative Researching*, 60.

Participant observation differs dramatically from phenomenology in that when one moves to what the researcher observed and experienced, a shift is made to the "researcher's reality" rather than the reality of those studied.[18] This difference in purpose and result informs the relative use of the differing methods described above within the present research context. Specifically, phenomenological methods are given preeminence because chief emphasis is placed on *participant* concepts and reasons for the appropriation of mystic practices. In keeping with this emphasis, grounded theory presented itself as the best system for analysis of data.

Data Analysis

The analysis of gathered data utilized grounded theory to answer the proposed research claim. In definition, grounded theory is "a methodology based on theory development from data that are collected and analyzed systematically and recursively."[19] One begins with data and then allows the data to shape theory naturally rather than imposing a particular theory on data which has been collected. This method appears to be ideal for almost any type of qualitative research because it attempts to circumvent problems of bias through allowing data to "speak for themselves." In this way, grounded theory was ideal for this research area, and it particularly complemented the phenomenological nature of the data gathering process. Such an epistemological fit operates as its own powerful rationale. So, data collection and analysis interweaves in a process of mutual induction.

Analysis itself proceeded through the constant comparative method, which is the continual comparison of all data bits that arise within the course of the study. This process allowed for the greatest possible validity given the constraints of the study since as much data as possible was recorded verbatim, providing for the need for low-inference descriptors.[20] All data was coded for commonalities, then coded for connections between different categories and subdivisions, then these interrelated categories merged to form a "storyline" (in this case a description of connections between appropriated mystic practices and theological anchors) that described the subject(s) of the study, and, finally, formed a comprehensive theory.[21] So, these methodologies

---

18. Boss, Dahl, and Kaplan, "Use of Phenomenology," 95.
19. Rafuls and Moon, "Grounded Theory Methodology," 65.
20. Silverman, *Interpreting Qualitative Data*, 287.
21. Leedy and Ormrod, *Practical Research*, 154–55. Cf., Jones, "Becoming Grounded in Grounded Theory Methodology," 176.

were employed to gather and analyze data in the study, but their applicability to the research subject also requires a few comments.

Empirical Rationale

While the "Contribution" section of the first chapter functions as the rationale for the study, the reasons and justifications behind the use of the particular methodologies outlined above is also necessary. To this end, this section offers an empirical rationale in three parts. First, a rationale for the use of qualitative methods over quantitative ones is necessary to lay the foundation for this study as a qualitative enterprise. Next, from a qualitative basis, the logic of utilizing the case study model of research design and grounded theory for analysis is tendered. Then, rationale discussions are presented for the major areas of data collection: interviews, phenomenology over ethnography, the limited use of participant observation, and the ethical issues raised by the research endeavor. Discussion of the utilization of surveys/questionnaires is not independent in this structure from the discussion on interviews since surveys were used primarily as an aid to the selection and focusing process of conducting interviews. While the empirical methodology of this study has been introduced generally, this section applies those principles to the specific situations met and researched within the current research enterprise.

Qualitative over Quantitative

Qualitative methods of research are ideal for the exact question of the study. Once more, the intention of this book is to explore the veracity of the main research claim: *The emergent church is appropriating Christian mystical practices by investing these practices with their own theological content.* Within this narrow purpose, quantitative methods do not provide the needed information to consider this issue. Quantitative methods provide statistics, numbers, and/or the distribution of characteristics or beliefs in a given population; however, they are not as useful when the given population or its attendant systems of practice or belief are not fully delineated or even settled into a final form, as is the case with the EC. Notably, qualitative methods assist the researcher most "at the stage where the problem is to know what the problem is, not what the answer is."[22] While the term *issue* would be semantically preferable at this point over the term *problem*, the principle remains

---

22. Dey, *Qualitative Data Analysis*, 52.

the same. To apply this principle specifically, qualitative methods allow for description of EC spiritual borrowing which is the essential task here rather than developing theory on the basis of a previously established description.

Qualitative research also "is characterized by studying human meanings which are to be interpreted by the researcher," and it is this aspect of studying *meaning* which makes qualitative research ideal for the present study.[23] While qualitative methods do not normally allow for a researcher to determine cause-and-effect relationships, particularly on a large scale, this potential weakness of qualitative methods is not applicable to the present study because the major claim does not intend to delineate an exact cause and effect relationship.[24] To reiterate, focus is placed here on *describing* the current level of spiritual borrowing in the EC through appropriation of Christian mystical practices, not *theorizing* whether this spiritual borrowing was present from the inception of the conversation or whether it will, or should, continue in the future. Therefore, it is evident that qualitative methodology is preferable for this research area and claim, but there are multiple avenues through which qualitative research can be conducted. As a consequence, a rationale for the selection of the case study model as well as the number of case studies is subsequently necessary.

Case Study

As noted above, case study design is characterized by the bounded nature of the research subject and by the types of questions which can be answered through this methodology. For the purpose of this book, an individual emergent church was the appropriate "bounded system" for an in-depth case study. An individual emergent church was large enough to yield considerable data and multiple participant perspectives leading to thick description, yet it was also small enough to allow for comprehensive study within the defined limits of the research project. Along with the basic rationale for the use of case studies, this model was also fitting for the study on the basis of what type of information was to be gathered and how it was to be analyzed. With respect to the basic logic of utilizing case studies, the main crux of the issue was the aim of discovering how ordinary EC attenders implement various mystic practices and why they do so. Then, the data gathered and analyzed through this method could be compared to literary claims for EC spiritual borrowing. Additionally, the analytic task meshed well with this possibility for research design. There are significant advantages to utilization of case

23. Riis, "Methodology in the Sociology of Religion," 235.
24. Leedy and Ormrod, *Practical Research*, 149.

study design with grounded theory. First, grounded theory works well with versatile methods for data collection—almost any intellectual output can be considered a potential source for evaluation.[25] This method also allows for a balance between evaluation of documents and personal interview/observation without combining it with other analytic methodologies. A final strength lies in the fact that this method has only one primary means of implementation, the constant-comparative method, which works ideally within the boundaries of case study design. So, the case study model and grounded theory mode of analysis are ideally suited for the research claim, but it is also necessary to provide reasons concerning the specific selection of case study participants.

Three emergent churches from different urban areas of the USA provided the context for the case study portion of the research for the purpose of discovering general theological anchors which different emergent churches have in common. This selective choice was made on the basis of a few important reasons. First, it was necessary to choose churches which identified as "emergent." While this reason might seem to be obvious and easy in the selection process, it was difficult in practice to locate churches that were willing to allow themselves to be labeled at all.[26] As a consequence of this difficulty, churches were located on the basis of their online participation in the emergent conversation, principally through blogs and web lists of emergent churches. Of the nineteen churches/groups that were approached for participation in the study, the resulting three were willing to identify as emergent for the purposes of the study and could participate within my time limitations. An additional limitation for selectivity was the fact that most USA EC churches are "concentrated in urban and suburban America."[27] I am not located near an urban center, so I had to choose churches on the basis of relative proximity to my location or relative opportunity to combine a research visit with a business trip. Three churches were selected from various urban areas in the southwestern region of the USA to allow for the maximum amount of difference on the basis of location while working within these geographic limitations. Additionally, *three* case studies were chosen on the basis of balance between the value of multiple perspectives leading to greater opportunity for discovering general theological principles and the value of limited size in order to achieve thick description of each case study church. Furthermore, this selection of multiple case stud-

---

25. Merriam, "Grounded Theory," 142. Cf., Silverman, *Interpreting Qualitative Data*, 201.

26. Multiple interview participants took umbrage at even being labeled as "members" of a "church," displaying disdain for both terms.

27. Bielo, *Emerging Evangelicals*, 26.

ies was coupled with the selection of multiple research instruments in order to provide a multi-faceted portrait of each case study church.

Data Collection Instruments

The use of multiple data collection instruments (surveys, interviews, and participant observation) offered two major advantages that justified their use in the present study. First, the utilization of multiple instruments allowed for the reduction of "inappropriate certainty."[28] Essentially, reliance on one method alone would leave unanswered methodological reasons concerning whether anomalous results were only a reflection of the relative weaknesses present in the chosen method. By utilization of three methods of data collection, this particular problem has been obviated. Second, using multiple instruments permits a certain amount of "triangulation" in which differing data perspectives can be compared and synthesized in order to return a more realistic depiction of the group under examination.[29] To this end, surveys/questionnaires, phenomenological interviews, and participant observation have all been utilized as data collecting tools; however, as mentioned previously, they have not been implemented equally. Surveys were chiefly utilized in conjunction with interviews, and they will be considered within that attendant rationale. Participant observation, as a more appropriate instrument for ethnographic research, will be considered within an overall rationale for the use of phenomenological methods over ethnographic ones while still utilizing both types. So, the rationale of the empirical methodology concerning the selection of data collection instruments can be grouped into discussion of interviews and benefits of phenomenology over limited ethnography.

Interviews were the primary data collection tool within this study for a number of reasons. First and foremost, as stated pithily by sociologist Jennifer Mason, "Interviews are one of the most commonly recognized forms of qualitative research method."[30] In line with noting the popularity of interviews, Robert Weiss provides an appropriate rationale for interview utilization in a qualitative case study by noting their ability to produce detailed descriptions, integrate multiple perspectives, describe processes, describe complex issues and events holistically, learn how events and issues are interpreted by participants, bridge intersubjectivities, and provide a frame for later

---

28. Robson, *Real World Research*, 370.
29. Ibid., 371.
30. Mason, *Qualitative Researching*, 39.

quantitative research.[31] Weiss' first five advantages for qualitative interviewing particularly apply to the present study. For these reasons, interviews were the primary research instrument, and surveys/questionnaires were only used in conjunction with interview methodology. Specifically, surveys allowed for a non-threatening way of identifying potential interview participants since the final question on the survey asked whether the person would be willing to participate in a formal interview.[32] Surveys also offered some structure to interviews in determining which mystic practices should be focused on during a particular interview.[33] Both interviews and surveys were used within the study from a phenomenological framework.

Multiple epistemological bases suggested a phenomenological approach as ideal. First, other sociological approaches to the study of religion tend to focus on individual belief as that which comes out of "concepts and classifications [that] arise from social relations."[34] While this viewpoint is useful when principally examining behavior within a social group, it would deviate slightly from the need to gather data about what individuals *state they believe* concerning behavior. Next, to articulate the utility of phenomenology in a positive sense, researcher Sharan Merriam concisely offers the underlying philosophical perspective of phenomenology by noting that "phenomenology focuses on the subjective experience of the individual."[35] As a result, the phenomenological researcher focuses neither on "the human subject nor the human world but on the essence of the meaning of this interaction."[36] Along with this focus comes the assumption that the individual has the ability to articulate meaning *accurately* within his or her everyday life although the terminology utilized may differ among individuals.[37] For the purposes of the empirical research informing this book, I approached the data collection instruments of surveys and interviews from this phenomenological perspective. By way of explanation and distinction from phenomenology, ethnographic epistemological assumptions also deserve some comment.

While participant observation was utilized in empirical research, it was only a minor data-gathering tool due to a practical difficulty and an

31. Weiss, *Learning from Strangers*, 9–11.
32. Please see Appendix A to view the questionnaire.
33. Please see Appendix B to view the interview questions.
34. Day, *Believing in Belonging*, 10.
35. Merriam, "Phenomenological Research," 93.
36. Ibid.
37. Cf., Boss, Dahl, and Kaplan, "Use of Phenomenology for Family Therapy Research," 85–86.

epistemological issue. First, ethnographic participant observation as a principal tool for data collection was not possible due to the necessity for extended periods of observation that I was simply unable to do in light of geographic and financial limitations.[38] Additionally, I was only able to spend 1–2 weeks of participant observation with each church which is not nearly enough time to utilize this instrument as a major data-gathering tool for the study. Second, and more centrally, the aim of ethnography would put it partially at odds with the empirical research goal of the study. To clarify, in the words of ethnographic researcher Geoffrey Pearson, "Ethnography is often said to be way of 'telling it like it is,' looking at the social world of the subject as it is seen 'from the inside,' telling stories as people might tell these stories themselves."[39] This approach favors the researcher's interpretations over any possible interpretations by the research subjects.[40] For the purpose of synthesizing multiple perspectives of social behaviors, this approach might seem preferable *unless* one is particularly interested in why research subjects *believe* they utilize a certain practice(s). Therefore, it is necessary to reiterate that this book is principally concerned with the *perceptions* of the individuals in the emergent churches studied. With this epistemological issue in mind, a question arises concerning the justification for including participant observation at all. Why not rely solely on phenomenological methods? Simply put, I found limited participant observation to be useful because it allowed me to raise questions which I observed in corporate spiritual activities that were not treated on the survey/questionnaire or interview schedule. Additionally, both ethnographic participant observation and phenomenological interviews raised some practical ethical issues with respect to the research subjects.

Ethical Issues

Whenever research involves particular persons and their descriptions of sensitive, and often private, matters of belief and spiritual practice, certain ethical steps are necessary in data-gathering and the presentation of research results. First, the churches themselves were not pseudonymized, but this direction was only followed after receiving express permission from the entire staff of each case study group. Consequently, the details provided in

---

38. See Robson, *Real World Research*, 187. The nearest emergent church is approximately a six-hour drive from my location.

39. Pearson, "Foreword: Talking a Good Fight," viii.

40. See Hammersley, *What's Wrong with Ethnography?*, 11–12. This perspective is evident by the subtle phrasing choice, "as people might tell," not "as people tell."

each profile will use the actual name and history of each case study church. Second, individual participants were pseudonymized through the use of random numerical designations to allow for anonymity when discussing matters as intimate as religious belief and spiritual practice. Third, ethical consent from each interview participant was received in the following manner. Initially, once permission for the study was granted by the staff of each church, a designated staff member would distribute paper versions and online instructions of the spiritual practices questionnaire. Interested individuals could then complete the questionnaire and indicate whether they would be amenable to an interview. I then contacted potential interviewees to set up an in-person or virtual interview. Finally, at the actual interview, I gave the interviewee a participant information sheet describing the study and an ethical consent form to sign before any discussion began.[41] In this way, the rights and privileges of each participating individual and group were respected at each stage of the empirical research process.

Church Profiles

Within the empirical phase of study, I visited three emergent churches in the southwestern region of the USA for two-week intervals during May-September 2011. Among these churches, I observed multiple services and meetings, interviewed thirty-eight members or regular attendees, and conducted documentary research on the podcasts and blogposts which composed their archives of sermons and public conversations. On these visits, I did participate within the various meetings and services, but I was careful to remain in the background in order to minimize the intrusiveness of my presence. At each meeting, the pastor or facilitator introduced me and briefly stated my research intentions, so participants were not left uninformed about my position as an interested outsider to the community. While one church offered me the opportunity to make such a statement personally, I deferred to the pastor's judgment concerning how to articulate my role at the church. While I was definitely perceived as an outsider in informal conversations and formal interviews, I was able to establish rapport by mentioning some aspects of my personal faith history. Like multiple interviewees, I grew up in an evangelical religious tradition (Southern Baptist), and I had become dissatisfied with it after going away to university. That common ground served to open up avenues of conversation and tended to relax my conversational partner noticeably. Often, I would go on to note that my personal faith perspective led me to the Episcopal Church. At that point, the interviewee

---

41. See Appendices C and D respectively for these documents.

would typically ask me what attracted me to Episcopalianism, and I had a few brief comments prepared which would take only a few minutes to say. These personal comments usually provided a perfect opening for me to turn the conversation around and ask "Would you tell me a little about why you first started attending the church in which you are now involved?"[42] The interview would then proceed along the schedule, yet the interviewee tended to retain a relaxed and conversational demeanor.

Additionally, before diving into extended descriptions of each case study EC church, it is essential to explain why neo-monastic communities were not studied since this group appears to be an ideal research subject for mystic practice appropriation and reinterpretation. As noted previously in the book, the EC, or *emergent* church, can be viewed as a single arm of larger developments. While the *emerging* church as a separate entity has been briefly introduced and dismissed as less conducive a social context than the EC for the study of mystic practices, there is another analogous context, or perhaps "cousin," of the EC which appears to be even more receptive to mystic practices: neo-monasticism. While the EC has not been silent on the possibility of monastic patterns and ideals affecting the conversation, they have not sought to apply the monastic tradition in a consistent way.[43] However, sociologists, such as James Bielo, have noticed and observed neo-monasticism as a group which does seek more engagement.[44] Neo-monasticism bears many similarities to the EC, but this movement also displays several notable differences such as no interest in church planting, a distinct appeal to Christians over 40, and greater multiculturalism.[45] They engage with the mystical tradition and, specifically, the monastic tradition for a pragmatic purpose. In the words of one of their most prominent advocates, Shane Claiborne, neo-monastics seek to be an answer to a question, for "[m]ost people know what Christians believe, but if you ask them how Christians live they do not know."[46] As a result, they take as their particular goal to show the "world" how Christians can live Christianity consistently in a postmodern context. So, if this group can indeed be separated tentatively from the EC, why not focus on this group instead?

There are four main reasons why neo-monasticism is not investigated within this study: two simply practical reasons and two larger epistemological issues. First, a limitation of scope was necessary for the thick description

---

42. See Appendix B for details.
43. Jones, *New Christians*, 209–10.
44. Bielo, *Emerging Evangelicals*, 99.
45. Sine, *New Conspirators*, 49.
46. Claiborne, "Mark 2," 31.

desired, and EC communities seemed to offer me greater potential for sociological engagement without extended participant observation. Second, the EC conversational "branch" was the first group that raised questions in my mind, so it seemed logical to follow this specific area of investigation rather than detour to a side group. Third, and more influentially, I wanted to investigate an environment markedly different than the one in which the mystic practices first developed. To return to the microbe analogy, I desired to study the "solution," or social context, that represented the greatest difference from the original solution, while still employing the "microbes" or mystic practices. Finally, and most importantly, my interest in congregations as case studies informed against scrutinizing neo-monasticism because "[n]eo-monastic communities do not become congregations. Instead, they encourage members to commit to local congregations as an extension of their commitment to the local community."[47]

Prior to proceeding to a discussion of each individual church, it is valuable to note that these three churches can be lined up on a continuum. On this conceptual continuum, on one end lies a strongly positive identification with the EC conversation, engagement with EC literature and/or authors, and a readiness to *embrace* the concept of postmodernity. On the other end, lies an ambivalent identification with the EC conversation, passing familiarity with EC literature and/or authors, and a readiness to *engage* with postmodernity while not necessarily embracing it. Each individual church profile offers a glimpse at the particular context in which each instance of EC spiritual borrowing actually occurs. In this perspective, the following profiles will present a basic description of each church and its history and offer the notable or unique qualities of each church as noted by interview participants. When quotations are utilized from specific participants here and throughout the study, interviewees are referred to by a designated number rather than by name in order to preserve the privacy of each participant. Churches will be profiled on the basis of chronological visit by the researcher. Sources for this information include interview data, website or blog entries, sermon recordings, and field-note observations.

Riverside Community Church

The first church that I visited was Riverside Community Church (RCC), located in the greater San Antonio, Texas (TX), area (approximately twenty miles from downtown San Antonio). The visit extended from May 21, 2011 through June 5, 2011. While visiting this church, I attended six corporate

---

47. Marti and Ganiel, *Deconstructed Church*, 20.

services (two services each Sunday morning), a mid-week small group meeting, and a church staff meeting. This church was by far the largest of the three (averaging two hundred members between the two services each Sunday). It was also the most typically suburban and affluent. Seventeen congregants were interviewed (including one over the telephone following the visit). Demographic information for interview participants was gathered on the following markers: age, highest education level completed, ethnicity, gender, profession, income, marital status, and number and age of children. Notable demographic characteristics include a higher than expected average age among interviewees of 47 (range 22-65), almost exclusive ethnic representation as "white" or Caucasian (16 participants), and an income noticeably higher than the national average (RCC average = $158,636; national USA average = $50,054).[48]

While the leadership of this church strongly identified as emergent, occasional resistance and/or ignorance to the term *emergent* was displayed among church members, and the term *emerging* was only slightly more preferable. Additionally, while the church did self-identify, particularly through the pastor, as interested in "ancient paths," the term that the pastor used to talk about spiritual and mystical practices, they tended to mean an engagement with the Hebrew Root movement[49] rather than a strong connection with the Christian mystical tradition. Viewed on the aforementioned continuum, this church comprised the far end toward *engagement* and away from *embracing*. In order to create a comprehensive profile of RCC, it is necessary to include the historical origin/development of the church and the notable qualities of the church, as mentioned by specific individual attendees.

Development of RCC

RCC has developed distinctively through its origin, its focus on home study groups, its many ministries, and its lack of a permanent meeting place. With regard to the beginning of RCC, it was a direct intentional planting of a church by an older church, Alamo Heights United Methodist Church. According to Riverside's website, "One of the things God asked them [Alamo

---

48. DeNavas-Walt, Proctor, and Smith, *Income, Poverty, and Health Insurance*, 5. These characteristics are actually quite typical of emergent churches, although participants tend to be slightly younger on average than in RCC. Cf., Flory and Miller, *Finding Faith*, 37.

49. The Hebrew Root movement is the creation of Ray Vanderlaan who stresses the need for Christians to attain a knowledge of Jewish customs since Judaism was the religion that Jesus practiced. Cf., That the World May Know Ministries, www.rvl-on.com.

Heights] to do was plant a daughter community. That daughter community is Riverside."[50] According to Interviewee 16, this step was not taken lightly; rather, "it was through a series of prayer times over a number of years." It also did not start as a major corporate gathering on a Sunday morning; instead, RCC first met in homes on Wednesday nights. Additionally, interviewees focused on the church retaining a sense of this small beginning, as noted by Interviewee 14 specifically comparing RCC to "a large Sunday School class." Home groups have remained a large part of their ministry, and, according to a church information brochure, other "connection ministries" have been added including a community coffeehouse (The Loft), a food pantry and thrift store, provision of meals to the elderly or unfortunate, and multiple foreign mission trips. These ministries occur in various locations since the church does not own a permanent building although several interviewees expressed concern over this lack, and one noted that he was on a church committee to find a "permanent home" for RCC. These developments help to present an overarching portrait of RCC with important developmental and historical ties noted, but participant comments extended beyond these basics to present a more well-rounded interpretation of how they view their church, its ministry, and its place in the EC conversation.

Notable Qualities of RCC

Interview participants had overwhelmingly positive things to say about RCC, and these comments concerning the unique attractiveness of the church can be grouped into a few major categories, including the influence of the pastor, the influence of community connections, and the place of the Bible, prayer, and social ministries within RCC. To begin, the most consistent influence on interviewee responses and emergent developments within RCC was no doubt their pastor, Scott Heare. Almost every participant allocated a lion's share of responsibility to the pastor for the innovativeness of the church. In fact, Interviewee 9 even recalled a moment in prayer concerning Heare that fittingly encapsulates congregants' perspectives: "So, I sat back and started to pray, and the Lord told me 'My hand is on Scott. I'm going to do a great work through him. Come up here and pray that it happens.'" The pastor's influence on the congregation is also eminently noticeable in how particular emphases of the pastor are assimilated wholeheartedly among the laity. For instance, only the pastor and his wife strongly advocated a direct engagement with the EC conversation among

---

50. Riverside Community Church, "Denomination," www.connect2riverside.com/denomination.

interview participants. Other participants voiced hesitancy to be identified with the conversation although they often noted that Heare was leading them in that direction. An additional emphasis of the pastor was in the Hebrew Root movement, and many interview participants had taken up this focus as well. It should be noted that this Hebrew Root influence tinted how many congregants approached appropriation of individual mystic practices within RCC, meaning that mystic practices were reinterpreted in a distinctly Jewish manner. For instance, the Jewish liturgical calendar was utilized more often than the Christian church year. While Heare's influence was primary in this church, it was by no means the only factor. The influence of a connected community was also very widespread among interview participants and in church communications.

Connectedness and community was at the forefront of the conversations among the members and attenders at RCC. Interviewee 15 stated this emphasis succinctly by noting "The buzzword there [RCC] is 'community.'" In a more comprehensive statement, Interviewee 11 explained the particular emphasis on community at RCC in this way:

> Riverside is a community that is genuinely trying to seek God in all they do, believes in the whole commandment of "loving God with all your heart, soul, and mind," and then "loving your neighbor as yourself" in community. It's always been a church—it's always been a community for me. It's always been a church that has defined itself as working to have a real [sic] strong Christian community that would be a witness in its broader community.

Additionally, when fully explained and described, the sense of community which interviewees noted focused on the acceptance that they experienced within the context of RCC whether that was in the Loft coffeehouse ministry, in progressions from other religious traditions (principally Catholic and charismatic), or in a willingness to experiment and ask questions in the spirit of the EC conversation. Interviewee 1 referred to this quality of acceptance in community poignantly through stating, "We are very much about sharing everything, about being able to open and [be] up front with each other about that we all have problems." Along with the major influences of the pastor and the RCC sense of community, many congregants also noted theological trends which attracted them to Riverside.

Notable theological characteristics among interview participants and other sources at RCC include an emphasis on the Bible, a distinctive stress on prayer, and a committed implementation of the biblical injunction to "love your neighbor." While one might expect for most Christian churches to emphasize the Bible in some respect, RCC congregants noted this distinction in connection with a humility surrounding it. Interviewee 17 was impressed by this emphasis: "When I found Riverside, it was like, boy, this is low-key. They consistently preach from the Bible." In connection to this general emphasis, multiple congregants noted the RCC aspiration to use both Old and New Testaments in creation of doctrine. Interviewee 4 referred to this emphasis as the main reason why she had chosen RCC: "The main thing that I tell my friends, like back at Bulverde [United Methodist Church], is that Riverside really focuses on keeping the Old Testament with the New Testament. It's important to know your roots." Another noted emphasis among RCC attenders and members is the church's view of prayer. In the words of Interviewee 5, "I think that Riverside really believes that prayer is going to do something. It's not a hope; it's an expectation." Prayer ministry is even included as a specific subsection of Riverside's corporate gatherings in which a "prayer team" will pray throughout the entirety of the meeting and be available for individual prayer with interested persons following services. A final theological trait which was noted by several interviewees was the active social ministries implemented by RCC. In reference to many of the ministries noted previously, Interviewee 17 asserted, "I think the distinguishing characteristic of the spirituality of Riverside is 'Love your neighbor as yourself.' There's a lot of people there that go out of their way to help others, and they tend to make it a point to be anonymous." Many of these distinctives were also quite visible to me when conducting the visit. While it should be remembered that this church represents the closest kinship with its evangelical ancestor among the case studies, yet individuals still felt free to experiment with various mystic practices which arise out of a Christian tradition quite different from their own. While RCC displayed some qualities in kinship with the next church investigated, there were also notable differences.

Emmaus Road Church

On June 18 and June 25 through July 1, 2011, I visited Emmaus Road Church (ERC) in Tulsa, Oklahoma (OK). This church met on Saturday nights because they had developed out of a Saturday night service at their parent church The Life Connection. Originally, ERC was a ministry to the youth of the parent church. I was only able to attend two services at this church because they had few activities going on during the middle of the summer. Approximately thirty to forty people regularly attended this church, and it was interestingly split among attendees in their twenties and several persons who were over sixty. At the time of the visit, ERC had recently established a permanent presence in downtown Tulsa by renting office space and converting it into an environment suited to their particular congregational desires. This group had many traditional earmarks of an emergent church service present in their meetings, including the use of candles, independent prayer and art stations, and a variety of seating options (pews, straight-back chairs, school desks, and recliners) intended to create a relaxed and eclectic atmosphere. Ten people were interviewed in this congregation, which represented a much greater proportion of attendees than in the previous church. Demographic information for interview participants was gathered on the following markers: age, highest education level completed, ethnicity, gender, profession, income, marital status, and number and age of children. Notable demographic characteristics include great disparity in ages among participants (average = 35; range = 16–68; no interviewees between the ages of 27 and 60), greater ethnic diversity (including Jewish, Iranian, and Latino), a lower average income status than the previous case study church, and a preponderance of single persons without children (7 out of 10 interviewees).

This church showed much greater acknowledgment of engagement with Christian mysticism. For instance, there was a specific position for a pastor of spiritual formation and liturgy, and one of their pastors had recently finished a seminary degree in sacramental theology. While this group was very comfortable with *emerging* terminology, many lay members were still hesitant to claim an *emergent* label, or any label for that matter. With respect to the continuum among case study churches, ERC represents a mid-point. Within this church, there are many marks of alignment with the EC conversation, yet there are notable qualities, and even prominent persons in the church, that do not fit into this mold. In order to create a profile for ERC in keeping with the previous case study depiction, the same areas of historical origin/development of the church and notable qualities of the church as mentioned by individual members will be traced.

Development of ERC

Unlike the previous church profiled, ERC presented a brief history statement on their website,[51] and it is beneficial to quote this excerpt in full although several comments made by interviewees will also be necessary to offer supplemental information. The history statement for ERC is as follows:

---

51. Emmaus Road Church, http://emmausroadtulsa.org.

> In October 2005, Saturday Night [the original name of ERC] began meeting as a new church service at The Life Connection Church in Jenks, Oklahoma. It was evident from the start that it was less of a "service" and more of a "community." Our relationship with "The Life Connection" (our parent church) has always been a healthy one. We still "connect" with them on a regular basis. In the summer of 2007, it was apparent that Saturday Night was called out as its own community. We also sensed that it was necessary to move to a different area of town. In November of '07, Saturday Night Community Church was formally commissioned as a church plant of The Life Connection. In February '08, after months of searching for a new worship space, Saturday Night moved into the Agora Marketplace at 51st and Memorial in Tulsa. In October '10, we have renamed ourselves "Emmaus Road Church" because we have resonated so strongly with the story of Luke 24. We will soon be moving into our very own space in downtown Tulsa [which happened just prior to my visit]. These are general highlights of major events that have happened in the life of our church. However, the most important part of our history is our own stories. Our community has celebrated marriages, dedications, new jobs, and new babies. We have also mourned losses, cried together, and seen some of our friends move away. You don't get to know a church by reading its website. We find God in the midst of our relationships.[52]

As the closing sentences of ERC's history statement assert, the stories of those within their own community best represent their history and development. Within the interviews for the study, the facts noted above were confirmed by participants; however, they also added notable comments of depth which support their historical statement.

In addition to the historical statement of ERC, many interviewees added comments concerning the description of the church, its affiliation, its common emphases, and important background concerning its separation from its parent church, The Life Connection (TLC). Concerning basic description, Interviewee 26 provided clarifying information on typical size of the congregation for a Saturday night meeting by stating, "On average, I'd say about thirty-five [is typical]." Additional descriptive comments were offered by interviewees concerning denominational affiliation with ERC as "non-denominational"; however, the pastor clarified the relationship as "independent charismatic" along with a non-denominational qualifier. Interestingly, there was some confusion about the length that ERC had been

---

52. Emmaus Road Church, "History," http://emmausroadtulsa.org/history.

in existence, but Interviewee 19 who had been a founding member noted equivocally, "I think right now, every time we say it, we're saying five years [in 2011]." From these basic descriptive and clarifying comments, a few interviewees proceeded to note deeper background information.

Interviewee 23 noted that ERC was focused early on matters of "artistic expression" and "reading poetry," and he asserted that these emphases have remained foundational issues throughout the duration of the church. Additionally, the pastor related that many ERC emphases had begun while he led the TLC youth group corporate services, and he also noted that "it was my supervisor's view that because we were doing some of those things [i.e., artistic expressions and reading poetry] that our youth ministry was not really growing at the rate that he wanted it to." At this point, the pastor continued by saying,

> He [the pastor of the Life Connection] told me I could have a separate youth service for that and remain on staff, but the main youth service needed to go to somebody else, or I needed to change the format for that. So, I went back to him, basically, with a counter-proposal, and at that time the church had grown to two services. It was overflowing, and I said "What if we started that service that you're talking about, but we opened it up to all ages?" We did some different things with it, and they were actually thrilled about that. The board approved that, so we moved forward with what we called at that time "Saturday Night at TLC."

This further insight into the development of the church may serve to explain the great disparity in ages among congregants, for many interviewees noted that they were either former members of the youth group at TLC (accounting for the young members) or that they had been volunteers to help with that youth group (accounting for the members who were over 60). A further note concerning development of ERC concerns the separation between ERC and TLC.

According to the pastor, ERC existed as a worship service of TLC for a little over two years; however, differences arose concerning overall spiritual emphasis. Specifically, the pastor related that a perception arose concerning the relatively radical nature of ERC within the larger TLC body by stating, "Any time we say words like 'social justice' or 'environmental stewardship' certain perceptions in this area of the country jump certain places." As a result, the two churches parted ways, although amicably according to all interviewees, and ERC was left free to develop its own distinctive traits.

Notable Qualities of ERC

Within the context of the phenomenological interviews, participants were introduced to the topic of discussion through the general question, "Would you tell me a little bit about why you first started attending the church in which you are now involved?" While personal reasons often arose in answer to this query, many general themes and trends appeared when interviewees sought to emphasize the uniqueness of ERC. These distinctive traits can be grouped into three major categories: community, expression, and eclectic methodology.

Community, the first major category, is a term that weaves in and out of the EC conversation, and it was often encountered by the researcher in the case study churches; however, ERC interview participants had very specific connotations connected to this term for the purposes of their church. Definitionally, Interviewee 20 succinctly stated, "We're just a very tight-knit group of people but not closed off. When new people come, it's not like they're not welcomed." In the spirit of this statement, an ERC view of community developed along two lines. First, interviewees offered multiple examples of how "tight-knit" they were as a church. For instance, Interviewee 18 stresses ERC community in the following example: "When my dog got killed [the pastor and his wife] and everybody was just there for me because I was a wreck. I didn't even answer the phone for three days, but it's really a community thing, it's like a family." In a more ongoing example, Interviewee 21 clarified his sense of ERC community in saying, "When I mean community, I mean that throughout the week I'm engaged with a lot of these people I go to church with; there's always a continual conversation." This sense of closeness was supplemented in interviewee conversations with a strong focus on acceptance and welcoming. When Interviewee 26 was recounting how she became more involved in ERC ministry, she confessed, "They sought me out. They made me feel like I was a part, and so I've only actually been there since January of this year, but I feel like I've known most of the people in the community for years, and I haven't." This sense of acceptance also extended to those who had experienced negative Christian reactions in the past. Interviewee 21 poignantly recounted, "She [a friend] invited me to come to Emmaus Road, because after that experience [of coming out publicly as homosexual] I felt very disillusioned with the Christianity that I saw up until that point. So, I felt that if my friend could accept me, she thought that there was a community that was also very accepting and Christian." A final example of this trend was quite notable for Interviewee 22 who asserted his stance as an atheist. When I asked if he still viewed himself as an integral part of ERC, Interviewee 22 responded, "I would say so. I [have] really come to love being a part of the Emmaus Road community, so that's why I consider myself a part of the church, but not of the Christian church per se." Apparently, ERC displays a sense of community that is so welcoming and close-knit that even oppositional theological beliefs do not seem to represent a barrier to full community involvement. This strong sense of community also is manifest within the ERC trait of expression.

Multiple sources noted that one of the foundational characteristics of the ERC community is its emphasis on expression. Interviewee 23 noted this focus concisely by declaring, "We had a lot of people who were unable to express their creativity in various forms in various church settings." The pastor noted this focus in sermon form on October 8, 2011, when stating that ERC was unique from its evangelical background through "engaging the right brain and the arts more intentionally with poetry and painting and music." Interviewee 19 echoed this statement by identifying the uniqueness of ERC as "our willingness to engage with art and provide a safe place for artists." Interviewee 24 placed this value for art in terms of comparison to the traditional Methodist church in which he was raised:

> If I went back to the church I grew up in, and I said "All right, here is [sic] some art supplies, and here's a canvas. Just draw and concentrate on experiencing God through art and what he's speaking to you creatively." The difference between where I grew up and am now is that Emmaus Road would go right to work. They would tackle that, and they'd be all over it. My folks' church, they would give it a shot, but it would be something very foreign and very uncomfortable because it's just out of the box.

This quality of readiness to "go right to work" was indicative of the ERC emphasis on expression, but it was equally a distinctive characteristic of their focus on eclectic methodology.

The distinctive quality in ERC which congregants noted as most closely aligned with the EC conversation was an allowance for an eclectic methodology. In the specific words of Interviewee 26, "our worship is nontraditional compared to a lot of other churches. I would say that it's eclectic; it's very eclectic." While this particular interviewee extended eclecticism only so far as worship methods, other parishioners saw a wider influence. In the words of Interviewee 19, ERC has sought "A reexamination of core beliefs, not to reject them, but just to reexamine that that's really where we are." Interviewee 27 positioned the focus on eclecticism within an overall concern for "balance" within ERC. Such a clarification concerning the eclecticism of methods and *not* theological content was also made by Interviewee 24 through a statement concerning the rejection of stereotypes: "I believe that we don't fit the stereotype, but part of what Emmaus Road is about is taking truths and reframing them in somewhat different language to make them accessible again." These major characteristics noted in interviews and field-notes form the context that allowed for ERC appropriation of mystic practices on an individual, as well as social, level. As expected, since this church moves closer to a typical emergent church as described in EC literature, more use and discussion of mystic practices arises. A willingness to experiment melds well with the eclecticism noted by interview participants. This focus on experimentation, acceptance, and free expression becomes even more noticeable in the final case study.

Church in the Cliff

I visited the Church in the Cliff (CitC) from September 4–11, 2011. This church was located in Dallas, TX, specifically in the Oak Cliff neighborhood, which is considered an "inner-city" or disadvantaged urban neighborhood within Dallas. During this visit, I attended a mid-week evening Bible study with seven persons present as well as two Sunday morning "conversations" with twenty to thirty persons in attendance. These conversations were very interesting, and they represent the general tenor of the church in rejecting the overtly one-sided monological sermons for a much more dialogical form of communication on a topic and accompanying scripture passage. This church was very active with respect to social justice and ecological issues within their community, particularly concerning urban farming and buying fair trade or locally grown items. Additionally, they greatly stressed inclusion with a focus on gender and sexual orientation inclusivity.

Within this community, I interviewed eleven persons, including one person who identified as a member of the CitC community but had never attended Sunday "conversations" [the term which the church preferred over "sermon"]. Notable demographic characteristics include the highest levels of education among participants in a case study church (one PhD, eight master's degrees), more balanced ethnic representation of the two major ethnic groups composing the region (Caucasian and Hispanic), a high percentage of individuals involved in non-profit organizations (45%), and a notable proportion of married couples without children (36%). Interview participants disliked the term "member," and CitC did not have a formal membership status of any sort. This disdain for labels carried over in many directions, unless they were allowed to coin the term/phrase themselves, such as "ecumergent," "Buddheo-Christian," and "a drinking club with a Jesus problem." This church had often had specific studies on many of the mystic practices noted on the questionnaire that are often quite alien to a Protestant evangelical context. With respect to the continuum among case study churches, CitC represents the pole of *embracing*. Within this church, there are substantial marks of alignment with the EC conversation, yet multiple interviewees still only hesitantly embraced this label due to their strong dislike for labeling. In order to create a profile for CitC in keeping with previous case study portrayals, the same areas of development will be traced: historical origin/development of the church and the notable qualities of the church as mentioned by individual interviewees.

Development of CitC

More than any other case study church, CitC has had a very checkered history in its origin and development as a church. Interestingly, I discovered that no one interviewee seemed to have the whole story concerning the origin and development of CitC. As a result, many interview participant comments are necessary in order to present the fullest picture of this church's many incarnations and the reasoning behind such transitions. Multiple participants knew that the church had existed in some form for ten to twelve years as of 2011. The original incarnation of CitC was named City Church, and it was located "in the Oak Lawn area on Hood Street right off of Oak Lawn Avenue," according to Interviewee 35. It was the impression of that interviewee that "it [CitC] was originally organized and founded by three Baptist churches, all of which were affiliated at that time with the Southern Baptist denomination, and there were no Baptist churches in the Oak Lawn area. So, they wanted to establish an outpost there." However, I learned upon further investigation from Interviewee 31, who was corroborated by the pastor, that the Alliance of Baptists first formed the congregation. The reasoning behind the start of a new Baptist church in an overwhelmingly Baptist area such as Dallas was for deeper reasons than location alone. In the words of Interviewee 37, "It was basically a church that was created [and] put intentionally into the gay part of town." This intention is not surprising since CitC was quite vociferous in its continued engagement with the LGBT community. The church moved to the Oak Cliff neighborhood of Dallas, TX, approximately three years prior to my visit, but this move did not seem to change this emphasis; rather, additional emphases were added to this original focus. With these interviewee comments pieced together, it is possible to see the origin point for CitC, but its development occurred through many unplanned progressions and crises within its history.

When I first approached interviewees concerning distinctive traits of CitC, many historical progressions were noted, but several crises of change also arose in conversation as discussion continued. For instance, as a neutral progression, Interviewee 37 noted that at one time eleven people had been ordained in their group; however, she also noted that this number was out of forty or fifty total attenders. To this statement, I remarked, "You say you were running 40 or 50. So it [the church] has gotten smaller?" Interviewee 37 thought for a moment then responded, "I feel like, yeah. We're smaller." When I followed this line of questioning to ask what changed in CitC, I received quite a lengthy answer to display many progressions and crises in the church:

> Vickie's [the first pastor] salary was underwritten by one of our sponsoring churches, and the term that they were going to sponsor that salary went away, and we just didn't have the money coming in. Now, our fiscal models actually never worked, which is interesting. I mean, really, we say we're going to do this, but we don't have a fiscal model that supports what this is. The next pastor that came in, in 2004, was Laura Fragen, and she came in 2004, and somewhere along the lines we got kicked out of the Baptist General Convention of Texas [BGCT] because we were open and affirming. We recognized the ordination of an openly gay seminary professor out at TCU [Texas Christian University], and when we recognized his ordination, BGCT was like "That's enough of you guys." So, we recognized that, and that process went through. And, somewhere along the way, probably about the time that we started, somewhere along the way we started losing our Baptist identity, and then when we moved to Oak Cliff somewhere in that process, Laura announced to us that we were an emergent church. And, not like "People, this is how it's going to be." It wasn't like that at all. It was like what we're doing, how we're interacting with art, all this stuff, this is what "emergent church" is. So, we had this thing called the emergent cohort. I went to a couple of them. There's another emergent church called Journey, that's up north, and we did a couple of things with them. We'd go to their stuff, and we were kind of snarky about it. They would come to our stuff, and they probably weren't snarky. I really do feel the emergent church is like junior high [school] for adults.

This concept of continual change through progression and crisis was also integral in the current pastor's experience in entering leadership. Specifically, she noted, "People were just busting out of the seams. There were just tons of young people, different kinds of people. So, I sort of ticked into it and didn't know what it all meant. At first, I thought I was just going to be part of the community, work somewhere else or whatever, and then everything exploded, and she [Fragen] left, and the church called me to be their pastor." In light of these comments, it appears that CitC is a church that is very much in flux, which is a typical characteristic of emergent churches. As a result of the ever-changing ebb and flow of EC conversation, many churches such as CitC would be expected to change dramatically as the people they wish to engage also change. Still, at the juncture when I visited, CitC offered many unique qualities and traits which interview participants sought to emphasize in their responses to interview questions. These responses serve to present a snapshot of CitC as an emergent church where there is ongoing appropriation and reinterpretation of various mystic practices.

Notable Qualities of CitC

As presented in official group meetings, electronic communication, and interviewee responses, CitC is unique on many levels, and they highly value their uniqueness. Such a high worth was placed on being unique that interviewees often had difficulty in finding common points between their church and the larger EC conversation. In fact, even though many in this church utilized the terminology of *community* extensively, this term was simply used as a semantic substitute for the term *church*, unlike the two previous case studies. As a result, *community* did not appear to be a significant term of *meaning* for CitC attenders. However, even with such a stress on being different from all others, CitC displays uniqueness in ways that map to two major adjectival categories: postmodern and embodied.

With respect to considerations of being postmodern, CitC bloggers [blogposts are used by CitC in lieu of sermon recordings on their website] quite avidly embraced this self-designation. For instance, one blogger assertively stated, "I may come across all savvy and postmodern [because] I really do love the complexity and humility that come with constantly 'not knowing.'"

CitC also avidly identifies with aforementioned postmodern traits, such as disdain for labeling. In fact, the pastor was quick to note, "I'm still, ironically, after pastoring 2 ½ years a sort of church that is in some ways so emergent, they don't even like to claim the word *emergent*." When asked concerning a more preferable term, many interview participants shrugged their shoulders to indicate that they had none to offer; however, Interviewee 30 suggested the possibility of "church through the looking glass." Similarly,

Interviewee 37 suggested the tongue-in-cheek description of CitC as "a drinking club with a Jesus problem." In addition to being postmodern in terms of labeling and categorizing, multiple respondents connected their postmodernity to a perceived difficulty for the church to retain a sense of permanent identity. Interviewee 37 noted that each time they moved to a new meeting location, the identity of the church shifted to fit the new environment of art gallery, community center, or theatre. So, in their sense of self, or perhaps *lack* of sense of self coupled with a deep concern about this lack, CitC group participants embraced popular postmodern emphases. They also connected their foci on conversation and inclusivity to this postmodern mindset.

As noted above, CitC refers to Sunday morning discussions between the pastors and gathered attenders as "conversations"; however, a high value placed on conversation among CitC regular attenders goes beyond this terminological issue. First, CitC interview participants view conversation as a primary marker for belief and common agreement. Specifically, Interviewee 38 made the interesting note that "the people in the community come together over what we agree on, and then the things we disagree on we hold in conversation." In other words, CitC persons see conversation as the appropriate place to hold their differences rather than allowing these differences to separate them and create barriers. Also, CitC values conversation for its ability to deconstruct. While terms particular to literary deconstruction are not utilized within CitC regularly, deconstruction emphases are noted in more basic language. As an example, Interviewee 37 succinctly related her feelings about the uniqueness of CitC by saying, "I really feel like in our community what is distinct for me is that you can find deep meaning in irony, and there's a place where you can play with stuff." In other words, deconstruction is approached by CitC conversationalists through the lens of irony, and no belief or practice is considered "too sacred" for this type of treatment and consideration. However, this deconstruction does have boundaries such as not carrying them over into any place where it might cause exclusion of persons or a non-welcoming attitude in their estimation.

The most consistent trait to be noted by CitC interviewees in connection with postmodern emphases was a high estimation for acceptance and inclusion. A call for acceptance and welcoming appears in every corporate gathering of CitC as well as in electronic forms of communication and interviewee responses. Specifically, they often repeat verbatim, "You are welcome whether you believe a little, a lot, or not." When I asked for clarification of this repeated phrase, two interview respondents offered very insightful clarifying comments although all respondents strongly asserted this statement as presenting the foundational perspective of CitC. The first clarifying statement concerned the extent of this welcome. Specifically, Interviewee 35 stated, "Everyone is welcome no matter who they are, whatever their background, whether they're Christian or not, whether they're Jewish, whether they're Muslim, anything. As long as they're comfortable in coming and being with us. I'm comfortable with that. And, we don't tell anyone what to believe. Each person believes what he or she wants to believe." So, the welcoming stance of CitC is meant to include absolutely anyone who would be interested in attending or aligning with the community in one way or another. In fact, Interviewee 33 admitted to me that "I actually never have gone to Church in the Cliff," and she was quick to add, "I'm fairly familiar with Church in the Cliff, and, honestly, I don't go to any church right now." Interviewee 31 provided the second clarifying remark by avowing, "I would say, first of all, that all are welcome, and that really does, I really mean that. When I say all are welcome, we practice . . . our communion is open table, which this is, honestly, the first church that I've been to where our theological value of hospitality trumps." As displayed in this quote and other interviewee perspectives, this sense of welcoming and including everyone was seen as distinctly postmodern and one of the few consistent markers of identity for CitC.[53] The other major category of description for CitC appeared to be in a greater state of flux than their postmodern designation.

A recurrent category of consideration and conversation within CitC centered on the term *embodied* as a modifier for their spirituality; however, an understanding of this term varied in order to include other concepts within it. For instance, one CitC blogger wrote, "Thus our bodies are spiritual, being the locus of transformation through the mind and heart and will. As embodied beings, we press against one another leaving impressions like pieces of soft clay." The imagery of this quote would seem to inform toward an understanding of *embodied* as interpersonal, resulting in social interactions of some sort, and, indeed, social action is a major characteristic of CitC. However, *embodied* has also been taken in ways which more directly impact the divine-human encounter within CitC. Notably, one blogger stated, "It just makes sense to me that God is on the move and somehow accessible as an *embodied experience*."[54] CitC interview respondents often connected use of liturgy and experimentation with familiar and exotic spiritual practices as indicative of this viewpoint. Both of these meanings were explicated illustratively by CitC interviewees.

53. While it would appear that this concern for absolute inclusion was very distinctive to Church in the Cliff, EC literary output confirmed that this concern is common among emergent churches. Cf., Snider and Bowen, *Toward a Hopeful Future*, 162–64.

54. Emphasis added.

With respect to *embodied* as a category of social action, CitC attenders were pleased to consider the ways in which CitC builds relationships within their group and with their larger community. For instance, with respect to intragroup relations, many respondents focused on the friendship and hospitality aspects of their gatherings. To refer back to the tongue-in-cheek description of CitC as "a drinking club with a Jesus problem," the respondent who used this explanation was quick to clarify that she meant, "in Church in the Cliff you can find a community that is not bound together by belief but is bound together by doing stuff together." Examples of "doing stuff together" ranged from hanging out at bars and having Bible studies at participants' homes to attending local theatre and music productions put on by attenders or friends of attenders. Additionally, Interviewee 30 noted strongly that they were focused on the local and small business community of Oak Cliff in which the church met and most participants lived. Several participants picked up this theme in noting their distinction from many other churches in which members drive for many miles to reach a church that is not connected to their local community or neighborhood. While discussion of the term *embodied* in this sense definitely highlighted CitC interest in social involvement, the other meaning attached to this term in interviews was much more directly related to CitC appropriation of mystic practices.

For CitC, one of the meanings attached to the term *embodied* focused on connecting an individual with God in a variety of possible ways, and interviewee comments tended to apply this meaning to how they used liturgy, the Bible, and a host of ever-changing experimental spiritual practices. First, with respect to liturgy, CitC participants were quick to note that the group used liturgy much more often than the religious traditions in which many of them were raised so that multiple interviewees first experienced CitC as slightly disorienting as compared with more familiar settings. In the words of Interviewee 37, "I showed up, my little Fundamentalist, Republican-voting self, showed up into the middle of this crazy liturgical, quiet, contemplative service." Other participants also noted this liturgical container as part of the corporate CitC experience. In fact, Interviewee 31 noted that, while most things change from meeting to meeting, use of the liturgy was "a ritual container to Church in the Cliff which stays consistent." Interviewee 30 picks up the "container" element to note, "the Holy Spirit meets us in these really ancient containers." However, it was quite interesting to note that this ritual aspect did not translate into prescribed forms of human-divine engagement.

With regard to the use of the Bible, Interviewee 28 was shocked that "they were actually suggesting that people put their own spin on the Bible."

The pastor brings this perspective into sharp relief on the church blog by stating, "these stories [from the Bible] are not meant to be taken literally, but are formative identity stories told again and again to create conversation and dialogue." So, looking at what CitC interviewees say about liturgy and the Bible in tandem, a picture begins to form of this group as one that values the ancient but as one that also participates and innovates with the ancient. This viewpoint extended beyond the spiritual practices of liturgy and use of the Bible. In fact, Interviewee 29 put all of the mystic practices considered succinctly into this framework by saying, "We can learn from all kinds of spiritual traditions and figure out what works within our context." As seen in this quote, CitC has two parts to how they assimilate spiritual practices in general. First, they firmly believe that they can learn from anyone, but, second, they follow this belief up with the view that they can modify practices to fit their context. So, as the church which most fully embraced postmodern identity and participation in the EC conversation, it will likely come as no surprise that this church had also experimented most with individual mystic practices. However, experimentation did not always lead to assimilation or even a detailed understanding of a practice for those who engaged it once or twice only within a corporate setting. Within the fifth chapter, focus on interviewee responses concerning individual mystic practices will display specifically the appropriation of mystic practices within the contexts of each case study church.

Summary of Chapter

To revisit the major questions of this chapter, the empirical design of this study can be demonstrated in a straightforward manner of answering the questions *what*, *why*, and *who*. The foregoing descriptions of tools used within empirical methodology served to answer the question of *what* for any person unfamiliar with the general use and application of qualitative research, case studies, surveys/questionnaires, interviews, and participant observation, as these were the combined methods in this study. Then, the rationale section offered an insight into *why* these particular methods were valuable for gathering the desired data. Matters of rationale focused on my specific interest in the *meanings* attached to behaviors rather than simply investigating the behaviors of the case study churches themselves. Descriptions of the three case study churches through their historical development and notable social qualities served to answer the question of *who*. Now, discussion can proceed to an in-depth consideration of empirical findings concerning EC borrowing of mystic practices. To this end, chapter five will present practical implementation of methods and detailed findings concerning exactly how EC participants *appropriate* mystic practices. Chapter six will then continue this empirical discussion by displaying the ways in which EC practitioners *reinterpret* these practices for their own theological context. In the final chapter, evaluation of empirical findings from chapters five and six will be compared with theological emphases analyzed from EC literature along with matters of conclusion, contribution, and recommendation.

5

Phenomenological Appropriation of Mystic Practices

SOCIOLOGICAL INVESTIGATION OF THE appropriation of mystic practices within the case study churches can be approached from two directions: phenomenological and theological. This bi-directional focus is possible as a result of the interview structure for this study.[1] Specifically, interview participants were questioned concerning *how* and *why* they utilize each practice. The answers to these questions formed the bulk of each interview and provided the basis for understanding the extent of appropriation of each practice on a concrete and abstract level. With respect to the research claim, it is notable that focus is chiefly placed on theological interpretation. While the study itself is sociological in nature, it is principally concerned with *theological content*. Explication of theological interpretation of mystic practices will be the subject of the sixth chapter. However, examination of the appropriation of practices on a phenomenological level provides the crucial foundation for observations made and conclusions drawn concerning EC theological connections. In other words, certain overarching features of *how* interview participants actually employ practices in their personal or corporate spiritualities, particularly crossing the boundaries of each case study unit, provide vital information concerning spiritual borrowing *in the EC*, not just in a single church. In keeping with this purpose, focus will rest chiefly on individual participants as the primary units of data gathering and analysis in this chapter rather than on each case study church or comparison among churches. Therefore, this chapter will introduce general categories and observed themes that arose within interviews concerning

---

1. While other media were utilized in the research process, such as participant observation, podcasts, and blog posts, these formats did not serve to offer new perspectives from what was revealed in interview data. As the stated sociological method for this study was phenomenological, interview data was used over any other source in order to allow for participants to speak for themselves most directly.

the tangible implementation of individual mystic practices principally for cross-case analysis, and distinctives of a particular church context will only be noted when directly impacting implementation.

All interview participants completed a survey listing twenty-one specific mystic practices in order to ascertain which practices were used and which were not.[2] Answers to this questionnaire provided the structure for each interview by designating which practices would be considered, and these survey answers also provided the structure for general categories of data analysis. While analysis of theological interpretation in chapter six will utilize the theological anchors introduced in chapter three, the phenomenological appropriation of practices presented in this chapter is better suited to a simpler process of classification. Precisely, practices have been grouped into categories for examination on the basis of descending order of widespread usage. With this numerical focus, practices can be grouped into five categories: major practices, divergent major practices, minor practices, divergent minor practices, and practices of passing familiarity. The categories of major and minor practices showed a convergence of definition and focus among EC participants. Conversely, divergent major and divergent minor categories are provided as a recognition that certain practices appear to be either major or minor practices among the churches, but these appearances are deceiving because analysis of interviewee responses clarified that they were appropriating divergent practices that were subsumed under one name. Consequently, these divergent practices were difficult to chart according to statistical usage. Statistics are provided with consideration of these categories, but interviewees occasionally used divergent definitions within the course of a single interview, which served to skew these statistics because I sometimes had to count an interviewee in multiple categories as a result. The phenomenological method employed in this study is responsible in part for the necessity of creating these divergent categories because participants were allowed to define and interpret terms for themselves. Divergent categories illustrate the ambiguity literally present in interview responses. In other words, this method allowed for recognition that semantic disparity concerning certain practices is a vital piece of data in itself. Additionally, certain practices are considered in tandem because multiple interviewees noted a vital link between two or more practices.

A further breakdown of particular categories may be helpful before proceeding to each discrete section for full exposition. Practices were statistically charted as major, minor, or passing familiarity with the usage ranges of 60–100%, 30–59%, or 0–29% respectively. The percentage of interviewees

---

2. A sample survey is available in Appendix A.

who utilize each practice will be provided in parentheses following each term. These percentages are based on any level of participation without stratification into personal or communal use.[3] Additionally, percentages are based on the responses of thirty-seven interview participants. One interview participant declined to fill out a survey on the basis of non-utilization of any practice, and several surveys were completed online by individuals who declined participation in a face-to-face interview. With these caveats in mind, major practices include Holy Communion (94.6%), silence (72.9%) and solitude (62.2%) considered together, and meditation (67.6%). Divergent major practices are centering prayer (89.1%), contemplative prayer (72.9%), and spiritual direction (72.9%). Minor practices comprise confession (59.5%), the liturgical calendar (56.8%) and liturgical prayer (48.6%) considered together, fasting (51.4%), and making the sign of the cross (32.4%). Divergent minor practices consist of the following: the Jesus Prayer (54.1%), practicing the presence of God (43.2%), pilgrimage (35.1%), and fixed-hour prayer (32.4%). Additional practices are utilized on the level of passing familiarity or according to personal idiosyncrasy. These practices include *lectio Divina* (24.3%), prayer labyrinths (24.3%), the stations of the cross (24.3%), icons (18.9%), and the rosary (16.2%).

It is important at the outset to reiterate that this study is phenomenological with regard to its empirical methodology. In other words, although the researcher buttressed several points through direct observation, the primary data component of this chapter and consideration of these practices is what the interviewees stated in their own words. In light of this situation, some practices which were not implemented as widely may receive more comment here because more description was often provided for those practices which interviewees considered most unique rather than ones considered most central to their churches. So, the first discrete section of spiritual borrowing in light of participant responses is the major practices which the case study churches implemented.

Major Practices

As discovered in the empirical research phase for this project, interview participants at the three case study emergent churches noted that Holy Communion (94.6%), silence (72.9%) and solitude (62.2%), and meditation

---

3. Interestingly, interview participants discussed categories of personal and communal use as well as regularity of practice with little connection to the categories they marked on the spiritual practices questionnaire (Cf., Appendix A). As a result, these categorical divisions were not applicable for analyzing the resulting data.

(67.6%) were the most common mystic practices borrowed for spiritual application. For the purposes of this study, major practices were categorized as those which more than 60% of respondents utilized in some form. In accordance with the division of questions on the interview schedule, interviewees distinguished their comments on the basis of *how* they utilize a particular practice from *why* they utilize that practice.[4] Unsurprisingly, respondents did not delineate all minute details of each practice; rather, they tended to focus on two areas: either what they viewed as essential characteristics or what they regarded as notable eccentricities of how that practice was utilized within their specific church setting. As a result, these practices will be presented similarly, focusing first on what interviewees considered to be most vital before proceeding to notable traits that were considered to be innovative or unique to their church of attendance. In keeping with the overall thrust of phenomenology, discussion will focus as much as possible on specific interviewee observations.

Holy Communion

The practice of Holy Communion was by far the most common mystic practice among participants, utilized by thirty-five out of thirty-seven respondents. This particular finding is quite unsurprising since it is one of the most common practices utilized by all segments of Christianity. However, the case study churches interestingly drew closer to each other in their essential structure for celebrating this sacrament even though they originated from disparate denominations. This directional trend is notable in the most basic characteristics which interviewees mentioned, particularly *when* Holy Communion was practiced and *how* the elements of bread and wine were distributed to those in attendance. Two out of three of the case study churches celebrate Holy Communion every week, which was in distinction from their originating traditions. Only one church, RCC, held to the traditional monthly celebration instituted by their denomination, the United Methodist Church. Participants noted the frequency of Holy Communion as both essential and unique. Interviewee 23 paradigmatically illustrates this viewpoint by saying, "It's really a place where Christ meets us, and we want to do that as often as possible. And so, we started doing that every week, which for my Protestant tradition is very rare." Interviewees often went into great depth concerning the importance of Holy Communion and the reasons for its practice; however, some participants noted this frequency without any further rumination on the topic, such as the succinct statement

---

4. See Appendix B for a sample interview schedule.

provided by Interviewee 35: "We do that every Sunday." Another interesting basic feature of how the case study churches implement Holy Communion is that they all practice intinction.

Intinction is the term designating the process in which the bread is dipped in the wine or grape juice (or, in the case of one church, grape soda) and then the communicant eats the bread without taking a sip directly from the cup. Multiple respondents noted this particular practice within their churches, including Interviewees 7, 19, and 31 who specifically used the technical term *intinction*. It is also interesting to note that this specific mode of Holy Communion was often not questioned by interviewees, but they did note that it was often different from the Christian traditions with which they were previously aligned. While the prevalence of Holy Communion, its frequency, and its mode were all basic common qualities within the case studies, participants emphasized the distinctive nature of this practice in these emergent churches as well.

Interview responses and researcher observations uncovered the notable level of variation in how Holy Communion was practiced within each church, and respondents were often quite comfortable and supportive of how different this practice might appear from observance to observance within their own churches. For instance, RCC often practiced Holy Communion in family groups and Bible study groups rather than only in a corporate worship service.

> We use it as a teaching tool in our family settings. We'll have a family night that we try to do where it becomes a place that it's a starting point, and we set the tone for the evening where we spend time together as a family and watch movies and we discuss how can we take, what lessons can we learn from those movies. What do those speak about our culture? What do those speak about who we are as Christians and what God wants for us? For me, that's partly communion. I would say communion is a big part of the Acacia groups. (Interviewee 3)

As another example of variation, Interviewees 14, 25, and 27 noted that they use Holy Communion personally on occasion. However, personal practice can be adapted to one's situation strikingly, as described by Interviewee 25.

> I do that at home sometimes. If I'm praying at home, I'll actually get a glass of water and some bread because we don't usually have juice at my house, but the whole point of it is that it is symbolic, so I don't think it really matters. It's not really often. I don't know. I'll be reading the Bible or something, and I'm like "Hmm, little church service, whatever."

There is also great variation in the elements used for Holy Communion. Most respondents noted that their churches varied between loaves of bread and communion wafers. They also noted a variation in utilizing grape juice or wine, and, as mentioned previously, one church utilized grape soda for Holy Communion, and they often used locally made tortillas as well. While these examples display quite a bit of variation, interview participants often sought to focus their discussions of this practice through the variations that they perceived in their liturgy. Specifically, liturgy associated with the celebration of Holy Communion was quite open to modification in the case study churches, according to Interviewees 24, 29, 30, and 38. So, the emergent churches studied all utilize Holy Communion, but they often vary its practice from observance to observance on the basis of where it is practiced, whom is involved, what is consumed, and what is said. However, interviewed individuals did note a particular point where consistency is strictly maintained.

While all case study churches practiced openness in Holy Communion, two of the three churches focused specifically on the words utilized to invite all persons present to partake in Holy Communion. Within the context of ERC, these words took the form of this hospitable invitation, "Regardless of your background or experience, if you desire to take in the grace of Christ, then come" (Interviewee 23). Many ERC interviewees evinced this sense of welcome as a part of their practice of Holy Communion, but CitC attenders focused on their welcoming words even more stridently. CitC participants stressed the welcoming nature of Holy Communion by the call for *all* to come, as noted by Interviewee 32: "I think everyone loves the words 'whether you believe a little or a lot or not, come, because all things are ready.'" The history behind this Eucharistic welcome was outlined by another interviewee in the words below.

> "Whether you're baptized or not, whether you believe a lot or not." Although, I will say, actually, that did change, since I've been going to Church in the Cliff. The "whether you believe a little, a lot, or not" used to be "whether you believe a little or a lot." And, we started including the "or not" part when we did a series, not this past summer, but the one before where people talked about the different traditions they came from. And, we had members of the church who talked about being agnostic or atheist, and we were also reading *Take This Bread* at that time, which was just about being this radically welcoming community. And, we decided that if we want to be radically welcoming, then that meant everybody. And so, that's when we started putting in the "or not" part of the belief statement. (Interviewee 29)

This practical emphasis illustrates how emergent churches utilize traditional practices in the service of their larger value on community even as the previous trait of variation in implementation of a practice illustrates how a traditional practice can be put in service to a larger value set on experimentation. While it is helpful to note the beginnings of these theological connections at this point, further delineation and explication of the theology behind these innovations in the practice of Holy Communion and other practices will be the proper task of chapter six. At this point, it is more directly applicable to take stock simply of the commonalities of the practice of Holy Communion among the case study churches. Specifically, these emergent churches display their distinctive emphasis on Holy Communion by frequent practice, utilization of intinction, variation of multiple aspects of implementation, and a liturgical welcome that is absolutely open to everyone. Distinguishing EC characteristics for spiritual borrowing also appear in consideration of the concrete aspects of the appropriation of silence and solitude in the case study churches.

Silence and Solitude

Silence and solitude, while separate categories on the survey taken by interview participants, were often considered together by the interviewees. This connection, as well as the places and times for these practices, were the major notable phenomenological characteristics of these practices pointed out by participants. Interviewees also discussed silence and solitude with a noted emphasis on the contextual nature of these mystic practices. Comments denoted a very strong link between these practices. Interviewee 16 aptly summed up this connection by admitting, "Silence is something that I really have to be away to do. I have to be far away." This comment illustrates the pragmatic basis on which these two practices were combined for interview participants in the case study churches. More in-depth discussion of the process with which each interviewee participated in silence or solitude steered in the direction of a consideration of when and where these two practices became important rather than what one might do during a specific time or in a specific place.

With regard to the time and place for silence and solitude, interviewees typically did not look to a scheduled event; rather, these practices were used on an as-needed basis. In the words of Interviewee 20, "I'd say it's a regular occurrence, but I don't ... it's not like Saturday before church, all day Saturday I'm not talking, and I'm sitting in silence and solitude before." In a brief disconnection between silence and solitude, a couple of interviewees noted that church services contained "moments of silence."

> We use it at church. I intentionally stretch out that moment after song, before I stand up, and I feel myself holding that. I feel the Spirit holding that, but I definitely [believe that] having that silence as a response to the psalm is really important. (Interviewee 30)

> I think, we're pretty regular about incorporating moments of silence, not, maybe, extended periods, but moments. So, where it's an invitation to just be for a bit, before we move on. (Interviewee 31)

The use of "moments of silence" was also occasionally noted on a personal level, but at that point these moments were once more connected to solitude. In this sense, Interviewee 12 described a personal experience which came the closest of any interviewee to describing an actual process of using silence and solitude as a regular practice. Specifically, he stated, "I was impacted very, very strongly by Psalm 46, I think, 46:11, 'Be still and know that I am God,' and I really got a lot out of that discipline of silence where you just don't think, don't meditate on anything particular, don't contemplate on a Scripture. You just sit silently with God." While the timing of silence often coincided with that of solitude, aside from the exception of church services, the places for silence and solitude varied.

The crux behind the reasoning of combining silence and solitude for many interviewees was the difficulty of being silent in the presence of others. As a result, many respondents focused their comments on the different solitary places where they found moments to be silent and alone before God.

> Solitude isn't something that I get a lot of. I've got four kids. They're all under eleven, so it's kind of an anthill when I get home, and I love my anthill. So, I stay up late at night. From about 10 at night until about 12 is when I'm alone. That might be watching a very artsy movie or ridiculous action film or it may be reading, but it may also just be [that] I run at night in the middle [of the street]. We don't have street lights out here. It's rural. So, I'll run at eleven o'clock at night and be outside and worship and be all by myself. (Interviewee 16)

> I used to really not like to be alone. I was . . . I'm very social, but, over the years, I've been able to start to appreciate having quiet time and having, now that my kids are both in school, I'll even use it if I'm going to do some chores around the house, turn on

PHENOMENOLOGICAL APPROPRIATION OF MYSTIC PRACTICES 137

> praise and worship music, shut the phones off, so nobody can call me, shut the computer off, shut the TV off, and just have quiet and worshiping in my spirit. Really, [it's] just calm time where I'm just thinking about God and just dwelling on his goodness and his attributes and that kind of thing. (Interviewee 1)

> I'd like to go on a retreat by myself. I've done that. While I was in seminary, I went to a Jesuit house for only a 24-hour silent retreat, but I loved it. (Interviewee 31)

> I do like to go camp out. I do like to be out by myself, periodically, in wild places, semi-wild around here. And, it's not really silent, but there's some real healing that goes on for me, and it's just sounds of nature. It's not human-generated kinds of things, unless a plane flies over, whatever. (Interviewee 28)

> For me, it's stealing away to my room and just sitting or in my car. That's definitely somewhere where I turn off the radio, and I sit in silence. (Interviewee 26)

These comments amply illustrate the ways in which interviews focused on the time and place where solitude and silence became valuable practices. Additionally, several interviewees made links between these practices and other mystic practices on the survey, such as meditation, centering prayer, contemplation, and practicing the presence of God. These connections often arose out of a manifest tendency for interviewees to view both silence and solitude as primarily contextual practices. In this sense, silence and/or solitude provided the necessary *context* for another mystic practice which was then the *content* of an intentional experience. In the apt words of Interviewee 24, "It [silence] goes hand in glove with everything. Yeah, but I don't practice silence just to practice silence." Within the scope of the interviews, it became quite apparent that this judgment could easily be extended to solitude as well. In summary, the phenomenological comments on the practices of silence and solitude focused on their connections, the times and places of application, and the contextual nature of these practices. As part of this contextual nature, many respondents noted that silence and solitude often provided the milieu for the practice of meditation, the final major practice denoted by interviewees.

Meditation

The practice of meditation was utilized by twenty-five of the interview participants, and, while this practice had many methods and meanings attached to it, three notable features tied definitions together for interviewees: communal, personal, and singular. The first common feature of meditation for interviewees was the ways in which this practice was utilized corporately. Communal meditation was also termed *reflection* or *guided meditation* by interview participants, and, in this sense, it shared some kinship with the "moments of silence" noted in the foregoing section. This type of meditation, however, necessitated a specific focus for meditation. Interviewee 31 recalled an instance which exemplifies this type of meditation in the case study churches.

> Recently, we did that at church. People walked. It was on anxiety, and you meditate on your anxiety. I had this Brillo pad, representing your anxiety like this steel wool and how conductive it is and how it fills up our soul. That's a whole other meditation, but, on the way in [to the church service], you walked in and you meditate on it, and when you left, you left it in a bucket on the way out, depending on what God could do in that space. It calmed their anxieties.

As illustrated by this anecdote, whether termed *meditation*, *reflection*, or *guided meditation*, interviewees viewed meditation in a group as an activity or occasion during which they were led to think deeply on an issue. In addition to this communal interpretation, the personal practice of meditation extended this perspective for many interviewees.

The second common feature of the practice of meditation among the emergent churches studied was utilization on a personal level. Personal use was the preferred category for implementation of meditation for a majority of interviewees who appropriated the practice. Descriptions of personal meditation began to focus more specifically on matters of process. Typically, respondent comments divided on matters of process into categories of passive meditation and active meditation. With regard to passive meditation, multiple participants noted their characteristic process. Interviewee 17 provided an in-depth example of this passive meditative process.

> My meditation is usually after my evening Bible studies. It's usually about 7:45, 8 o'clock, and I just like to disengage from everything else that's going on. Turn off everything in the house, but the air conditioner these days [I] like to turn all that off, and particularly the lights, and I try to spend a full ten minutes, meditating on God's word. That's a challenge for me. My mind definitely drifts. So, what I find myself doing is constantly saying, "Wait a minute that has nothing to do with meditating. Get

out of that. Go back to where you're supposed to be." That goes on for ten minutes, and I try to do that every night.

While quiet, still forms of meditation were quite popular, other respondents coupled their practice of meditation with particular activities which helped them to focus. Interestingly, these activities were rarely of a religious nature. Popular combinations involved music and gardening. Interviewee 29 provided insight into his full process of an active meditation.

> I do my own—I call it my "gardening meditation." Which I thought was kind of weird until I read about people doing walking meditation, and I thought "Well, okay, it's not so weird." I know what my tasks are beforehand, so I don't have to stop and think about what needs to be done now. So, I can slip into this more meditative state rather than a getting-chores-done state, and it's always a contemplation of life and death, really. I mean, I don't think of it in those terms when I'm doing it, but it's just always meant working with whatever is in front of me, whatever plant or slug or whatever I'm dealing with at the time, and I'm not even sure how to really describe it, because there's thought, and it's always kind of a sustained theme, I guess, on the life of the little plot of land that I'm tending about how that's a microcosm of everything.

These two forms of meditation, active and passive, differed in their process widely among interview participants, but they were vitally linked through the major connecting feature of meditation which set it apart for respondents from other similar practices: a singular focus for one's thought.

The third, and most distinguishing, common feature for the practice of meditation among these emergent churches was a singular focus of thought within that practice. Several respondents noted that such a focus might be a passage of Scripture. Interviewee 12 described representatively his meditative focus in this manner.

> We've talked about a practice where you will come across a Scripture, for example, or a phrase that comes into your mind, like "God is good." You'll just [say] "God is good, God is good." You'll meditate just on "God is good" and not trying to understand the meaning of it or the significance of it to my life. It's just a meditation on Scripture or the phrase.

While Scripture was a popular focus, other potential foci were noted as well, such as a literary character or the world of nature. These different points of attention were the most notable points of connection among interviewees with respect to how they practiced meditation. However, there was a notable undercurrent among interviewee perspectives that connected the practice of meditation with Buddhist meditation or yoga. Participants who made these connections tended to center attention on an "emptying" process for meditation rather than a "concentration" method. Interviewee 34 relates this process in the following way.

> I do yoga. It's a physically demanding yoga, but it's still a very meditative thing for me at the same time. It's just, as you're going, it's 105 degrees, hour and a half practice, and so it's very, very physical. So, a lot of times, your meditation is breathe, just let go of the struggle and everything like that and just think about breathing regularly and properly and not panic breathing or holding your breath.

While perspectives on meditation through the lenses of non-Christian religions offer an interesting contrast to other interviewee responses, they did not constitute a major trend with respect to phenomenological appropriation of meditation. Instead, interviewee comments concerning the implementation of meditation focus on common features of group *reflection* or *guided meditation*, personal eccentricities of passive and active meditation, and, most importantly, the binding phenomenological element of focus on a singular topic, trait, or Scripture for deep concentration.

Divergent Major Practices

Moving on from major practices, three practices appeared misleadingly to be practiced by a majority of respondents: centering prayer (89.1%), contemplative prayer (72.9%), and spiritual direction (72.9%). Upon closer inspection, these practices were not easily chartable, but they were significant. To elaborate, the apparent status of these practices is the result of semantic divergence concerning these practices. Succinctly stated, interviewees diverged into two and sometimes three different definitions depending on how they understood these terms, so much so that the participants' responses had little convergence when read together. In light of this circumstance, discussion of these practices must begin with comments concerning the disambiguation of definitions. Once lines of meaning have been fully separated, it is possible to see that these practices were not appropriated in a major way. However, it is also difficult to know exactly where they fit because while the participants converged on a common term, they diverged on its meaning. Simply stated, these practices often have vague names which allowed participants to connect multiple meanings and/or innovate their own meaning for an unfamiliar term. Nevertheless, the practices retain their importance for EC interviewees even if it is difficult to chart them on the spectrum of importance statistically. Once these lines of definition are clearly drawn for each practice, progress can be made concerning explication of common features of these practices as pointed out by multiple interview participants. Notable unique responses will be considered at the end of discussion on each practice. As mentioned above, focus at this point will rest heavily on *how* each practice is utilized through frequent reference to verbatim responses of individuals interviewed.

Centering Prayer

Interviewee comments on the practice of centering prayer displayed a genuine lack of consensus in how the term was defined, necessitating disambiguation of meanings prior to discussing matters of appropriation. Due to these divergent definitions, this practice is not major nor is it minor because it technically diverges into three separate practices. This circumstance may be due in part to broadness of interpretation or to the questionnaire supplying the term *wordless prayer* as a possible synonym for those who had not heard of centering prayer. As a result, interviewee comments tended to show one of three divergent understandings of centering prayer: simply praying silently (24.3%), praying through actions (13.5%), or praying as listening to God rather than asking for something (51.3%). Interviewee quotations will illustrate this semantic divergence in greater depth below. While significant differences persist, certain commonalities within participant discussion of the practice were also visible. Many respondents connected centering prayer to a focus on breathing in prayer as a means of "centering oneself." Others made a point to mention that their practice of centering prayer was not limited to a specific time or context. Finally, multiple interviewees implemented centering prayer through a general process either performed individually or as part of a group. So, while centering prayer was the subject of great definitional divergence among interview participants, convergent features of the practice across case study churches include a connection to breathing, no specific limitations of time or context for the practice, and a general process through which the practice is embraced on a personal and corporate level.

Despite the aforementioned commonalities, centering prayer was defined by most interviewees in one of the three divergent ways: praying silently, praying through actions, or praying as listening to God rather than asking. With respect to the first definition, interviewees followed the pattern of Interviewee 15 who succinctly admitted, "When I see wordless prayer I just mean praying not out loud." While each of the interviewees who defined centering prayer in this way was quick to note uncertainty about its definition, subsequent responses displayed a lack of any familiarity with the term. This lack of familiarity informs the study concerning the divergent nature of the frequency of this practice, for several individuals would have likely not listed centering prayer as a practice if they had not been allowed the latitude of defining the term for themselves.

Other respondents defined the "wordless" aspect of centering prayer as praying through one's actions rather than through words. These respondents connected centering prayer to different activities which held personal meaning. For instance, Interviewee 11 comments on this connection by noting, "That's what I focus on a song. Sometimes, if you've decided to just sit and sort of soak in the words of that song or whatever the image is that is being conjured." Interestingly, participants noted that the "centering" aspect of the prayer according to this definition related to the feelings which resulted from the activity, and they also noted that the activity to be used as prayer would likely change for each person who desired to pray in that manner.

A final way of defining centering prayer among interview participants was focused on prayer as listening without asking God a specific request. Individuals who defined the practice in this manner focused chiefly on what centering prayer is *not*. Interviewee 7 described this approach thoroughly.

> This is my understanding of centering prayer, and that idea of focusing in, letting God begin to . . . just being open to him and saying "God, what is it that you would speak to me?" I want to clear out everything and be still long enough to listen. So, that's my understanding of centering prayer. So, that I'm not going in with some preconceived idea of what I want God to tell me or going in with a Scripture text, which in my mind would be a different kind of prayer idea.

It is in this final sense of non-petitionary listening that multiple respondents began to connect with the definition of centering prayer considered in EC literature, which was derived from the practice so named by Thomas Keating and M. Basil Pennington. Multiple interviewees followed this vein of definition with varying levels of detail, often simply defining centering prayer as "just listening" (Interviewee 19). While it is evident that there was little consensus of definition for centering prayer, there were common traits associated with this practice across case study churches and interview participants, even those who described a unique version of the practice.

Although little commonality existed with respect to the definition of centering prayer, multiple interviewees connected this practice to one's breathing and through that action to the concepts of calming or relieving anxiety. Specifically, they noted the calming effect of focusing on breathing, particularly with the goal of first slowing one's breath then concentrating on the rhythm of inhalation and exhalation. Interviewee 3 mentioned this process most concisely by stating, "I use it [centering prayer] often. I would say I use it quite a bit in a lot of different settings. So it often just starts with breathing techniques just to calm my body down and get to a place where there's not a lot of unnecessary anxiety." Interestingly, whatever definition respondents used for centering prayer, part of the "centering" aspect of their intended prayer was a conscious connection with physical breathing, as illustrated in the representative comment above. Breathing possibly became more important to these individuals because of the lack of specificity in timing or context of the practice.

While centering prayer could be sectioned off as a discrete activity by most interview participants, the times and contexts of this practice were viewed as quite fluid by EC attendees. For instance, Interviewee 12 artfully asserted a sense of complete freedom for when and where to implement this practice.

> I think [centering prayer can be practiced] at the beginning of a service at church. It could happen at four in the morning when you can't sleep, when you sit down and your mind is wandering over a lot of things, and you say "You know, I just need to center in and focus on the Holy Spirit's presence and see where that leads me." So, I think it can happen in a lot of different contexts.

Other interview participants supported this open framework for practice with the addition of a few personal preferences. With respect to time, Interviewee 31 noted that there were no specific limits other than internal ones: "I think one of the keys to centering prayer for me, at least how I learned it through Keating and all of that, is creating a space that's long enough to really let go." Interviewee 21 added a comment that enhanced the need for enough time to focus on the basis of personal variability by saying, "And, it's a little bit harder for me to concentrate because I feel more active. That's why whenever I participate in centered prayer, it usually comes about when I'm more tired and exhausted, either after I work out or after work." Therefore, while there were no general limits on the time for centering prayer, multiple EC adherents asserted personal limits that each one must set for him/

herself. Issues of personal boundaries for centering prayer also extended to contextual matters. As Interviewee 19 admitted, "I guess the masters could walk around and just do it. I can't do that. I've got to find a quiet place with no distraction." So, context matters for EC appropriation of centering prayer as it pertains to each individual; however, it is fascinating that aside from personal boundaries, there are few, if any, limits on context.

As already discussed, the practice of centering prayer among EC interviewees has no firmly set limits of time or context, but respondents went even further in asserting the freedom of context for appropriation by noting that not even a solely Christian context is necessary for this practice. Interviewees 21 and 34 found the practice of yoga to be a very conducive context within which to practice centering prayer. While a yogic context was a notable connection for these interviewees, it was not the only context for centering prayer noted within the case study churches that had roots outside of the Christian experience. As another example, Interviewee 30, who claimed what she termed a "Buddheo-Christian" perspective, readily asserted that her concept of centering prayer rested most deeply in her experiences with Buddhist meditation. In this vein, she understood centering prayer and Buddhist meditation to be essentially the same process of "a kind of emptying out in acknowledging, noticing the thoughts and letting them pass, and then it's this deepening down to the bottom of the river experience." However, other respondents were careful to point out that they saw a distinction between centering prayer and the non-Christian contexts presented above. For example, Interviewee 23 distinguished types of centering prayer by noting, "In some forms of Eastern spirituality, centering prayer is to empty one's mind, and I think in Christian spirituality it's to empty one's mind in order to fill it with Christ." Contrasting perspectives on the interplay of centering prayer with contexts outside of Christianity were interesting for the scope of the context of EC assimilation of centering prayer because they display that among the case study churches even supposedly opposing theological positions can be equally attached to the "container" of centering prayer. In addition to matters of time and context, interview participants also noted common features of the process of practicing centering prayer on individual and communal levels.

Interestingly, while the definition of centering prayer differed among interview participants at case study EC churches, the process for individual use of centering prayer was described in a markedly similar fashion. The process itself was most succinctly described by Interviewee 23 who stated, "Centering prayer for me is to focus on Christ, on who he is, on quieting myself, and . . . I don't know . . . clearing my mind of my anxieties, which is easier said than done." As the interviewee admits, this process is easier to say than to do, yet he offers the two categorical actions which other respondents used to describe the centering prayer process. First, multiple interviewees noted the principal aspect of centering prayer as a progressive focusing on God although that characteristic did not map equally to all three definitions. Specifically, an aspect of focusing maps most strongly to the third definition, listening to God. While the primary action of centering prayer for many EC practitioners was a developing focus on God, a secondary emphasis was laid on the reaction and experience of the one praying. Interviewee 3 agreed with Interviewee 23 concerning the calming effects of centering prayer by noting, "So, it often just starts with breathing techniques just to calm my body down and get to a place where there's not a lot of unnecessary anxiety." Additionally, Interviewee 36 referred to this aspect of the practice of centering prayer through its suitability for his own personality: "I'm an introvert, and so being able to just sit in a room by myself quiet for half an hour is pretty nice." While most respondents considered the centering prayer process in an individual sense, others connected centering prayer to a group context as well.

Semantically, interviewees did not connect the term *centering prayer* with a corporate practice of the same name; rather, they described group centering prayer in terms of "moments of silence" or "reflection" offered in their particular emergent churches, connecting centering prayer and meditation. As an initial example, Interviewee 23 described a group centering prayer time in the following manner: "A lot of times [the spiritual formation pastor] will have something she comes up and presents, and then she'll say 'Let's just sit and just be for a while and not feel like we have to answer something or anything like that.'" The exact particulars of group centering prayer differed among the churches studied, but other respondents made the same connections as Interviewee 23 between these moments in corporate services and the practice of centering prayer. As another example, Interviewee 32 noted, "I think for me a lot of times, when we do have a time of silence [in church services], it results in a time of centering prayer for me, if that makes sense?" This usage was not entirely limited to just one type of communal context. For instance, Interviewee 8 related the process of centering prayer, as he understood it, in the context of large corporate worship *and* smaller home groups. While the content of centering prayer may vary, it seems that there was great utility in centering prayer for multiple corporate contexts. So, centering prayer may be variously defined among EC case study churches, but its features of a fluidly defined sense of focus, fluid context, yet a general set format were common among those interviewed.

This dichotomy between definitional divergence and practical commonality was mirrored in interviewee responses concerning the practice of contemplative prayer. Such a circumstance should not be entirely surprising, since some respondents saw little difference between centering prayer and contemplative prayer. By way of example, Interviewee 19 said, "I've read different fans [of these two practices] that describe it different ways, and sometimes people call them the same thing. Sometimes, people say contemplative prayer is what you do after centering prayer so, in my mind, I can't even differentiate between the two of them." While not all respondents agreed with Interviewee 19, there was definite overlap between the two practices considered in interview conversations.

Contemplative Prayer

As noted above, contemplative prayer is a divergent major practice for the same reason as centering prayer: the great breadth of its definition among the case study emergent churches. The definitional disparities, however, were much more stark with this practice. Still, its explication in terms of divergent definitions and common features can proceed in a similar fashion. First, clarification is necessary concerning interviewee understandings of the meaning of the word *contemplate*. For most persons, the modern sense of *contemplate* as intense concentration was implied, and any differences that were manifest in interviews resulted from a difference *in subject matter* on which one was to concentrate. Following initial discussion of definitions, comments may turn to points in common among interviewees. There were three principal areas of contact among EC practitioners. First, one way or another, many respondents (27%) connected contemplative prayer to the use of the Christian Scriptures. Second, contemplative prayer was often (27%) viewed as a contextual practice to be combined with other mystic practices for the content of an experience. Third, other interviewees (18.9%) avowed that contemplative prayer was not a practice per se; rather, it was an experience which happened to a person in God's timing. In this third definition, EC respondents came closest to understanding contemplative prayer in an analogous way to the mystical tradition. As such, it seems to be almost a "trick question" to even include contemplative prayer on a list of mystic *practices*. In fact, contemplative prayer was only included on the spiritual practices questionnaire which interviewees filled out because EC authors encouraged the appropriation of it as a practice in literary conversations. Therefore, a close investigation of *how* contemplative prayer was practiced within the emergent churches surveyed will take into account semantic issues, scriptural connections, contextual associations, and the relative role of each individual in initiating the practice.

Unlike centering prayer, interviewee definitions of contemplative prayer had a common point of contact in their basic understanding of the word *contemplate*; however, definitions diverged markedly from that point. Concerning a basic definition of the word *contemplate*, most interview respondents implicitly or explicitly understood this term as simply an intense form of concentration. As applied to prayer, this understanding of *contemplate* practically appeared in the proceeding manner: "To contemplate over something is, in my mind, to say 'All right, God, here are some things that I would like for us to talk about together.' So, I don't want to move away from these things. I don't want to get sidetracked" (Interviewee 7). The above quotation states explicitly what other participants implicitly understood as the meaning of the word *contemplate*, as shown in their subsequent conversation on the topic. While this basis allowed for a little more convergence among interviewee statements for contemplative prayer as opposed to centering prayer, respondent understanding of the practice branched in several directions from this initial point.

Multiple interviewees linked contemplative prayer specifically to intense concentration on a passage of Scripture for various purposes. As a representative example, Interviewee 9 explained his process of contemplative prayer. "I could read a Scripture passage and just pray over that. I'll do that a lot. I'll read a passage, and I'll just be like 'Okay, Lord, I'm just going to pray over this until you give me or reveal to me a knowledge about it.' There, I'm contemplating the Scripture." As this participant comment exemplifies, the appropriation of contemplative prayer included a new way to treat Scripture and a sense of "enlightenment" that could be variously interpreted or recognized by practitioners. While many interviewees noted this involvement with Scripture in the sense of going deeper into a particular passage, others linked Scripture to contemplative prayer in a different manner.

As a second definitional branch, interviewees connected contemplative prayer to an imaginative engagement with Scripture in which they did not so much wish to gain deeper knowledge of a passage but deeper *experiences*. By way of illustration, Interviewee 3 mentions this imaginative engagement succinctly, "Picturing myself in different scenes within the text, that sort of stuff, that way I can relate in [sic] a different level with what I'm reading." Interviewee 21 agrees with this perspective but goes into a bit more detail, particularly with relation to separating contemplative prayer from centering prayer.

> Whereas centered prayer seemed quiet and meditative, I thought of contemplative prayer as thinking about a specific thing or guided. I used to have this podcast that I listened to occasionally

called "Pray as You Go," and sometimes a person will say "Imagine yourself, say, put yourself in the place of a certain disciple, listening to Jesus' words. How would you react?" So, that's what I think of contemplative prayer, as more guided.

As is evident from interviewee comments, both of these branches interpret contemplative prayer through a connection with Scripture, yet that is not the only link which respondents made within interviews.

A final definitional branch connects contemplative prayer with self-evaluation. In this sense, contemplative prayer is turned inward as a tool of discovery for the individual practitioner. While this definitional branch was a decidedly minor one, interview respondents still occasionally viewed contemplative prayer in this way, as is evident in the following explanation by Interviewee 17: "To contemplate. It's like, for me, occasionally, we all do self-evaluations. I know I do, and many of the believers that I know do that also. Sometimes, when I contemplate what I'm doing and what I think I could be doing, there's a huge gap there." So, EC practitioners added self-evaluation to connections with reading Scripture as another branch of meaning for the term *contemplative prayer*. These three definitional branches move from a basic understanding of contemplative prayer as intense concentration in very different directions; however, some points of convergence among those interviewed from different case study churches still remains.

The first major point of contact for the practice of contemplative prayer among interviewees is quite apparent from the semantic issues previously mentioned. Specifically, many interview respondents connected contemplative prayer to the reading of scriptural passages. It is most likely that this connection was primary because of the semantic link between the word *contemplate* and *contemplative prayer*. As a result of needing content to contemplate in the sense of intensely concentrate, it appears that the EC located their concentration on Scripture more than anything else. In such a situation, Scripture offered a ready-made source for concentration. While the Bible was the primary source of content for contemplative prayer, EC interviewees did not necessarily limit this point of contact simply to Scripture. For instance, Interviewee 29 widened the scope of potential subjects/aids in contemplative prayer.

> With contemplative prayer, I usually either pick a reading, or sometimes I'll be reading about the life of a saint. It's still sort of meditative, but it's meditating upon that one thing. I tend to have that focus, and it's not as wordless. It's more of an imbibing of the words I've read or the story or even, sometimes, just an image, [be]cause I love medieval artwork. Sometimes, I'll just

> contemplate an image, and it—I don't know—I'm not sure how to explain it really, but I feel like, again, it's sort of a tie to the past and a sense of identifying.

In other words, there are many options for content within contemplative prayer, but the need for some specific content was common among all interviewees who practiced contemplative prayer. Scriptural passages only happened to be the most popular media. To be fair, many interviewees saw the Bible as a place to meet God, or themselves, so while the Bible was the subject of intense concentration, the aim of the process was not Scripture itself, but to meet God or themselves. In distinction from the understanding of multiple options for content in the context of contemplative prayer, interviewees often saw contemplative prayer itself as a practice which occurs in the context of other mystic practices that have been appropriated and implemented.

Contemplative prayer has already been connected to scripture and self-evaluation, yet interview participants linked contemplative prayer with many other practices as well. For instance, contemplative prayer was linked to meditation by Interviewees 27 and 29 above. While a potential connection between contemplative prayer and meditation may seem obvious, respondents made less obvious connections as well. Illustratively, Interviewee 24 associated his personal practice of contemplative prayer with the act of journaling.

> Contemplative prayer is something that I've tried. I'm not sure if I've been successful at it in any way because I'm a fidget, and my thoughts wandered quite often. It's helpful for me to have very tangible things, and I'm aware there are ways to add concrete things to contemplation, and so I'm trying to work on that. Right now, I have a prayer journal, and it helps me if instead of thinking my prayers or saying them out loud, if I write prayers down.

As another example, Interviewee 21 connected utilization of the stations of the cross with contemplative prayer in noting, "We did the stations of the cross for Holy Week, and we incorporated some of those practices like specific, guided prayer into some of the stations." Other interviewees connected contemplative prayer to several practices depending on the specific circumstances. The connection of contemplative prayer with other practices was often quite elastic for interview participants. This elasticity of contemplative prayer was even stretched to the point by one respondent that this practice became synonymous with the term *mysticism*, meaning "the part of your relationship with God that is indescribable, outside our understanding in the contemplative prayer sense" (Interviewee 19). This potential range for connection, perhaps, creates the necessary conditions for the final point of commonality among interviewees concerning contemplative prayer.

Some interview respondents understood contemplative prayer as an enlightening event that *happens to* a person rather than an action or habit that is intentionally practiced. For instance, in the context of praying, Interviewee 16 illustratively connected contemplative prayer to occurrences of something entirely unexpected.

> We may pray for an hour or hours, and in my experience, because I have been able to experience, we lived in England, so I got to experience a lot of the silent, beautiful, kind of, majestic stuff. You know, you're in St. Paul's Cathedral, or you're in these incredible places, and you're just in silent awe. You can't really say anything, so why try? It's overwhelming. But, at the same time, I've been at a home where what we're going to do is just play some music, worship for a while, and then pray until we quit, and that's an hour and a half later. There are chunks of silence along the way, but there's also Scripture. There's just kind of prophetic prayer which just means people just saying what they feel God's putting there. As far as contemplative, engaging prayers are almost always around the uncontrollable. When the mystery hits us, we try to find a place to enter it and take part.

As might be supposed, the nature of this unexpectedness made it quite difficult to "practice" in the traditional sense. From this perspective, participants asserted that contemplative prayer happens within the context of other mystic practices or, possibly, in the midst of actions which have no connection to mystic practices at all. The point of contact which interview participants most often noted in connection with this view was the timing and activity of the Holy Spirit. As seen from these descriptions, contemplative prayer in this definition is not so much a practice as an event, and concomitantly it could not be practiced regularly because it depended on God's timing. This factor may explain why contemplative prayer only *appears* to be a major practice. Consequently, contemplative prayer did have major points of contact among interviewees in a similar manner to centering prayer, yet both practices still suffered from a broad scope of divergence. It is this definitional issue which obstructs any possibility for these practices to be major ones for EC respondents, even if they appear to be so according to survey data.

Spiritual Direction/Spiritual Friendship

Spiritual direction or spiritual friendship was marked by many interviewees on the spiritual practices questionnaire. However, participant responses within interview contexts revealed that these two terms, listed as synonyms on the spiritual practices questionnaire, were in fact viewed quite differently by respondents and, therefore, represented two very divergent practices for EC participants. Precisely, spiritual direction was understood to mean a one-on-one relationship in which the director formally guides the one directed. Conversely, spiritual friendship was interpreted in a much wider sense to individuals or groups which offered interviewees any type of guidance, counsel, or discussion on matters deemed to be spiritual. Resultantly, an ensuing consideration of method or process for spiritual direction and spiritual friendship can best be accomplished through specific investigation of these two divergent practices.

Concerning spiritual direction, EC interviewees (24.3%) defined this practice essentially in terms of one-on-one meetings with spiritually knowledgeable individuals. Within this context, respondents divided their remarks according to whether they sought spiritual direction through the pastor of their church or through another individual whom they deemed qualified to dispense appropriate counsel. Multiple individuals remarked about the approachability of their pastors over sensitive issues. For instance, Interviewee 18 colorfully noted, "He [the pastor] won't let me get by with much, and I bitch a lot. A lot of times, our Wednesdays are bitch sessions on my part, but I want to know what's real, and he knows how to listen." While this sentiment about listening was common among interviewees who sought out spiritual direction from their pastors, a few participants commented on some difficulties arising from this relationship. For instance, in light of the nature of a pastor's relationship to his or her congregation, Interviewee 28 noted that spiritual direction was occasionally offered unbidden, "I have met with [the pastor] at least a couple of different times, and I don't know if I asked for spiritual direction, but she gave it to me." Another interviewee remarked that certain disparities between the experience of the director and the one who is directed can be a difficult obstacle to overcome.

> You can always go to your pastor, but not always. It's kind of hard with some pastors [due to] age differences because the experiences aren't there. Even our last pastor, same age as I, but his experiences were quite a bit different, and [I] wasn't into a situation where I knew he'd understand, and I think most spiritual . . . even though I think God can direct you, even if a spiritual

director doesn't. If they have some background that's like you, it helps. (Interviewee 27)

In situations where pastoral direction might not be desired or applicable, several respondents turned to the process of seeking out an outside spiritual director.

When interviewees sought out an individual specifically to act as a spiritual director, they often came to this process with a higher level of intentionality. Specificity of the spiritual direction process in these circumstances extended at the very least to a more rigid time structure. For example, Interviewee 3 said, "I also have a spiritual director that I meet with once a month, usually, to try and sort through things that I might be trying to deal with or trying to make decisions on." As an additional example, Interviewee 30 remarked that she met with her spiritual director "every six weeks." A regularly scheduled meeting was a common element of spiritual direction when interviewees met with a designated director; however, some respondents noted a temporary possibility for scheduled meetings with a spiritual director over a specific issue. Participants who practiced regular spiritual direction saw their need and process as a little more open-ended.

While this type of spiritual direction, its process, and area of need generally resulted in positive experiences for interviewees, there were some notable dissenting opinions surrounding negative experiences with spiritual direction. For instance, Interviewee 38 relates the following discomfiture: "It's sad. Honestly, I feel guilty. I felt guilty, because I couldn't do what she [the spiritual director] was asking me to do, the prayer and the reading and the writing. That didn't fit for me, and I felt guilty—I don't know—I didn't want to go back to her and say 'I couldn't do it.'" Even though negative experiences were recounted by a few interviewees, they were also quick to note that they did not eschew the entire practice of spiritual direction; rather, they regarded these matters as failures of the specific circumstances or method of implementation. In both pastoral and non-pastoral forms, multiple interviewees connected with the term and displayed an appropriation of the practice of spiritual direction, yet most respondents preferred the term *spiritual friendship* and the methods surrounding it.

Interview participants resonated more often (48.6%) with the term *spiritual friendship* than with the term *spiritual direction*. Additionally, those who practiced spiritual friendship noted its synonymous status with the term *accountability* as well as how it could be practiced in formal groups and informally with friends. With respect to terminology, multiple interviewees connected or placed spiritual friendship in the larger area of accountability.

In speaking of his church's practices and procedures, Interviewee 6 delineates the lines of communication in such a view of accountability.

> They [his church] have accountability partners, especially people that have had issues with drugs or alcohol, pornography or adultery, or whatever. They always seem to team-up with somebody to kind of keep each other in line or something. I've never had one. I've never had an accountability partner myself, and there's also mentor relationships in the church too, where an older lady will disciple a young woman or same thing with a man and young man. I see a lot of that going on.

This semantic connection or replacement is not surprising because *accountability* or *accountability partner* is the primary term under which spiritual direction and spiritual friendship is implemented in evangelical contexts. In this terminological hold-over, the case study EC churches displayed that not all points of contact with evangelicalism have been sundered. In addition, whether under the term *spiritual friendship* or *accountability*, multiple respondents noted the appropriation of this practice in their churches through either formal groups or informal friends.

Some interviewees favored the process of receiving spiritual guidance through formal groups that were associated with their church of attendance. However, it should be noted that interviewees did not comment that these groups were typically created to fulfill this specific purpose. As a representative example, Interviewee 4 described her group spiritual friendship.

> I meet weekly, every Monday, I meet with a group of six other ladies for our Emmaus reunion accountability group, and we always start with a centering prayer. We basically [discuss] the focus is whether during the past week you talk[ed] about your study, your prayer life, and then you either talk about an incident where you've felt was your closest to Christ moment or you can discuss where you felt God was calling you to discipleship or where you knew God was calling you to discipleship, and you said "No, Lord, not me" and hid behind the pickle barrel.

While this illustration emphasized the positive benefits of meeting in a group to discuss spiritual matters, Interviewee 12 remarked that the type of personal spiritual guidance often expected from a spiritual friendship situation might not be ideally suited to a group which is set up for more general spiritual teaching purposes.

> I keep doing it, but I got to tell you, Dann, it's been the biggest source of disappointment and hurt to me in my spiritual life.

> So, I keep doing it, and I think it has enhanced my spirituality, [be]cause I've had to struggle so much more, [be]cause once you start going down a road with other men or families together, invariably what I've seen is you start breaking down walls and become vulnerable to each other, and then invariably some things happen where you get very, very hurt by other members of the group.

This particular episode highlights the potential disadvantages of seeking spiritual guidance through a formal group. In light of this potentiality, other interview participants preferred gaining spiritual insight and direction on personal matters through loose associations with friends.

Among respondents who preferred the term *spiritual friendship*, a marked partiality was evident for interpreting this process in an informal manner. As a result, such an understanding of spiritual friendship was not often considered as an intentional practice to be appropriated as much as a series of serendipitous occasions to be welcomed. Interviewee 1 described her process, as much as it can be considered a process at all.

> I have, I would say, several women that I loosely disciple. It's not anything that's set in [stone]. "We meet every Tuesday for an hour type thing." It's more [that] a lot of them know what I've gone through with my husband and other issues that I've had my oldest son was very sick for a long [time]. So, a lot of things, I've just been through a lot. There are younger women that know the things I've been through that come to me, like "How did you deal with this? How did you that?" I, likewise, I have women that have been through things that I find myself looking up to, or who I consider very godly women, further along in their faith than I am, more mature in their faith, like [the associate pastor], who I know I can say, like "I'm struggling with this," and I know [she] will really always be there to talk to me. Again, it's not a formal relationship, but they're friendships that we're gaining spiritual teaching [or] wisdom from.

In addition to the non-intentional nature of the practice as understood by this respondent, it is interesting to note from the quotes above that this type of spiritual guidance is often designed to proceed in multiple directions so that one person is at times in both the role of spiritual director and spiritual directee. It can also be noted that interviewees tended to have a less defined *practice* of spiritual direction as it moved more toward this open-ended friendship; although, this manner of interpreting the mystic practice was much more common than a formal relationship with a spiritual director. So, interviewees were utilizing spiritual direction, but this practice, if defined in a more specific way than having friends with whom one discussed spiritual matters on occasion, turned out only to be practiced by a few persons on a level beyond that of passing familiarity.

Minor Practices

While the practices in the previous section casually looked like major practices but proved to be divergent, this section will consider those mystic practices which were appropriated in a clearly minor way by the emergent churches studied. Specifically, these practices range from a 30% to 60% participation rate among interviewees. Aside from statistical categorization, these practices also grouped together on the basis that they were often introduced to interview respondents through the current church of attendance but then offered as options for personal practice or as lesser options within the context of corporate meetings. Minor practices include confession (59.5%), the liturgical calendar (56.8%) and liturgical prayer (48.6%) considered together, fasting (51.4%), and making the sign of the cross (32.4%). In much the same manner as major practices were presented, minor practices will be explicated by first focusing on what interviewees considered *primary* to each practice, then notable *exceptions* or standout examples will be discussed. Throughout this entire section, focus will remain on *how* each practice is implemented with particular emphasis on explanations in interviewees' own words wherever possible.

Confession

The most common minor practice among those interviewed was the practice of confession. Confession also provides an interesting microcosm through which one can view the EC facility with taking an interest in a mystic practice and combining it with their own practical spin. Interviewee comments reveal this progression through five points of description. First, EC interviewees uniformly noted the informal nature in which they employed the practice of confession. In transitioning to this informality, as a second point, respondents often noted their understanding and practice of confession from their various religious upbringings. Next, they then discussed the various communal and personal uses of confession employed in their respective EC contexts. Fourth and fifth, notably minor, points are evident in some participants' preference for newer terminology over traditional *sin* language and the experience of one interviewee in implementing a positive form of confession. These points of description combine to provide a full portrait of how the case study churches implemented and innovated the practice of confession in their local contexts.

The informal nature of confession was consistently mentioned by interviewees. While many participants were not particularly clear concerning what they considered to be a "formal" context, they often alluded to the formal context for the practice of confession as popularly connected to Roman Catholicism in which a priest serves as personal confessor for an individual congregant. In fact, Interviewee 16 referred to this situation explicitly although somewhat lightheartedly.

> My confession looks like this: the senior pastor of the church that birthed us will hear my struggles periodically, and it's not a formal thing. Although, every once in a while, we'll laugh and, you know, say "Forgive me father, for I have sinned." In all honesty, that's kind of a half-tease. I mean we're obviously teasing our Catholic friends, brothers, and sisters, but, at the same time, with a little bit of a tip of the hat, that this is something that they've done for a long time, for better or worse.

So, one of the major common points of contact for the practice of confession among interviewees was a distinction from this Catholic practice, and this distinction turned out to be made often on the basis of religious upbringing.

Multiple interviewees noted that their informal practice of confession in their current church grew out of a dissatisfaction for the practice of confession implemented in their childhood religious tradition, as noted strongly by Interviewee 4 in relating, "I always thought that the Catholic church's sacrament of confession was absurd when I was going through it in first grade." However, multiple respondents noted more positively that some emphasis on confession within their church of attendance was welcome, either as a significant change from evangelical churches or as a favorable connection to confession from their religious upbringing. One such positive connection was offered by Interviewee 38 in the following terms.

> Growing up in the Episcopal church, there's a place in the liturgy that's a formal confession, and I sort of like that, because you don't have to try and figure out what to say, because I struggle with "Oh God, what am I going to say?" But I, when I do talk to God with words, I'm very informal, because that also feels the easiest for me.

Such positive or negative connections to confession for each interviewee understandably often led to a relative preference for either communal or personal types of informal confession.

Corporate confession took three major forms for interviewed EC practitioners. First, respondents noted that there were often moments set aside during worship services for confession. This type of congregational confession still retained an element of privacy through individuals confessing to other individual persons rather than simply noting their shortcomings before all who were gathered there. While this first form of group confession retained individualistic elements, other forms emphasized the group dynamic. As a second form, interview participants delineated a practice of group confession in a smaller setting than weekly worship services. For instance, Interviewee 8 related the practice of confession in his emergent setting to the context of a formal group, particularly, his small group. "Part of the time tonight is a time of confession towards one another. Where we talk about life and how things are going, [we] and also confess the things that are going well and not going well and walk through all that." This vignette displays the interesting confluence of a formal group meeting with an informal focus on confession. Other interviewees who enjoyed a small group context for confession preferred an informal group as well as an informal focus. As a representative example, Interviewee 26 stated this predilection in the following manner:

> My friends are really good about practicing this "confessing one to another." Then, in that, holding each other accountable. [illustration of the conversation process] "Hey [Interviewee's name], how are you doing?" "Well, okay." "I'm praying for you." "You can do this just keep focusing on God." Whatever it is, or "Here are some verses that I think will really help you with this, or a quote that I heard, a song that I heard." Whatever it is that, wherever the truth of God is that, again will ultimately point us back to him.

In this way, group opportunities for confession existed in the studied emergent churches through various means with varying levels of informality. Additionally, participants also discussed corporately encouraged confession on a one-on-one basis.

This one-on-one focus was more in line with the evangelical heritage of the EC in which this type of confession practice is typically subsumed under the category of accountability. With regard to this type of communally acceptable confession, interviewees noted several personal emphases.

> I believe that confession is something that can be given to any trusted person in the community of faith. And so, I think what evangelicals might call "accountability," that would be, I think, that's a form of confession, of somebody really being honest with who they are, their struggles and their triumphs, and this is really who I am, this is the vulnerability of who I am. (Interviewee 23)

> Confession is regularly used by me, and it's more in the context of sort of an honest relationship, generally with people that I respect at some level as a spiritual mentor. Whether, usually, they're just older women that serve as godly women that are in some way, shape, or form mentoring. Although, they can be also peers, so confession to me is very, very important. If I have transgressed in some way, I really take to heart the "confess your sins to one another." (Interviewee 11)

It is interesting to note the varying criteria among the quoted selections concerning whom one desires to be one's confessor, even in an informal sense. While corporate options for the practice of confession extend to congregational settings, small groups, and one-on-one encounters, interviewees did not note communal forms of confession as primary within their respective church contexts.

The principal form of the practice of confession noted by interview respondents was a individualistic utilization of the practice between the practitioner and God alone. Multiple respondents affirmed a strong preference for this type of confession. As a representative example, Interviewee 13 described his process of confession: "Personal confession, sure. When, sometimes, I'm lying there in bed, thinking I should have done this and I should have done that. I ask forgiveness for those types of things. They seem to keep coming up over and over." As seen in this respondent comment, this personal form of confession tends to take a very informal shape, and it is practiced by EC interviewees at practically any time and place. Interestingly, while most respondents strongly favored communal forms of mystic practices, even when those practices were not historically or typically communal, this particular practice was manifestly individual for interview participants. In addition to this major interpretation of confession as personal and private, interviewees evinced minor emphases worthy of comment.

Among minor issues and remarks made by EC interviewees, two observations stood out from the rest, specifically semantic desire to replace *sin* language in confession and the desire to flip the practice of confession to focus on positive actions. First, as an interesting undertone to some interviews, respondents manifested a strong dislike for the term *sin*. The term *struggle* was interposed by interviewees from different churches and backgrounds in place of traditional *sin* language. One of the pastors from the case study churches outlined illustratively this terminological change.

> I don't know how many people would say that they're coming to my office to give a confession. They would probably say that they're coming to share a struggle or to need help, but then I have to use that practice myself. I have people that I go to that— I have to—that I'm in regular relationship with, but I ultimately think that the best confession is taken out of relationship.

This desire for a more positive consideration of the practice of confession continued for some respondents beyond the semantic level to the entire scope of the practice itself. One interviewee noted that she had taken up the practice of confession with the novel twist of "confessing" to God all of the things she had done correctly in a week. "We had to see that was part of our spiritual formation, to go through and say 'Yeah, I actually did this [positive action] this week, and that was good.' What will God call on me to do the next week? It's positive reinforcement" (Interviewee 27). In these standout cases, interviewee comments display how deeply EC conversationalists can appropriate and reinterpret a mystic practice with regard to their specific circumstances. In a less striking way, participant emphases on informality, communal options, and the prominence of individual confession also displayed how the practice of confession had been appropriated in the case study emergent churches.

Liturgical Calendar/Liturgical Prayer

Another minor practice which was used to varying extents within each emergent church studied was the implementation of elements from the liturgical calendar, or church year, and liturgical prayer, or liturgy. These two practices are discussed in the same section because many respondents described implementation of the two practices jointly within the interview context. While the use of the qualifier *liturgical* may have predisposed some interviewees toward such a connection, many noted an inextricable link between the two practices. In fact, Interviewee 38 stated this relationship artfully in the following manner: "It's kind of separate, yeah. Although, it's sort of similar like the liturgical calendar takes me through the rhythm of the year, and the liturgy and the worship take me through the rhythm of that worship service." Throughout each interview, this quality and value of *rhythm* offered through these practices came to the forefront over and over again. So, in the overall context of rhythm, interviewees discussed the liturgical calendar in terms of extent of assimilation and ties to the lectionary. Similarly, liturgical prayer was considered through the level of practice and innovation in each of the emergent churches.

Use of the liturgical calendar varied significantly from church to church and in relative importance to each interview participant. On one end of the spectrum, some noticed any implementation of the days and seasons of the church year as a departure from the evangelical heritage from which the EC emerged. For instance, Interviewee 36 declared this development concisely by saying, "It's not that big of a deal to me except for the special things because growing up Baptist, you don't have Lent. You don't even have Good Friday really. You have nothing. Basically, growing up in my church, you had Christmas and Easter and Fourth of July." As this lack of use of the liturgical calendar was quite common in interviewee religious backgrounds, a modest emphasis on the seasons of Advent and Lent in preparation for the holidays of Christmas and Easter, respectively, was seen as a significant change within the case study churches. All three churches that were studied emphasized the seasons of Advent and Lent in a way more strongly than the evangelical tradition from which they arose. In addition, on a lesser level, these churches put into practice other elements from the church year.

Interview respondents often commented that the liturgical calendar was utilized in their churches through focus on days and seasons in addition to Advent and Lent. Observance of the seasons of the church year was typically practiced with an emphasis on a sense of innovation and in a spirit of exploration of the unfamiliar. Interviewee 23 enthusiastically displayed this spirit in the following comment.

> For me to go through Advent, for me to go through Lent and Easter, Pentecost to go through these seasons, ordinary time, which is an awesome concept for somebody who didn't grow up in that. To hear that, it's hilarious, but it's great that "Now, we're in ordinary time." Recognizing that there's something incredibly amazing about the ordinary, and God in the ordinary, it's just really, really great.

This interest displays the sense of novelty and progressive implementation of the church year which drew these EC practitioners to further use. Engagement of the seasons of the church year practically worked out in many of the churches through their corporate worship services, such as how Interviewee 37 noted changes in the church décor.

> I love the liturgical calendar. I love feast days and saint days. I like for colors to be right. I really, really need when it's in green time, for us to be in green time. I need when it's Advent, I need things to go purple or blue, even though that wasn't the way I was raised. That was one of the first things I fell in love with at City Church [original name of CitC]. I need our candle color to be right. I don't know why that matters to me.

As seen in the above comment, these changes were seemingly minor but had profound impact on individuals who came out of Christian traditions that had few ties with the liturgical calendar and few, if any, tangible connections to specific seasons within the course of communal worship services. Interviewees were also quick to mention when their church emphasized the celebration of specific saint's days although this celebration was unevenly appropriated on the basis of topical interest.

Participants noted minor specific uses of the liturgical calendar through the celebration of specific saint's days, and a few interviewees even noted the implementation of non-Christian liturgical calendars. With regard to the observance of particular saint's days, there was particular emphasis on this practice at CitC where choices for celebration were based on inclusive themes. As a result, they celebrated the feast days of Mary Magdalene, Brigit, and Hildegard of Bingen. As noted, these selections for saint celebrations were based on the inclusive interests of CitC; however, it is also worthy of note that an emphasis on the Virgin Mary was not displayed in this church. When I asked about this omission of the premiere female saint, interview participants evinced confusion on the omission, citing a possible connection to Catholicism as the reason for not focusing on the mother of Jesus Christ. As another minor extension of interest in the liturgical calendar, RCC participants expressed their interest in portions of the Jewish liturgical calendar as the liturgical rituals that Jesus himself would have celebrated. One participant vividly captured this interest in his comments on the liturgical calendar.

> I grew up with [the liturgical calendar] as a Methodist. It was always a part of things, but again until I had that realization about community that's when the liturgical calendar really blew up for me. Studying in Israel, you study the Parashah [particular sections of the first five books of the Bible divided topically]. You understand the rhythms of the Parashah, and then you understand that when Jesus went to Nazareth [Luke 4:14–30]. When he read that [in the synagogue], that was part of the Parashah. He knew the Scripture going in. When he showed up, so did they. They'd been studying it for the whole week, and

> somebody had memorized it that sat aside for Jesus to sit in the Moses' seat and speak out. There's this whole world of that. When I started to realize that for me it was that there was this God-given rhythm, through the festivals which are connected to the seasons of the world. The Parashahs are all part of those festivals, connecting us to a larger experience of humanity that God has actually created. I started to think about how all those rhythms were incredibly important, and they again were communal. (Interviewee 16)

So, in minor emphases specific to certain churches, the case study churches were utilizing the liturgical calendar eclectically for their own topical interests. In addition to celebrations and church decorations, interviewees also noted the role of the lectionary in their corporate church meetings and personal lives.

In many ways, the primary element of application of the church year in the emergent churches studied was the inclusion and utilization of lectionary readings. Multiple interview respondents noted the value of the lectionary in corporate meetings and in personal devotions. However, it is also important to note that the use of the lectionary was not viewed as a rigid structure. For instance, in CitC, the pastor used Sunday lectionary readings as a selection to choose from on the basis of topical interest. In ERC, use of the lectionary was frequent, but it was just as common to deviate from this source, as described by the pastor below.

> I'm getting ready to start a series this summer, and we're still in the season of Pentecost. We recognize we're in the season of Pentecost. We talk about that, but I'm doing a sermon series that isn't necessarily going along with the lectionary, and I think that's okay. I recognize, hey, we have a leading to go in this direction, so we'll do that, but we also recognize the rhythms of our faith. So, we're trying to find this third way where I don't have to preach the lectionary every week, but it's there.

In other words, interviewees were often aware of and excited about use of the lectionary, but the extent of its utilization was definitely on the individual church's or person's own terms. Liturgical prayer was viewed similarly in case study churches.

Liturgical prayer, or liturgy, was often used in connection with the seasons of the liturgical calendar and/or the readings of the lectionary. In similar fashion to the employment of the liturgical calendar, liturgical prayer had many different levels of engagement as reported by interview participants. First, some respondents noted the use of liturgy in a very minor way within corporate church services. Interviewee 7 made this connection through the use of litany by recounting, "Some of that I marked as litany also—that litany—draws on the liturgy but, maybe, paraphrased, but it's all sort of call and response ideas." Such a level of use did not seek to employ liturgical prayer in a comprehensive way; rather, it was a potential method for ministers to use in order to engage the congregation.

A second level in which liturgical prayer was implemented in case study churches often began as an introduction to liturgical forms of prayer for the express purpose of offering it as an *option* for personal use or as a minor element in communal worship. For instance, Interviewee 21 speaks to the option of liturgical prayer in the following circumstances.

> We'll go through the liturgical calendar, like through Lent and Advent, and [the pastor] will let us know about other events going on, and sometimes I know [the spiritual formation pastor], she's sometimes even made little booklets with devotional prayers for each day and the season that we can follow, and I've used those.

As this comment shows, liturgical prayer was not viewed as a vital element of a worship service, but it became an option or an experimental avenue for operating communally and experientially in worship within an EC context. This second level of potential implementation was often connected by interview participants to fixed hour prayer as well. In fact, this relationship was so strong among certain participants that several did not understand how they could be separated at all. Interviewee 27 gave this perspective a clear voice when I questioned the difference between fixed hour prayer and liturgical prayer, using the examples of the Daily Office and the Book of Common Prayer. To this query, Interviewee 27 answered, "Oh, I see them as the same." While this second level of use of liturgical prayer was common among the case study churches, one church moved to a third level of engagement with liturgical prayer.

Interestingly, interviewees from CitC talked about their own *creation* of liturgy on a weekly or monthly basis. While some interviewees were active in the process of liturgy composition or revision, all interview participants from this church knew that the liturgical prayers utilized in services were often created by other attendees.

> The liturgy, that's one of the things I enjoy about Church in the Cliff, the words. And, sometimes, we have people that are great at writing those words, and then sometimes we borrow from other resources and what-not. (Interviewee 32)

> I get a lot [of liturgical prayers] from Rex Hunt. [The church liturgist] and I write a lot. I enjoy that. It's fun. It's really important, an aspect I enjoy a lot. The writing, crafting. I remember being startled when I first came to the community, [the previous pastor] said "[The church liturgist] writes really good liturgy." And, I remember thinking "Can you just write liturgy? Isn't all the liturgy that exists already down?" It was really confusing to me, and I asked her about that. So, that was my own journey [of] what makes for liturgy. (Interviewee 30)

These innovations and changes were often tied to the strong emphasis at CitC on gender inclusivism and perception of chauvinistic bias in existing liturgical prayer sources. When the chief liturgist of CitC was queried about the process of inclusion attached to these changes, she responded in the following manner.

> Obviously, the one that affects me most directly is gender inclusive, and it's also, I think, one of the most visible in the texts. If it's all "he, he, he," and God is a man, it's hard for me to relate to that, especially when I'm so much thinking about it. And, that's probably part of my own growth is being—making—space to allow that to be there, while still being critical about that. I just can't hold those together yet.

So, interestingly, the attraction for most interview respondents to both the liturgical calendar and liturgical prayer arose out of the desire for a practical rhythm to church worship occasions and the larger scope of the calendar year; however, innovation was not only permissible but often encouraged, or even vital in the case of CitC. In many ways, these changes resulted in a rhythm that was still quite unique to each specific faith community. Fasting was another mystic practice employed in a minor way within the studied churches with a strong communal emphasis that was still tied to the local community context.

Fasting

The appropriation of fasting as a mystic practice among the emergent churches in the study was inconsistent across the spectrum of churches. While interview participants from ERC and CitC participated in fasting on an individual basis alone, members of RCC had a major emphasis on fasting within their congregational community. In addition to inconsistent usage, many respondents discussed fasting in terms of their process of implementation, focusing on the methods and circumstances of fasting. Most interviewee comments divided equally on these aspects of techniques of fasting and conditions in which one might fast.

With respect to the methods of fasting, all varieties included some form of abstention, but they varied on the basis of the extent of abstention. Three forms of fasting could be delineated from interviewee comments: complete fasting from all food, Daniel fasting, and fasting from a specific food or activity. With respect to a complete fast, only a few individuals asserted that they had ever undertaken a lengthy fast of this type. For instance, Interviewee 14 noted that he once participated in a 21-day water-only fast; however, he noted that this fast was not conducted for solely spiritual reasons; instead, he was part of a study which was measuring potential physical benefits of fasting. Complete fasts as noted by other respondents tended toward a shorter period of time. For example, Interviewee 16 related the following personal practice: "We've done, I personally, have done. The ancient rabbis and John Wesley, oddly enough, fasted two days a week. So, they fasted on different days, and I've done both." While complete fasts had been utilized by respondents at certain times, less strenuous fasting was much more common.

One of the major types of fasting that interviewees implemented was what they referred to as a "Daniel Fast." This terminology refers to the biblical passage of Daniel 1:8–20 in which the eponymous character of the book and his friends abstained from all sustenance other than vegetables and water for a time. This type of fast was quite typical for the called fasts in RCC, particularly in connection to community prayer. Concisely, Interviewee 16 outlined this connection: "We didn't know what we would do about a building, so we did a Daniel fast as a community." Little practical reasoning behind the mechanics of this type of fast was offered by participants due to the presumed self-evident nature of how one would eat only vegetables and drink only water. The final type of fasting as noted by interviewees allowed for the greatest personal interpretation.

Multiple interview participants marked on the spiritual practices questionnaire that they participated in fasting, and they then explained their use of this mystic practice through abstention of a particular food or activity for a specified period of time rather than more comprehensive dietary restrictions. Those who abstained from a particular food often chose a food that had some addictive qualities for them, such as caffeine. In keeping with this "addictive" criterion, individuals who discussed giving up a particular activity tied their selection of activities to those which seemed to have addictive properties for them, most principally television viewing. Consequently, fasting could extend practically to any food or activity. The circumstances in which fasting may be employed as a spiritual practice also extended for interviewees to multiple contexts.

Situations in which fasting was enacted among interviewees stratified into three main categories: church-called fasts, Lenten fasts, and personal fasts. As mentioned above, RCC was the only church which participated in church-called fasts, yet this practice stood out in the minds of many interviewees as a very distinctive practice of their church from their previous religious contexts. The response of Interviewee 11 is demonstrative of respondent comments in this regard.

> The only times I've ever fasted really are actually in the Riverside context because the community was fasting for land, decisions regarding land or buildings, decisions about missions, African missions. Fasting in preparation for that [referring to African missions]. Things like that. It's usually tied to what we would consider a big decision being made or some sort of big event is happening, but I rarely ever elect to [fast] on my own volition, choose to fast. Obviously, I'm choosing sometimes, but it's usually within the context of a group of people that are also doing it.

As seen from the above comment, it was quite typical among interview participants to have only one context in which communal fasts had been encouraged. While the other churches in the study were not in the habit of calling a communal fast for a specific prayer reason, they did tie the liturgical calendar, particularly in connection to Lent, to participating in an individual fast.

Respondents from ERC and CitC often noted use of fasting in connection with the observance of Lent. This factor likely corresponds to the increased emphasis on the church year within these two case study churches. In connection to this type of circumstance for fasting, participants remarked on ties with the larger Christian tradition.

> We just didn't do Lent in the church I grew up in. when I joined Church in the Cliff, and I've been through three Lenten seasons now. There's just this sense of the tradition. There's this weight behind it [that] makes me feel like part of this community, and not just the Church in the Cliff community, but the 2,000-year-old Christian community. (Interviewee 29)

> Fasting is very infrequent for me. I do it every Lent. I pick up something that is, well, to backtrack a little bit, this year I became convicted of the way I'd viewed fasting previously and that it was incorrect. I used to [view] fasting just in terms of giving something up, and that was the extent of fasting, giving

> something up. This past year, for Lent, someone I heard from somewhere, maybe it was one of my Anglican people heard from somewhere, the idea of fasting can be seen in terms of taking something on. (Interviewee 24)

These respondent comments are notable in the sense of connection with different Christian traditions; however, it is even more significant to see how Interviewee 24 reinterprets the practice of fasting as not only a tie to the liturgical calendar but also as a basis for innovation and experimentation in order to personalize the practice of fasting. The final situation in which interviewees practiced fasting also emphasized this customization aspect.

Multiple interview participants did not utilize fasting on a communal or liturgical level, but they combined communal fasting with a vibrant personal practice. Their personal practices of fasting were usually tailored to their specific tastes, interests, and purposes. These respondents were often quick to explain their methods and point out that they practiced fasting on their own terms. As a detailed example, Interviewee 5 described thoroughly her practice of fasting.

> For me, fasting puts me back in control like I'm not subservient to the food anymore, brings myself back into perspective. I don't think that's the way fasting is perceived by a lot of people. I think a lot of people do fasting to get some spiritual enlightenment. For me, it's more of [that] I need to reverse that hold instead of the food being here and me being below, I need to put myself above that, and I'm in control of this. Eventually, I wind up moving back to where I'm watching my cooking shows again and doing stuff, and then I'll wind up doing another fast. Those fasts are usually vegan fasts that I'll do where I'll just eat vegetables. I would generally say that they're pretty long-term. I don't do real short fasts. I'll do a forty-day vegan fast and during that time I'm very consciously aware that I'm doing it for my own spirit, that I'm gaining control back over myself.

So, personal fasting had great variability for interview participants even to the level of a personal dieting choice. While interviewee responses about methods of fasting and circumstances varied greatly and the practice itself is employed unevenly across the case study churches, the key to this practice in an EC context is its implementation in all forms of customization, especially in light of the rarity of the practice of fasting in the evangelical context from which the EC emerged. The practice of fasting benefited from the tangible nature in which participants could comment on its implementation in both process and conditions for practice, and the final minor practice also shares this benefit.

Sign of the Cross

Just less than a third of respondents (32.4%) reported utilizing the sign of the cross either personally or in a group setting. With respect to *how* this practice was utilized, interviewees did not spend much time in discussion. In fact, multiple interview participants physically made the sign of the cross within the interview to illustrate how they implement the practice rather than use any words to describe it. However, there were a few interviewee opinions on other aspects of the process. Respondent comments on utilization of making the sign of the cross focused on when this practice was used in a religious context and how they first came in contact with the practice.

With respect to when interviewees reported using the sign of the cross, comments divided into two simple categories: within worship services and outside of worship services. As part of worship services, respondents noted utilizing this mystic practice when they personally felt obliged to do so rather than in connection with specific liturgical words or actions, as is the case in other Christian traditions. Interviewees noted these particular circumstances, but they were quick to point out that there was also no place in a worship service within their respective church settings that this practice would be discouraged. Time and choice of implementation rested solely with the individual. Additionally, other respondents noted the utilization of this practice during times and activities that are not generally associated with making the sign of the cross. For instance, Interviewee 30 related, "I've been drawn to that. I find myself now doing it, like I did it today, when I clicked 'send' on the e-mail." Interviewee 27 remarked that she implemented this practice many times a day, but, since she did not desire to call attention to herself, she clarified, "A lot of times—I won't physically do it—I'm mentally doing it." So, while the optional status of this practice was stressed by multiple respondents, making the sign of the cross was a potential practice based on personal preference for any situation inside or outside of the communal worship context.

Comments on the practice of making the sign of the cross also tended to include the source of introduction to this practice for each individual. Origin points for this practice grouped into two areas. Either interview participants were familiar with this practice as a result of personal religious upbringing in a tradition that encouraged it or they had been introduced to the practice by a person from such a tradition. Illustratively, Interviewee 38 connected making the sign of the cross to her religious background by saying, "I used it a lot when I was a practicing Episcopalian, and I carried it with me for a long time. I think that's another thing about emergent church. People just accept you for whatever it is that you bring." Interviewee 38's closing sentences mention an important common thread in the appropriation of mystic practices by the EC, specifically that individuals are encouraged to bring whatever practices they find beneficial to the conversation.

Other persons who made the sign of the cross a personal practice had come across contexts in which that practice is common even if they did not grow up in that tradition themselves. Interviewee 29 depicted this process in the following vignette.

> I did my undergraduate work in San Antonio. That was the first time I was ever around a largely Catholic community, and my friends would invite me to go to family gatherings, weddings, funerals, whatever that were held in Catholic churches, and that's, well, obviously, I'd seen people do it [making the sign of the cross] on TV before, but it had never really meant anything to me. And, I guess, the thing that I got from my friends was that it was almost a way of—they never told me this, but this is what I got from them—that it was a way of physically reminding themselves that they were in a sacred space.

Interviewee 29 also noted that this practice became personally valuable as a result of its kinesthetic value: "I'm a kinesthetic learner, and movement is one of the ways, I guess, that I learn and also express myself, so it's both of those at once." So, the source of this mystic practice for EC appropriation was more directly through modern Christian traditions which utilize the sign of the cross than practices previously discussed. Interestingly, this provenance could arise from personal background or familiarity gained through family and friends. Either way, this practice could be employed in interviewees' respective EC contexts to some extent. In fact, these issues of provenance and employment could easily be extended to each of the minor practices here discussed.

The foregoing minor practices serve to explicate which mystical practices were reported to be utilized, either personally or corporately, by 30% to 60% of EC interviewees. Practices considered in this section included confession, liturgical calendar, liturgical prayer, fasting, and making the sign of the cross. From these comments, it can be seen that the implementation of these practices and understandings connected to these practices can vary widely. However, all of the practices discussed fit within this category through their common placement as encouraged options for personal practice or infrequent use in communal church contexts. In addition to these minor practices, there are a few practices which appeared to fit within this category according to statistical measurements on the spiritual practices questionnaire, but they actually were not employed to this degree due to significant variations in definition on the part of interview respondents.

Divergent Minor Practices

In much the same vein as the above section on divergent major practices, there were a number of practices which appeared to be minor practices in the case study emergent churches when only statistical data from the spiritual practices questionnaire were consulted. Similarly, due to the phenomenological focus of the study, respondents were encouraged to put definitions in their own words to avoid superficial convergence based on lack of options for definition. So, these divergent practices may be more difficult to chart, but they more accurately represent interviewee theological thought. Four practices which appeared to fit within the minor category were actually divergent: the Jesus Prayer (54.1%), practicing the presence of God (43.2%), pilgrimage (35.1%), and fixed hour prayer (32.4%). As a conflation of meanings for these practices predominated in the interview context, the first step in description of *how* each practice was utilized will consist in clarifying lines of definition. From this basis, discussion will ensue concerning common features of the practices among case study churches. Unique circumstances which do not follow the general flow of use for each practice in an EC context will be noted, when applicable, at the close of the section on that particular practice. Emphasis in each section will continue to remain on verbatim descriptions of interview participants.

Jesus Prayer

The most common divergent minor practice according to questionnaire and interview responses was utilization of the Jesus Prayer. As might be expected, the major issue that caused a mis-measurement of the relative use of this practice in terms of the spiritual practices questionnaire was the semantic vagueness of the term *Jesus Prayer*. Definitionally, semantic differences can be grouped into three categories in which respondents understood the Jesus Prayer variously to mean the Lord's Prayer/Our Father (18.9%), any prayer addressed specifically to Jesus Christ (8.1%), or the Jesus Prayer of Eastern Orthodox extraction (29.7%). Moving on from these semantic issues, this practice lends itself to few comments concerning *how* it was utilized in differing contexts. With respect to issues of context, interviewees noted corporate and personal uses of this practice with personal uses predominating. In these ways, interview participants reported use of the Jesus Prayer primarily on the level of personal value no matter the definition.

The definition of the term *Jesus Prayer* was understood variously by interviewees. These multiple understandings can be classified into three kinds: the Lord's Prayer, a general understanding of praying to Jesus, and the Eastern Orthodox Jesus Prayer. First, several respondents noted that they understood the term *Jesus Prayer* on the spiritual practices questionnaire to be synonymous with the Lord's Prayer or the "Our Father." Interviewee 17 goes into detail concerning the importance of this prayer: "Isn't that the prayer that when the disciples asked Christ 'How do we pray when we pray?' Well, that's why I think it's important. It certainly covers all the bases that Christ thought was important, so to me that's why it's important. That's the one prayer that Christ gave us word-for-word." This interpretation was common to multiple interviewees, and, when I introduced the Eastern Orthodox Jesus Prayer to these participants, few had come in contact with it previously. Additionally, none of the respondents who viewed the Jesus Prayer as the Lord's Prayer and also were familiar with the Eastern Orthodox Jesus Prayer used the latter as a regular practice either personally or communally. While the Lord's Prayer definition was a significant semantic branch for interview participants, some respondents interpreted the term *Jesus Prayer* in a very literal sense.

A minor definition of the Jesus Prayer among interview participants was to view this practice as praying directly to Jesus, as opposed to praying to God the Father or the Holy Spirit. When interpreted in this sense, Interviewee 5 discussed this activity as a major prayer practice of her personal spirituality.

> For me, I tend to forget about Jesus sometimes and get really focused on God himself, the Old Testament God, and I have to bring myself back. Sometimes, it's actually a chore for me to have to go back and read New Testament stuff. I love Old Testament stuff. So, it's like "Oh, yeah. There's this whole part with Jesus, and I need to read that too." Praying around Jesus is a way to bring him back into my life, invite him back in and say "Look, I know you're God, but you existed as a man in the form of Jesus, and I need to bring you back in."

While this type of response was not common, it did constitute a minor deviation from the main definitional divide of this practice between the Lord's Prayer and the Eastern Orthodox Jesus Prayer. As is evident from above comments, interviewees often meant various practices when they marked the practice of the Jesus Prayer on the spiritual practices questionnaire, but several respondents did actually intend to mark this mystic practice as a utilization of the Eastern Orthodox Jesus Prayer in either a communal or personal sense.

When interviewed, multiple participants confirmed that they utilize to some extent the Jesus Prayer as originated in and promulgated by the Eastern Orthodox Church. Within an Eastern Orthodox context, this prayer consists of the repeated phrase, "Lord Jesus Christ, son of God, have mercy on me, a sinner." Having originated out of a desert hermit context, the Jesus Prayer was often repeated countless times throughout the course of a day in the midst of all types of activities. While multiple respondents asserted that they employed this practice in some way, it is notable that variants of this prayer were also utilized. For instance, Interviewee 4 affirmed that she utilized a Roman Catholic variant stating, "Lamb of God, who takes away the sins of the world, have mercy on me." As an additional example, Interviewee 23 stated that he utilized a form of the Jesus Prayer which included all members of the Trinity. When interviewees used the Jesus Prayer of Eastern Orthodox extraction, they explained their method of use in corporate and individual circumstances.

The Eastern Orthodox Jesus Prayer was used in a communal context only by ERC. Such use of this prayer as a community was not as part of a typical corporate worship act; rather, this practice was introduced and taught within a communal meeting with the understanding that it could be employed personally if congregants felt the practice was valuable for their individual spirituality. It is also notable that this practice was introduced in ERC in tandem with the use of an Eastern Orthodox prayer rope, which multiple interview participants equated to the Roman Catholic rosary. Upon such introduction, ERC respondents often asserted their intention to implement the Jesus Prayer on a more regular basis. As a representative example, Interview 26 recounts the following instance:

> We had done it [the Jesus Prayer] in church once during one of our services. I want to say it may have been during Lent. It was read collectively, and, again, because I didn't grow up with liturgy or written prayers or stuff like that, the only consistent prayer I knew was our Lord's Prayer. It was very much this, again with that woman from the church who I connected with, I was talking with her about a lot of frustrations I was having and a lot of "me, me, me, me." I kept saying "I want to focus on God, and I just don't know how to bring that back down, and I don't know how take my eyes off of myself and my own wants,

my own desires, and put them back on the source." So, she said "Well, one thing that works for me is the Jesus Prayer," and I was like "The Jesus Prayer?", and she was like "Look on the web" because she has a blog that she writes. I went on there, and I read through it, and I read the history of it, and it's something that here within the past three weeks that I've started doing.

This vignette artfully illustrates how a communal introduction to the use of the Jesus Prayer had led to a personal use of the mystic practice, and most interviewees followed this type in appropriating a solely personal use of the Jesus Prayer.

EC interview participants recounted the circumstances of their use of the Jesus Prayer at times and places that benefited their personal sense of spirituality. Some respondents were quite articulate and intentional in their assimilation of this practice. For instance, Interviewee 27 focused on the versatility of the Jesus Prayer by stating, "You can do it while you're doing the dishes or mowing the lawn, and I've heard of people being able to carry on conversations and still be praying it." Interviewee 24 agreed with this versatility and added the personal preference of emphasizing different words in the prayer each recitation as a means of centering one's mind and spirit. Other interview participants integrated this practice in their personal spirituality in a more minor role, as an optional prayer practice to rotate with others on an as-desired basis. Interviewee 32 articulates this role in mentioning, "That's just something that is meaningful to me, I guess, in my personal spiritual life. Again, not scheduled, but it comes as needed." However, whether as a major regular practice or a minor occasional one, the Jesus Prayer was overwhelmingly utilized on a *personal* basis among those interviewed. In fact, the Jesus Prayer was very close to being practiced only on a personal level since the only communal context, as noted above, was that in which a community learned together how to utilize the Jesus Prayer individually. So, the Jesus Prayer was practiced on a personal level by a few interviewees regularly or occasionally, but this practice appeared to be used more often statistically due to semantic divergence on the meaning of the term *Jesus Prayer*.

Practicing the Presence of God

Another notable divergent minor practice among interviewed EC participants was practicing the presence of God. This mystic practice was approached in EC literature as being that which primarily derived from the book *The Practice of the Presence of God* by the 17th century French monk and mystic Brother Lawrence. While multiple participants (21.6%) did connect this practice to Brother Lawrence, other respondents (18.9%) interpreted the term more generally as an awareness or "feeling" of God's presence in various contexts. As a result of this semantic divide, the course of discussion for this practice will consider the comments of interviewees in descending order of statistical usage. Additionally, considerable space will also be allotted to the difficulty of explaining the *process* of this practice because, as Interviewee 16 pointed out, practicing the presence of God is "like practicing breathing." According to this perspective, practicing the presence of God is much like contemplative prayer. It is difficult to consider either practice as a "practice" due to a strong correlation in defining them as an activity or event which cannot be limited to a discrete place, time, or intention of the participant. Also, as with contemplative prayer, this practice was only included on the spiritual practices questionnaire because EC literary conversations included it as a practice for appropriation in EC spirituality. So, practicing the presence of God can be most advantageously explicated in terms of relative connection to Brother Lawrence and of the difficulty of assigning a "process" to this practice.

Many interview respondents first came into contact with practicing the presence of God through an introduction to *The Practice of the Presence of God* by Brother Lawrence. In light of this literary link, these interviewees tended to describe the *how* of this practice through specific reference to Brother Lawrence's written work. Interviewee 24 amply illustrates this path of description.

> Probably about a year and a half ago, I read that book [*The Practice of the Presence of God*] as a devotional exercise, and I found it to be revolutionary for me in that whatever I do, wherever I am, God can be present. I can worship God through that, I can serve God through that. And so, I would put this for me in the same category as [or] similar to contemplative prayer and that I'm trying, and I haven't mastered it, and I may not ever, but I love the idea of God being present in everything that I do and me being able to experience God's presence in many, many different things. So, his teachings of particularly humble acts of service. Doing the dishes was his [Brother Lawrence's] thing. That he could find God in doing that and experience joy in that. That is what I took from reading the book, so I tried to see that in my own life, realize that there is no such thing as a purely physical activity, that all my activities, everything I do, has a spiritual dimension to it.

The comment above latches on to the germ of Brother Lawrence's concept—that one can practice awareness of God's presence in any and every activity. Such a practice enjoys tremendous latitude for implementation, and this facility of practice was a notably attractive quality to many interview participants. However, this quality also made it quite difficult to describe one's actual process of enacting this practice.

In many ways, practicing the presence of God could easily be termed the quintessential mystic practice under consideration, since it is quite easy to track the historical origin and development of the practice to compare and contrast with present-day application in an EC context. However, practicing the presence of God is also quite difficult to explain in terms of what one actually *does* in this practice. Multiple respondents noted this factor and commented on its difficulty. Interviewee 19 highlighted this difficulty by admitting, "I can't say that I got [sic] any 'practice' of that where I do such-and-so four times a day. It's just more of an awareness of the concept and, every once in a while, during my work day, I try to, as much as I can, praise him [God] in what I'm doing." As this comment illustrates, it is quite difficult to answer the question, "*How* do you use practicing the presence of God?" Each respondent noted the primary pieces of their process as, first, common everyday activities which one must attend to and, second, an awareness of God's presence. As seen in this response, the addition of "awareness" is the only action that can be added to normal everyday life, and this "awareness" is not easily quantifiable. In contrast, other respondents who understood practicing the presence of God to be a sense of feeling God's presence were often able to delineate a more specific process.

With respect to interpreting practicing the presence of God as fostering a feeling of God's presence in particular situations, multiple respondents were able to explicate quite a sophisticated process for recognizing this feeling. For instance, one participant explained his process of feeling God's presence through the means of dreams.

> I had a dream. I guess it was three weeks ago where in my dream, he [God] said that he was going to come visit, and I remember in my dream getting excited and going to my sister-in-law. I remember vividly, who lives down the street, and going to various people in the family, saying "He's going to come to my house. What should I ask him? I want to ask him how we get to heaven." They seemed disinterested, and I remember being really disappointed at the tail end of the dream, because there I was all excited about his coming into my presence, actually, physically coming into my presence. What's interesting is about five nights later, we're within a small group, and we meet together on Friday

nights, and we met at 9, and we went 'til 2:30 in the morning. There was a guy who was from India, and he's very spiritual, very. He's [the] closest thing I'd consider to an apostle, just very prophetic, very in tune, knows Scripture inside and out, just an amazing individual. Well, that night, not knowing about my dream, not knowing anything, that night he prophesied. He said "Keep the doors open. He will be coming for a visit." So, it's kind of weird that in every book that I ever read about prophesying it always says that he'll [God] confirm it through another source. So, when I mention the presence of God, I'm talking about I'm hoping and I'm praying that maybe that will sometime in my future, I will have a visitation either from angelic sources or from him. I just [believe] it's biblical. It's happened through history. (Interviewee 10)

This vignette displays this particular interviewee's sense of feeling God's presence as connected to dreams and prophecy as well as how he uses repetition of a message as the method to corroborate these means of communication. Another respondent was even more explicit concerning her "tests" of the presence of God, particularly with regard to use of the Bible: "I'll ask God to show me a specific Scripture that has something to do with what I'm studying, and I fully expect that the Scriptures that he leads me to are the [right] ones, and they're random" (Interviewee 5). So, the above interviewees focus on ways to check whether the presence they have felt is truly God's presence. Another interviewee focused on the physical reactions which he experiences whenever he feels the presence of God by stating, "It's different ways that I know God. One would be an inner peace. I can feel an inner peace. When I feel the inner peace, I know God's there. Sometimes, it's physical. I get weepy" (Interviewee 9). While these processes for testing God's presence or physically feeling this presence are quite intricate, respondents tended to be less clear on the "practice" aspect that was indicated in the term *practicing the presence of God*. In fact, only one respondent who did not connect practicing the presence of God to Brother Lawrence offered any clue toward a "practice" aspect by connecting God's felt presence to "those times in service where just that sense of 'I can't speak, and I just have to *be* right now'" (Interviewee 26). Through this interviewee's comments, one can gain a sense that a focus on feeling God's presence could be connected to an experience of communal worship or at least to specific prayers. Additionally, the differences noted here in interviewee method of implementation according to the level of appropriation of the teachings of Brother Lawrence becomes even more striking when moving to a discussion of purpose for practicing the presence of God, as will be more fully discussed in the next chapter.

Pilgrimage

Thirteen interview respondents reported use of the practice of pilgrimage on the spiritual practices questionnaire. This situation resulted in a 35.1% rate of utilization of this practice across the spectrum of interviewees, leading one to assume that this practice would fit within the context of the minor practices section. However, in light of conversation on this topic, it became manifest that there was no standard definition for this practice among participants. In fact, interviewee comments can be grouped into three divergent classifications depending on the general theme to which they coupled the practice of pilgrimage. Respondents categorized pilgrimage as chiefly dealing with place (18.9%), group (16.2%), or time (21.6%); however, a few respondents used two out of three aspects to offer a definition (accounting for the disparity in statistics). While this stratification would seem to completely sunder each definition of pilgrimage from the others, one common trait among all responses still rose to the surface. Interviewee 8 summarized this aspect in a short practical definition of pilgrimage, "I'm defining pilgrimage as a journey towards Jesus intentionally." In other words, all definitions and understanding of pilgrimage as a spiritual practice within the case study churches contained an aspect of "journey" or moving away from everyday aspects of living in order to connect with God in some way. As stated previously, practical divergences of *how* pilgrimage was implemented among interviewees hinged on the areas of understanding pilgrimage according to place visited, according to group association, or according to time spent in solely spiritual pursuits.

Many interview participants understood the primary aspect of "journey" within pilgrimage to be focused through a specific place or places to be visited. This facet of understanding pilgrimage is the one in greatest connection to the historical concept of pilgrimage to holy sites, and the places denoted by interviewees often coincided with traditional pilgrim destinations, particularly Israel. Pilgrimages to Israel were often associated with interviewees from RCC. As noted in chapter two, this church had a special affinity for the Jewish heritage of Christianity, so it is unsurprising that their first example would be a trip to Israel. Other interviewees retained a sense of the necessity of place, though not quite as specific, but also coupled a sense of place with a specific purpose in visiting. For example, Interviewee 38 connected multiple "coming of age" mission trips performed in the CitC with the mystic practice of pilgrimage. So, for this interviewee, the necessity of going to a new place was combined with one's purpose for going in order to call a trip a pilgrimage. For other interview participants, an engagement with particular groups provided a primary purpose in an understanding of pilgrimage.

In the comments of multiple interviewees, an understanding of pilgrimage was primarily associated with a group or organization that sponsored a spiritual event in a particular location. As a result, this understanding of pilgrimage was often synonymous for those interviewed with the terms *retreat* or *conference*. Interviewee 8 concisely illustrated this viewpoint in saying, "I define pilgrimage as I just got back from a Walk to Emmaus." In connection with Interviewee 8's comments, multiple respondents connected the practice of pilgrimage to the Walk to Emmaus program[5] while others, who had also participated in Walk to Emmaus, understood this activity as a retreat and did not view it as synonymous with pilgrimage. A definition of pilgrimage that hinged on group associations turned out also to be somewhat problematic because ERC referred to certain church-sponsored retreats as pilgrimages. Consequently, use of pilgrimage appeared somewhat skewed from the questionnaire data because several ERC respondents linked the term to their church retreats; however, in the course of discussion, they noted a divergence between a "proper" pilgrimage and their church's particular use of the term. While most respondents defined pilgrimage through this aspect of group association, a few participants focused more strongly on an aspect of time as the primary element in pilgrimage.

As a minor category, a few interviewees emphasized the aspect of taking time away from one's ordinary routine as primary for the practice. With respect to this stress, some respondents only discussed a time element while others connected time with a moving away from one's typical physical context. Concerning a time-only element, Interviewee 11 simply said, "The pilgrimage thing, for me, is just setting aside a time." Most other respondents who focused on a time element in pilgrimage clarified that they intended that time as a time to get away from everyday distractions and responsibilities. For instance, Interviewee 24 explained his process of pilgrimage in the following way.

> I'm an introverted person, so I experience God in solitude. Well, I guess, I should say more easily than in other ways. So, for me, pilgrimage in the past has taken on, and I enjoy nature too, so

---

5. Walk to Emmaus is a Christian retreat in which participants "attend a three-day experience of New Testament Christianity as a lifestyle." Cf., The Upper Room, "About—Walk to Emmaus," http://emmaus.upperroom.org/about.

> I'll do a camping trip. I'll get out. I'll go somewhere. I'll camp with dedication; set aside to maybe tackle a particular issue that's God has brought to my attention. But, this idea of going somewhere to be spiritually present in that place for sure.

As can be seen from this interviewee quotation, the places can vary, but the element of a specific period of time is a necessary component along with "going somewhere." In this respect, multiple respondents connected this sense of time with the sense of place as considered previously. So, each of these definitions of how to practice pilgrimage was not necessarily mutually exclusive of the others, but quite a bit of variety existed from person to person in how he or she implemented this practice in an EC context. A similar variety of definition and application, according to personal preference, existed in the practice of fixed-hour prayer among EC interviewees.

Fixed-Hour Prayer

The final divergent minor practice to be discussed is fixed-hour prayer. The divergent qualifier for this practice is particularly accurate because all respondents began their discussion on the subject by noting that the example offered on the questionnaire (i.e., the Daily Office) was either wholly unfamiliar or only known or practiced in the most cursory way. In light of this circumstance, further probing concerning the exact reasoning that the participant marked this particular practice. While notable unique characteristics were offered by interview respondents, each of them affirmed that the term *fixed-hour prayer* was interpreted in a very general sense to indicate simply that one prayed at about the same time each day. So, it is within the scope of this broad definition that interviewees explained their assimilation of the practice of fixed-hour prayer. The differences among participants are wholly confined to individual methodologies for practicing a regular prayer time and personal preferences for variations in content rather than a specific divergence in definitions that can be quantified statistically. In other words, there were as many definitions as participants.

Of the interviewees who marked this mystic practice, many of them related in the interview their personal idiosyncrasies of setting up a regular prayer time. Comments in this regard ranged from the laconic to the verbose. For instance, Interviewee 13 simply said, "Regular time, for me, after I'm laying down in bed. Turn the radio down, shut the light off, and all that." On the other hand, Interviewee 7 described the following detailed process.

> I would say that's, for us and our household, for my wife and I, that's Scripture time, and we don't do—I think of—the monks and how they would have their Matins and Lauds and their Terce and whatever. I don't have those things. However, and I can't say that it's always, it's ritualistic with every single day, but we do in our household, try to set aside, for example, a morning time where we're in word and we are in prayer. We're doing as a matter of fact, starting again with this Acacia group, we're going to be doing a daily Bible [study] and with that there's a section that leads you through prayer and through [a] devotion piece into a scriptural study piece. We're about to move into that as a whole Acacia group where we'll be every morning together as a family, as an Acacia family, doing that, as opposed to whatever everybody's doing separate and apart from each other right now. Which some have better practices than others in keeping that steady thing going, but this will be a way that we can do that together as that small group family and make that a regular morning practice. For some it will be a teaching moment where we really, hopefully, get some of our Acacia family interested in doing that on a regular basis.

As these quotations display, the practice of a semi-regular prayer time was popular among several respondents, but the actions performed in that time or exactly when or how long one would pray constituted a very broad range of options. Additionally, while interview participants occasionally referenced some particular sources for prayer content, they did not have rigid rules or structures for implementation. However, multiple respondents did remark that they utilized some form of set prayers, at least from time to time.

Several interviewees said that they had used set prayer content according to personal interest or experimentation. It was this aspect that fit with the overall EC characteristic of experimental eclecticism, and it was practically worked out in the spiritual lives of interviewed individuals by trying different types of prayers. For instance, two respondents noted the use of short set prayers personally chosen by them for a specific context.

> I definitely don't have a fixed prayer other than praying with my children at bedtime. We do have a fixed prayer that we'll pray together. So, I guess so, yeah. That's a fixed prayer. Every night, I'm saying the Shema and the Lord's Prayer. (Interviewee 12)

> I would start the day with a morning prayer or a series of prayers, I guess. One was I paraphrased the Lord's Prayer. I pulled a prayer off of a Catholic website that was devoted to devotional prayers, and they had a morning prayer that I liked,

and they also had an evening prayer. So, for a time, when I was doing this, I would wake up, roll out of bed, onto my knees, and I would pray my morning round of prayers. And then, at the evening, the last thing I did right before I crawled into bed was the evening prayer. (Interviewee 24)

In addition to these examples, many respondents had experimented with some form of the Daily Office from sources either based off of *The Book of Common Prayer* or *The Divine Hours* by Phyllis Tickle, which is in turn based on the Daily Office. One respondent even noted that he had experimented with the Daily Office, but he had opted for a simplified form in light of problems with navigating readings.

> My problem with this is I'm all over the map. I can't figure out how to use the Daily Office book to save my life. Really to me, the best one that I've found, which is not really the Daily Office, but it's Daily Office-esque, is commonprayer.net. It's one of those authors who you'd probably recognize his name if you've heard it, Scott-McKnight-type or somebody like that. Anyway, it's not the Daily Office, but it's kind of "The Daily Office for Dumb Evangelicals." (Interviewee 19)

Throughout each interview conversation on fixed-hour prayer, interviewee comments focused on the aspect of experimentation which is evident in the selected comments above. This feature of experimentation with mystic practices, particularly mystic practices which do not have a significant communal component, was even more pronounced in the final section: practices of passing familiarity.

Before proceeding to the final section of practices, it is useful to reiterate that the foregoing comments on the Jesus Prayer, practicing the presence of God, pilgrimage, and fixed-hour prayer highlight an interesting feature of the interview data. Specifically, these practices appeared to be used in a minor way among interview participants, with a 30–60% usage rate, but the practices proved to be unchartable once interview data was consulted. Still, divergent minor practices among respondents seldom enjoyed wide usage in a corporate context, but they were occasionally major personal practices among interviewees. The phenomenological methodology of this study has brought these issues into sharp relief through verbatim participant perspectives. However, a few practices still remain that were used by way of experimentation but were not used as significant practices by even a minority sampling of interviewees.

Practices of Passing Familiarity

The final section to be considered within this chapter consists of practices which interviewees were occasionally practicing or had been introduced to in the context of their EC of attendance. Practices that fall within the scope of this category, along with their statistical usages, are *lectio Divina* (24.3%), prayer labyrinths (24.3%), stations of the cross (24.3%), icons (18.9%), and the rosary (16.2%). As with other statistics concerning practices, it should be remembered that these numbers take into account any usage whatsoever, and many participants noted using a particular practice in this section only once. While an occasional participant found one or more of these practices to be foundational for his or her spiritual life, such a situation was not the norm for the group. Unlike the previous section, these practices did not generally suffer from the disadvantages of ambiguous definitions. As a result, discussion of these practices will only emphasize the circumstances surrounding the use of each practice and its practical methodology, as noted by interviewees. While the next chapter will answer questions of *why* and the reasoning behind utilizing practices, this section will round out the theme of this chapter in focusing on *how* these practices were integrated into the contexts of the examined emergent churches.

Lectio Divina

Lectio Divina, or simply *lectio*, was noted by respondents as either introduced by their church or utilized in an occasional way on a personal basis. Interviewee comments concerning *lectio* centered on two areas. First, several respondents remarked about methods in which this mystic practice had been employed in their EC setting, including its differentiation from other similar methods of engaging Scripture. Second, others focused their comments on the particular contexts in which this practice might be utilized by themselves or their respective emergent churches. Through these emphases, interviewees asserted that *lectio Divina* was considered to be one of many optional practices for Bible study in communal or, more usually, personal contexts.

For most respondents using *lectio*, this practice was a method in which to engage biblical materials in ways beyond historical or intellectual readings. Interviewee 8 provided an extended explanation of how *lectio* moves beyond literal methods of reading. "I try to let it be more of a soaking in: This is personally for me; this is not something I'm giving away, but this is something that's for me. So, I want to digest his words, and I want to understand all that. So, it's not something I'm necessarily giving away." As can be seen from this interviewee comment, it was difficult for practitioners to define fully what they actually did methodologically in the process of practicing *lectio*, but they returned again and again to the centrality of Scripture and the need to read passages repetitively and meditatively. It is also interesting to note that respondents from different churches all used the term *soaking* as a metaphor to describe the practice of *lectio*.

While the basic methodology of *lectio* was described in a generally similar manner among interview participants, some respondents disagreed over the use of imagination in this mystic practice. Some respondents acknowledged the use of one's imagination in *lectio*, but they disagreed on its essential connection to this mystic practice. For instance, Interviewee 27 noted a preference for the use of imagination but noted that this practice was not intrinsically part of *lectio*.

> Another type of reading that I like is [what] one teacher called "imaginative prayer," or "imaginative study." Where you take that Scripture and you set yourself into the place of one of those characters within it. And then, you try to experience it, and you try to see what you hear and see and smell and feel and everything and emotions, and how do you think you would have responded if it was you to Jesus saying that, and how do you really wish Jesus was responding to you? Some of those ways, that's not quite *lectio Divina*, but I think it's of value.

Historically, an imaginative process might be more accurately connected to Ignatian methods of Bible study, and this interviewee seems to be aware of the disparity. However, other respondents viewed the role of imagination as primary to, if not the totality of, the practice of *lectio*. For example, Interviewee 28 states that *lectio* is that "which is essentially contemplating on Scriptures and putting yourself in the scriptural context." Interestingly, this interview participant also goes on to draw links between *lectio*, as imaginative Bible reading, and hypnosis. While respondents disagreed on the role of the imagination in *lectio*, their overall procedural explanation of this practice did not differ on any other major point. In fact, the only other points of difference in interview conversations on the implementation of *lectio* were confined to the context in which it was practiced from church to church.

According to the scope of interview responses, *lectio* was utilized among case study emergent churches in three primary contexts. First, many respondents noted the assimilation of this practice on a personal level in engaging scriptural texts. Those interviewees which utilize *lectio* as a personal Bible study practice tend to group it with other optional Bible study practices and methods as well. A second context for the use of *lectio* among respondents was noted particularly in CitC because this church created a *lectio* "station" for communal gatherings on an occasional basis. One respondent described the process of creating and using this station in-depth.

> We had a room set up for *lectio Divina* upstairs, and one of our Hebrew Bible scholars helped to lead that. So, we had a handout explaining it, and then opportunity to just participate in those texts. I think it was the lectionary passages for the week and engaging those in ways that are different, I think again, than having to sit through and think "Well, what does this passage mean to me?" (Interviewee 31)

While the use of a specific station for *lectio* was unique to CitC, the other churches noted the integration of *lectio* methods as part of introducing biblical passages to younger persons. For example, Interviewee 32 described this process.

> I actually use that with the kids sometimes. I mean, I make it more kid-friendly. Instead of just listening, they listen the first time, and then I tell them to put their imaginations in the story. And then, we listen again, and usually I do it with stories. I don't think every story lends itself to that, but stories that have a lot of sounds, I'll read it through again, and they'll make sounds that go with the story, the sounds they hear. They'll go through it a third time, and we usually act it out.

The relative importance of the imagination aspect to the utilization of this practice is apparent in this example as a means to provide multiple modes of engagement for children and youth. So, whether viewed in a personal context, as an occasional station, or in engaging particular age groups, *lectio Divina* was valued by the respondents as a way to look at a biblical passage from a new angle. While *lectio* was used practically for this perspective in relation to study of the Bible, prayer labyrinths were occasionally used in a similar fashion with respect to prayer.

Prayer Labyrinths

If one word might be used to sum up interview participant perspectives on the use of prayer labyrinths, it would likely be the qualifying term *sporadic*. In other words, no respondents claimed frequent or regular use of this practice in their particular church context or elsewhere. However, use of prayer labyrinths in the past for these individuals was significant enough to create an impression or to offer a new angle on ways to pray. Interestingly, no interviewee offered an in-depth description of the physical construct of a labyrinth; rather, they focused on experiences in walking a labyrinth with occasional reference to building materials or to helping in the building process. With these issues in mind, the use of prayer labyrinths was uniformly regarded by interviewees as one possible prayer practice, yet participants differed with regard to whether they had participated in a prayer labyrinth outside of the context of their current EC of attendance or within it.

Quite a few interviewees who marked use of prayer labyrinths on the spiritual practices questionnaire remembered introduction and/or utilization of a labyrinth apart from the context of their current church of attendance. For instance, Interviewee 30 fondly recalled, "My first experience of it [prayer labyrinths] was very meaningful to me. I was on a retreat for people who were faith-based community organizing, and it was at this monastery in Kentucky. The monks had made a labyrinth of wild flowers." While most interviewee comments centered upon similar memorable experiences linked to prayer labyrinths, some respondents went into greater detail concerning personal use of the labyrinth. For example, Interviewee 3 noted time and focus elements as integral pieces of the labyrinth aside from the obvious physical walking element: "It gives you that time to focus as well, so you're going through and you have your questions, and you'll come to a different point and sit there and think about it for a while. Maybe do a little journaling while you're there. That's usually the form of it all." It is interesting to note that this interviewee connected the process of walking a labyrinth to the practice of journaling along with the more common connection to prayer. While the above interviewee responses are paradigmatic concerning notable instances and procedural reasons for using a labyrinth, they do not connect these uses in a significant way to their current EC context. Other respondents noted how prayer labyrinths fit into their particular emergent milieu.

As might be expected from a practice in this section, not every church was utilizing prayer labyrinths as part of their communal meetings. In fact, only CitC implemented prayer labyrinths as part of their services. While labyrinths were not a regular part of meetings for CitC, some interviewees noted how they were employed within this specific EC context. Interviewee 29 described this process in detail.

> We create them sometimes in church. I say "We," it's [the pastor] or [the associate pastor] will create them, and then they're part of the worship service. We had one just two or three weeks ago, I guess, up on the stage in the Kessler [Theatre]. But, [the

pastor] and I have actually talked about designing one, if we ever have land that the church can use. We want to do a wild flower one. And, we want to leave it, so even after the flowers have bloomed and gone to seed and died, we want it to be, again, a meditation on life and death to some extent, the mystery of the seasons of life.

While this interviewee focused on the impermanent nature of CitC labyrinths and the desire for more permanent possibilities, there was quite a range of sentiments within this one church concerning the use of this mystic practice ranging from mild disinterest to enthusiastic curiosity. The majority of participants were intrigued by it; however, other responses were not so positive. For instance, Interviewee 35 remarked, "Two or three Sundays ago, they put a labyrinth up there, and you could walk it. I didn't walk it. I think I was one of the few, that's just me. It didn't mean anything to me." However, for most respondents, positive interest or curiosity was the primary feeling which they connected with this sporadic practice, particularly curiosity about a prayer practice which engaged the participant on a physical level. In keeping with an interest in the physicality of spirituality, a similar response of interest and curiosity was displayed by interviewees in talking about the utilization of the stations of the cross.

Stations of the Cross

The stations of the cross were employed at two of the three case study emergent churches, excluding RCC, in connection with celebrations of Good Friday, leading up to Easter. In fact, Interviewee 27 succinctly summed up all matters of conversation on the subject in her interview with the terse statement, "Well, we basically just use them [stations of the cross] at Easter at the church." Additionally, participants from both churches numbered the stations at twelve rather than the more traditional fourteen. While the Easter context for implementation might naturally seem to lead to a link between this practice and observance of the liturgical calendar more generally, no interview respondent made this particular connection. In lieu of a liturgical connection, interview participants considered use of the stations of the cross through their dramatic experimental adaptations in their churches. Consequently, this practice which would seem to be overtly communal, had a particularly individual focus for most interviewees whether from the perspective of an individual creating one of the stations or of an individual experiencing the stations. Therefore, EC interview participants differed markedly on their comments concerning the stations of the cross depending on whether they haled from ERC or CitC.

Primary focus for assimilation of the stations of the cross as an Easter practice for ERC rested on the opportunities that existed for artists within that church to express themselves and, in turn, for other congregants to experience the stations of the cross uniquely through artistic interpretation. Multiple persons spoke to the perspective of enabling the artist to create an expression of the events surrounding the crucifixion of Jesus Christ. Interviewee 20 demonstratively noted this connection by stating, "I love to go. It's always very powerful and moving and gives people who are a little more creatively inclined than me to [have] a chance to express themselves within the church too in a very physical way." While the previous comment focused on the perspectives of the artists of ERC and their opportunity to create, other remarks focused on their experience of the stations of the cross as a participant going through each of the stations. Interviewee 19 emotionally related the experience of the stations from this standpoint.

> You weren't just walking by looking at exhibits. You had the cross and nails, and you had to nail nails in the cross. That was one of the most powerful things, because the whole time, everywhere else you were, every other station you were, you were hearing this constant bang, bang, bang, going on in the background. By the time I got through with it, with the whole thing, I was a wreck, just listening to that.

So, whether from the perspective of artist or participant, particular emphasis was placed on the physicality of the stations of the cross as a worship experience. While a strong element of physicality or movement was noted by several respondents, ERC participants were still walking among fixed expressions of the stations of the cross. CitC carried the theme of physical movement with regard to occasional implementation of the stations of the cross to a new level.

CitC interviewees noted as one of their most unique spiritual practices what they termed *DART Stations of the Cross*. In this practice, DART is the acronym designation for Dallas Area Rapid Transit, the local mass transit rail system. CitC played off of the double meaning of stations between the two, seemingly disparate, components of their unique assimilation of stations of the cross. According to Interviewee 30, CitC connected the stations of the cross to specific, quick celebrations at chosen train stations within the Dallas transit system.

> We do it on Good Friday. And, it's a moving meditation. The whole idea is the train car is like your chapel and the urban

landscape, and we also print out these meditation cards that have original art paintings and meditations or poetry. And so, you flip them as you ride, and then it all fits together, and the last time we did it, at every station, train station, correlates with a station of the cross, and at the three where Jesus falls, we got off, and we did a—what did we call it—I think we called it a moving meditation or something. These were the different things. One, you got the elements for communion. [Second], we told people to bring art supplies for homeless artists that we work with that this non-profit works with that we wanted to support, and there was something else for the third one. And so, we did that, and at the end we gathered to do this guerilla communion. So, it's kind of a community art project and a contemplative Lenten practice.

As may be glimpsed in this lengthy description, this unique celebration of the stations of the cross was deeply meaningful to participants on the level of physicality of participation, freshness of perspective, and connection to local city context. In these multiple levels of meaning, interviewees from CitC asserted that this practice had great value for an embodied spirituality. So, while the stations of the cross were not used as a very common ritual practice across the spectrum of case study churches and interviewees, this mystic practice did have a particular impact on those who had participated in its celebration, often out of proportion to extent of use. A likely point of connection for this level of impact is the value attached to increasing the physicality of spirituality. Interviewee 23 manifested this value as a bridge to consider the use of icons in connection to the stations of the cross by noting, "We've had some intentional times at church, especially when we do like a stations of the cross service, something like that, then I will reflect on icons."

Icons

The importance of the physical element among the studied emergent churches allowed for greater experimentation with stations of the cross than would be expected in churches arising from an evangelical heritage. Similarly, this focus on the physical allowed for experimentation with icons; however, icons did not seem to impact interviewees in as significant a way as the stations of the cross. While it is noteworthy that icons are even a spiritual option among the case study churches, they have not been incorporated to a large extent. Indeed, icons were only considered by interviewees in two contexts: a background option for corporate worship and a personal option for experimentation.

In a communal context, icons received occasional use only at ERC. Within this context, they were utilized in one of two ways. First, they were intermittently used as a background during corporate meetings, as noted briefly by Interviewee 21: "I noticed at Emmaus Road, sometimes, whenever they'll have a projection on the screen, maybe with a song or a Scripture, maybe while [the pastor] or someone else is sharing, there might be an icon back there." In addition to this modest use, a second way in which ERC utilized icons was through their prayer station. Interviewee 24 noted the availability of this option in the following terms: "I was thinking of our prayer station that we have off to the side. Yeah, and so there is one there. And, that's part of the experience, if someone goes over and decides to use that station." While this interviewee noted the accessibility of this option, he never attested to availing himself of it. As these uses display, there was not much intentional engagement with icons on a corporate level in the emergent churches studied, but there was a slightly higher level of usage of this mystic practice on an individual basis.

On a personal level, multiple interviewees noted some experimentation with icons. For one respondent, experimentation included creation of an icon. He related this experience in the following way: "I actually made an icon. Because we have a prayer station at Emmaus Road. I just out of fun, decided to make an icon" (Interviewee 21). While this option seemed open to anyone at ERC, other interviewees from this context only noted use of icons already created rather than participating in the process of icon creation. These respondents noted the focusing aspect of the process of using icons, but they tended to restrict this aspect to the context of personal prayer. Interviewee 33 approached this perspective by explaining, "They're [icons] just certain things that I use that just remind me of the things that fill my spirit or give me strength spiritually. When I'm praying, I won't sit directly in front of things or anything, but there's just certain things that I'll use when I'm praying in my home." Through this perspective, it is apparent how interviewees could experiment with how icons might fit into their own personal prayer practices. Interestingly, it did not appear that they felt limited only to traditional religious iconography; rather, the use of any image within prayer seemed to be subsumed under the term *icon*. Still, freedom of interpretation reigned in tandem with freedom to practice with respect to icons. This emphasis on liberty to experiment was also notable within discussion on the final practice: the rosary.

Rosary

The final practice for discussion as a practice of passing familiarity is the rosary. As might be expected from its placement, this mystic practice was implemented least within the case study emergent churches. In fact, many interviewees who did not mark this practice were also not even familiar with the term. Additionally, it may be noted that some individuals who did mark the practice of the rosary clarified that they actually utilized an Eastern Orthodox prayer rope or Anglican prayer beads rather than the more common Roman Catholic version. So, with respect to engagement with the rosary, all of these variants are included in light of their synonymous nature in the views of interviewees. As far as assimilation of this practice, participants responded that they utilized it in one of two ways: personal experimentation or cherished childhood tradition.

With respect to personal experimentation, individual interviewees commented on ways that they included this practice in their daily lives. Interviewee 27 provided a representative example of this process even though the specifics of implementation varied from person to person.

> We've made our own [prayer beads] at church, and I've made one, and I've used it at times that usually what I've done instead of using the Catholic prayers, there's some that I found that are from the Episcopal church, and then I actually sat down and wrote up some different prayers of my own. Now, when I use them now, I basically don't use the rosary. I'm just going through them. I know what they are, and, again, a lot of that is done at night, when I'm in bed and can't sleep. It's a real good way to fall asleep. One of two things happen. You either spend time with the Lord, or you fall asleep, one or the other. So, there are certain Scriptures that I'll say within it, like the Lord's Prayer and the Apostle's Creed, and I've even added "Hear, O Israel."

Additionally, Interviewee 27 asserted more than once in the course of conversation on the subject of the rosary that she freely interpreted or re-interpreted this practice, as it suited her. This freedom of interpretation is very much in keeping with the focus on experimentation evinced by interviewees interested in this practice. Also, as a singular occurrence, Interviewee 23 mentioned that ERC had a specific meeting in which the rosary was explained to all congregants by an Episcopal priest. While these circumstances reveal a passing interest in this practice for the means of providing options for experimentation with spiritual practices on a personal level, interviewees that claimed significant use of the rosary tied such use to their religious upbringing.

The most visible usage of the rosary among interview participants was among those who were raised in the Roman Catholic tradition. These respondents linked their particular practice to their past rather than specifically to their present EC context. For instance, Interviewee 4 recalls her personal foundations in this practice.

> My dad is staunch Catholic. [He] was an altar boy and then after him and my mom got married, the priest was not well, and my dad and another guy basically would help carry him or help him move from place-to-place. My grandfather always led the rosary, and we recited it. My dad's sister at the early service always lead the rosary for Most Precious Blood church. It's not something so much that we practiced at home, but I would say for a lot, probably from about third grade through probably high school that was my evening prayer.

While these ties to upbringing might seem to invalidate their appropriation into an EC context, the significance of Interviewee 4's comments should not be glossed over lightly, for this practice and the connection to the past that it offered was understood to be just as available in the new EC context as it was in her childhood context. As a result, this comment shows the liberty that those in an EC context enjoy by bringing those practices which they view as personally valuable into their new religious context, even if that is not a practice appropriated by the majority of persons in their new EC context. In fact, they can bring a practice not only for personal use but also for potential introduction to other persons in an EC who might then assimilate the practice according to the value of experimentation, as noted earlier. In this sense, even the practice of the rosary, minimal as it might be, highlighted emergent themes of experimentation and eclecticism which were just as present in the practices which enjoy widest usage. Therefore, as descriptions of process and methodology are now complete, attention can turn to matters of theological themes with respect to the reinterpretation of mystic practices.

Summary of Chapter

To reiterate, this chapter has explicated one direction for investigation of the appropriation of mystic practices within the case study emergent churches. Specifically, interview data has been presented phenomenologically in order to make the perspectives of the interviewees apparent. Additionally, as noted multiple times above, focus for this chapter has rested on how interview participants answered the question of *how* they utilize each practice. This appropriation of practices on a procedural level does inform the observations and conclusions of the researcher; nevertheless, participant answers to the question of *why* they utilize each practice remains the overall focus of the book because this sociological study is principally interested in the *theological content* with which these emergent churches are investing the practices. Still, investments of this nature require social context to be understood, and the way in which a practice is assimilated can be a significant clue to its ultimate meaning for practitioners. For these reasons, this chapter has demonstrated respondent perspectives on how twenty-one mystic practices are being integrated procedurally in the social contexts of the three case study congregations.

Considerations of the practical implementation of the practices led to grouping them into five categories discussed in descending order of widespread usage across the spectrum of the churches. With this focus on usage, practices were grouped into five categories: major practices (Holy Communion, silence, solitude, meditation), divergent major practices (centering prayer, contemplative prayer, spiritual direction/spiritual friendship), minor practices (confession, liturgical calendar, liturgical prayer, fasting, making the sign of the cross), divergent minor practices (the Jesus Prayer, practicing the presence of God, pilgrimage, fixed-hour prayer), and practices of passing familiarity (*lectio Divina*, prayer labyrinths, stations of the cross, icons, the rosary). While these categories were provided simply for a basis to view data clearly, the primary data component for investigation of each practice within its category was what the interviewees stated for themselves in their own words. Adherence to this standard was notably apparent in the necessary creation of two divergent categories to allow for discrepancies of definition among interviewees concerning particular practices.

In review of all that has been stated on each practice in this chapter, it might *seem* that the mystic practices as a whole have been appropriated with varying levels of usage, integration, and adaptation in the case study churches with *no* overarching purpose tying this assimilation together. However, there are notable theological anchors undergirding use and reinterpretation of mystic practices within these EC contexts. While this chapter benefited from a straightforward presentation of each practice, conceptual meanings attached to the practices can be more clearly examined in relation to the theological anchors supporting their use in the next chapter. Interestingly, while the case study emergent churches did map the appropriated practices to similar anchors as those noted in chapter three, there was some variance. Empirical results also varied from EC literature in exactly which practice tied to which anchor.

6

Theological Reinterpretation of Mystic Practices

As noted within the previous chapter, the structural framework of the phenomenological interviews allows an empirical consideration of EC appropriation of mystic practices from two angles. Specifically, chapter five explicated the appropriation of mystic practices with respect to questions of exactly *how* each practice was assimilated by individuals within the social context of three emergent churches. In this chapter, appropriation, reinterpretation, and theological investment will receive full description and delineation through interviewee answers to the question of *why* particular practices were appropriated in their own church contexts. At this juncture, the research claim of the study comes to the forefront. While the previous chapter provided invaluable procedural information, this study is principally a sociological investigation of the *theological content* with which EC Christians invest mystic practices. So, questions of *why* each practice has been appropriated into the spirituality of an EC practitioner and his/her church setting are even more vital than questions of *how* each practice is utilized.

In order to follow the inductive approach of grounded theory to answer questions of *why*, the structure of this chapter will diverge in part from the categories introduced in the previous chapter. Specifically, chapter five displayed interviewee comments on all twenty-one practices through the simple framework of five categories delineated on the level of usage: major practices, divergent major practices, minor practices, divergent minor practices, and practices of passing familiarity. Within each category, practices were discussed in a descending order of usage. While these simple categories are also employed within this chapter, they will be set within larger sections, listing theological anchors of EC spirituality which have been adapted from the list introduced in the third chapter. The practices will be assessed according to these major anchors to show how the anchors both allow appropriation of these practices and necessitate theological reinterpretation of these practices. It should be noted that some practices will be considered more than once because they map to multiple theological anchors for EC interview participants. Additionally, not all practices will be considered under each theme for the obvious reason that some practices will only be connected to one or two anchors rather than to all of them. Therefore, this chapter will consider theological reinterpretation of mystic practices in the case study churches through interviewee comments which mapped to the anchors of community, experimentation, embodied spirituality through social action, and embodied spirituality through physicality. To briefly reiterate previous definitions, the anchors are the unique theological themes which aid the EC in the appropriation of mystic practices, and they are also invested into practices as part of the process of reinterpretation.

Before proceeding to a full discussion of interview respondent comments in the theological framework of EC anchors, two qualifying comments concerning these anchors are necessary. First, one of the major questions answered by empirical research was whether all theological anchors/themes identified within literary research were present in actual case study situations. As the terminology at the end of the foregoing paragraph indicates, findings within empirical case studies did map to similar theological anchors but not exactly as denoted within EC literature, which were community, relevance over tradition, mystery, contemplation with action, and embodied spirituality. To delineate further, the anchor of experimentation within the case study churches replaces the anchor of relevance over tradition. While a connection between these two anchors is apparent, as a focus on relevance over tradition would naturally lead to experimentation, it is necessary to change terms in order to reflect the theological weight which interviewees placed on experimentation itself. Mystery, the third literary anchor, was not a significant anchor for the appropriation and reinterpretation of mystic practices in the case study churches. Additionally, embodied spirituality has been split into two separate categories. Although this separation was noted in consideration of EC literature, it was so strongly emphasized in interviewee comments that these categories required complete separation. Also, the contemplation with action category was subsumed within the anchor of embodied spirituality through social action. These qualifying issues offer boundaries for the scope of discussion in this chapter because focus is maintained on unique theological anchors which link to appropriation and reinterpretation of mystic practices, not to *all* EC theological anchors which are valuable for a *general* EC spiritual theology.

The second major qualifying issue is that these theological anchors are not mapped to practices in an attempt to exhaust all possibilities of theological connection for EC respondents. For instance, many respondents commented on the purpose of practices as, at least in part, dealing with a connection to or relationship with God. However, this anchor is not considered in the proceeding discussion because conceptual focus is placed on the theological anchors which are unique to the EC social context or uniquely interpreted/emphasized by the EC. In addition, the anchors listed here do not deal with EC spiritual themes in general but with those themes that allow for EC appropriation and reinterpretation of mystic practices. As an outflow of this emphasis on *unique* anchors, discussion centers on the values which allow for inter-tradition appropriation and reinterpretation of practices. According to this line of reasoning, a theological anchor of relationship with God is *not* unique because both the original (mystical tradition) and destination (EC) contexts hold this anchor in common. In connection with these slight changes among categories, it is also important to keep in view continually that these theological emphases are not only what *allow* EC participants to appropriate practices but they are also the theological values which the EC *invests* into their reinterpretations. For example, in the case of icons, the EC is not appropriating the use of icons as much as they are appropriating *what they perceive* the use of icons to be. So, with these caveats in mind, discussion can now progress to a delineation of practices that map to each theological anchor. Within the discussion on each individual anchor, consideration will proceed according to categories of usage introduced in chapter five.

Community

In light of the foregoing comment concerning the *distinctive* and *unique* nature of EC theological anchors for this discussion, one might legitimately raise the question of community as being unique to the EC. After all, many Christian traditions, as well as other religious traditions, have a high regard for community and its role in spirituality. While this question is quite relevant, community is considered as a *distinctive* theological anchor for the EC on the basis of its specific galvanizing role for EC spirituality. EC literature emphasizes community, and it is also quite apparent in empirical research that this anchor is stressed to the point that communal practices are appropriated and reinterpreted to become frequent and prominent in emergent spirituality. This prominence is reflected in which mystic practices are appropriated and how they are reinterpreted. Additionally, many individual practices are integrated in a way that they become communal practices, or, at least, they become practices which prepare the individual for life in community. With respect to interviewee comments, community was the theological anchor most often noted by name in interviews. With this trait of emphasizing community in mind, interviewee comments can be investigated concerning how particular practices and larger categories mapped to this theological anchor.

Major Practices

The anchor of community allowed for the appropriation of major practices, principally Holy Communion. With respect to the major practices researched in this study—Holy Communion, meditation, silence, and solitude—it is quite easy to see that most of these practices would not naturally map to an anchor on community. While meditation, silence, and solitude were interestingly not understood as solely individualistic enterprises,[1] which serves to emphasize how highly these emergent churches held community to be, interviewee comments definitely focused on the applicability of the practice of Holy Communion for this theological anchor. The essential value which EC participants placed on community made the practice of Holy Communion particularly attractive; however, the nuances of this appropriation can only be fully understood in light of actual participant perspectives.

By way of reiteration, Holy Communion was by far the most common practice appropriated in the case study churches and among interview participants with a 95% utilization rate. Additionally, this practice is notable because it was used by respondents within their previous evangelical contexts as well; however, in the process of appropriation, interviewees noted specific differences with the implementation of Holy Communion in their EC context. Principally, EC participants remarked that Holy Communion was used more often than in their previous contexts and there was more variety in mode of practice, yet intinction was the preferred method. From the basis of these unique aspects of appropriation, the question of whether interviewees were reinterpreting this practice can be approached.

Simply put, yes, interviewed individuals revealed that their churches were reinterpreting Holy Communion according to the theological anchor of community. They approached this reinterpretation through emphasis

---

1. For instance, Interviewee 29 stated the following with respect to solitude: "In an odd sort of way, I realize my connection to others more when I've chosen to be alone, chosen to be away from them."

of content already present in the practice and in investing new theological content into the practice. From the perspective of emphasizing theological content already present, Interviewee 21 provided a representative comment on the value of Holy Communion as a means of drawing congregants together in a tangible ritual. "There's a lot of young people there and a lot of older people there. I guess people that I wouldn't normally hang out with or associate with, but every time I see people, I see all of us come together, that's what I consider Communion." The strength of emphasis on community through the tangible nature of Holy Communion was also noted by respondents as the reasoning behind such frequent practice of it. Particularly, two out of three case study churches practiced Holy Communion every week which was a significant point of departure from the denominational traditions from which they had emerged.

A second major communal emphasis illustrated how interviewees invested new theological content into the practice of Holy Communion as they reinterpreted the practice in light of the primacy of relationship in the EC. The pastor of CitC provided some detailed reflection on this issue.

> Two big pieces I brought from the church I was part of in Boston, one, is a version of our welcome, which I think almost has become our mission statement, that was written by the pastors of the church I was part of in Boston, and most people in Church in the Cliff probably don't even realize that. I went through a season of experimenting with different welcomes, and that one just really stuck. The other piece is at the end when I say what I got from Hope church was "whether you're baptized or not, whether you believe a little or a lot." So, that was what I said for the first year and a half, and then we have some in our community, [personal name], who's married to our childcare minister, who claims identity as an agnostic-atheist. We did this whole series last summer "Filling the church-shaped hole," and the people told their stories from different perspectives. We had agnostic Sunday, and it was the best one. And, he—I think in the context of that Sunday [or] maybe a Wednesday night, somewhere pretty public—said for a long time he sat there and listened to that and didn't know how to participate [in Holy Communion], because we were still saying "believe a little or a lot," and he didn't feel like he even believed a little. So, in that moment, we just "believe a little, a lot, or not." And, I think, I said that for agnostic Sunday, and it became really clear that that was really important that I keep saying that, and so I do.

This extended quote explained the process in which one church, CitC, modified their liturgy and *theological standards of belief* with regard to the practice of Holy Communion in order to accommodate their high value on relationship for all persons in the community. So, in this specific story, it becomes apparent that such value is placed on community that other beliefs become secondary in status to it. In other words, the essential answer to the question "Why do you use the practice of Holy Communion?" is provided through a realization that, for the EC, theology changes on the basis of relationship *not* relationships change according to one's theology. So, this practice shows that a mystic practice can be appropriated and reinterpreted on the basis of relationship, *and* this high value on relationship is invested by the EC into each practice that they appropriate. While an emphasis on Holy Communion beautifully illustrates the theological anchor of community, an opposite development highlights the role of community with respect to divergent major practices.

Divergent Major Practices

Divergent major practices of centering prayer and contemplative prayer were very rarely mapped to the theological anchor, or unique theological theme, of community. Understandably, these practices were not viewed by many as having any communal element, and, as a result, they were practiced individually. However, a notable undercurrent of interpretation framed "centering prayer" as prayers which a community can be centered upon and, in this sense, still found a way to include a communal mindset in a practice which is seemingly exclusive to a personal context. Representatively, Interviewee 16 related, "For me, a centering prayer is traditionally a prayer that becomes, really becomes, a common ritual in a worship service that is an identifier for a community." So, while centering prayer was appropriated and reinterpreted chiefly according to other anchors, any connection to the anchor of community made this practice attractive, even if such connection necessitated reinterpreting centering prayer from a type of prayer to center oneself to a type of prayer that centered a community on common rituals.

While most interviewees did not make such communal links, it is telling that the practices of centering prayer and contemplative prayer were located in the particular category of *divergent* major practices. In other words, the fact that EC participants had a difficult time defining these practices may have contributed to the lack of possibility for mapping them to the theological anchor of community. While these divergent major practices lacked a significant communal component for mapping to the anchor of community, spiritual direction mapped more readily to this unique theological theme.

As with other divergent practices, spiritual direction was defined variously by interviewees. These definitions display diverse levels of appropriation, and they also offer different options for reinterpretation. To reiterate from the previous chapter, interview respondents identified the practice of spiritual direction according to whether they connected more with the term *direction* or *friendship*. Spiritual *direction* was interpreted as more formal, more intentional, and occurring in a hierarchical mentor and disciple relationship. Conversely, spiritual *friendship* was understood distinctively as more informal, more spontaneous, and occurring on a basis of equality as spiritual topics came up for discussion among friends. Within the interview data, a notable preference was evident for the latter definition as the principal means of appropriating this practice. This uneven preference between terms illustrates avenues of reinterpretation which occurred in the case study settings.

Reinterpretation of spiritual direction in the case study emergent churches proceeded subtly according to matters of emphasis rather than complete innovation of new theological content. Specifically, spiritual direction was appropriated on the basis of the value of community in small permutations to aid individuals. For instance, in the words of Interviewee 21, he appropriated spiritual direction in order "to feel that I'm not alone." So, even when participants actually meant spiritual *direction*, as they interpreted it, they meant one-on-one meetings *in terms of relationship*. However, it is notable that these relationships were seldom interpreted in a mentor/disciple type of relationship. Also, whenever possible, interviewees opted for understandings of spiritual direction that focused on group settings rather than one-on-one encounters. Spiritual direction was regularly reinterpreted in terms of individual persons coming together as equals to offer mutual spiritual direction and comfort. This way of reinterpreting community as an exchange of guidance among equals through spiritual direction was even more evident when this practice was employed through groups in the case study churches, as noted by Interviewee 6 below.

> We get together outside of church in small groups with the same people. I think there's like six families in our group, and there are several of those [groups] in the church, and in those groups, we usually do some sort of dinner together and have some sort of Bible study or just carry on a conversation about what the sermon was about Sunday morning and just discuss it amongst ourselves. Hammer out our differences, and then we share prayer requests and things like that, so it's not necessarily

a disciple/mentor relationship as it is group support. That sort of thing. [If] Somebody's down in the group, as a group we pray for them [sic] and help them with whatever they need, whether somebody's having a baby in the group, then everybody pitches in and brings them meals for a week. So, just a close-knit extension of the church kind of deal.

This passage emphasizes the EC tendency to reinterpret communal situations in order to invest them with an even stronger emphasis on community. So, participants invested community by appropriating spiritual direction in ways that *heightened* emphasis on community, and communal minor practices were treated similarly.

Minor Practices

While minor practices of an overtly individualistic nature, such as making the sign of the cross, were not discussed by interviewees according to the anchor of community, most minor practices received considerable explanation to tie them to a high value placed on this theological theme. The customization of confession, the liturgical calendar, liturgical prayer, and fasting invests these practices with a theological sense of the *breadth* of community. Theological stress on these practices often connected to the anchor of community through a matter of scope as a nuance of reinterpretation.

The appropriation of the practice of confession in chapter five was the most common borrowing of a minor practice within the case study churches. Phenomenological interview data revealed that while this practice was appropriated and implemented in these EC contexts, confession was typically viewed as an informal matter that tended to be employed in a group rather than individual context. Specifically, interviewees noted that they most often practiced confession in the context of worship services and small groups, but they occasionally had made one-on-one connections for the purpose of confession or "accountability." Additionally, interview data revealed a distinct preference for replacing "sin" terminology in confession with the term "struggle." These specifics of appropriation serve to guide an answer to the question of whether these churches were reinterpreting the practice of confession in light of the anchor of community or not.

With respect to confession, one may observe that interviewed individuals and the larger EC contexts with which they associated were reinterpreting the practice of confession for their particular circumstances. In a similar manner to the progression of reinterpretation of Holy Communion, EC participants were reinterpreting confession through twin paths of emphasis and innovation. Concerning matters of emphasis, while the practice of confession naturally contains a communal element, multiple interviewees extended the scope of confession to a wider participant inclusion. Interviewee 16 explained this viewpoint with particular reference to interpreting the book of Leviticus.

> The most important part of confession is the community. For me, Leviticus is the fifth gospel. It's a book about sacrifice and confession on behalf of the community. Every time you burn one of those animals you have to publicly say why. You also have had to gone to the person who you sinned against and ask them for forgiveness before you come to the temple. Then, you have to have a bunch of friends help you get the animal there, and then they hand most of it back to you. So that you basically have a celebratory barbecue. So it's become a really fascinating thing for me with confession.

As this comment illustrates, for interview respondents, the practice of confession hinged on the matter of relationship for appropriation and reinterpretation in much the same vein as the discussion surrounding Holy Communion. Close inspection of confession highlighted a new nuance for the anchor of community. Specifically, confession hinged on relationship in the context of a group as much as, or more than, any single individual. Notably, this was the primary way of mapping confession to a theological anchor that was offered by many interviewees.

A lesser emphasis within the interview data provided a very interesting perspective that moved EC reinterpretation of confession beyond emphasizing content already imbued within the practice. Interestingly, interviewee comments revealed that there was little mention about the applicability of categories of sin or God to the practice of confession. Therefore, this practice, which has traditionally been interpreted as a penitent practice concerning seeking God's forgiveness and absolution of sin, has been reinterpreted by the EC to focus less on sin and more on the relationship with others in community brought about through confession. Again, this development shows the degree to which EC participants are willing to invest their own theology into these practices. While participants extended the communal focus of confession which already had a communal element, they also reinterpreted confession to minimize any theological content which might get in the way of building relationships.

Focus for EC interviewees on the theological anchor of community was brought into sharp focus by considerations of *why* the liturgical calendar had received great emphasis in their churches. As noted in the previous chapter, the liturgical calendar was appropriated to varying degrees by the case study churches, and the level of use even varied from person to person. However, all permutations of use included an awareness of the major seasons of the Christian year (Advent, Christmas, Epiphany, Lent, Easter, and Pentecost) and a deeper recognition of the celebrations of Advent and Lent. Many interviewees went even further to remark about deeper appropriations of the liturgical calendar through the language of connecting to the ancient Christian community. These nuances of appropriation reveal analytic pathways for answering the question of whether these emergent churches are reinterpreting the practice of the liturgical calendar.

Concerning reinterpretation, yes, the practice of the liturgical calendar is being reinterpreted according to the anchor of community, yet this reinterpretation is more subtle than with previous anchors. In fact, respondents marked the liturgical calendar through connection of this practice to the rhythms of the community. As a result, a sense of *rhythm* served as a significant emphasis and theological characteristic of community which was already present within the practice of the liturgical calendar when appropriated, as identified by Interviewee 24 in saying, "I see the calendar in terms of putting people on the same page, individually and corporately, so we can experience the seasons and the ebb and flow of church life together." As seen in this quote, rhythm stood out as a trait for EC participants that was uniquely present in the liturgical calendar. This understanding of rhythm made the liturgical calendar a suitable subject of appropriation on the basis of the anchor of community. While the meaning behind the liturgical calendar for EC interviewees was stated in terms of the rhythms of community, they understandably tied this practice to the rhythms and seasons of the year as well. Interviewees also conversed over the sporadic deeper appropriations of the liturgical calendar mentioned above, but this aspect of appropriation mapped more specifically to the anchor of experimentation.

In great similarity to the appropriation of the liturgical calendar, the practice of liturgical prayer was appropriated by interviewed individuals and their respective emergent churches on various levels. Particularly, major appropriations followed the lines of inclusion of litany or responsive readings in worship services as well as offering lectionary passages as potential options for pastoral sermon choices. Deeper, though minor, appropriations were encouraged as a matter of personal emphasis. Only CitC took a deeper appropriation on a communal level through the process of liturgy creation for their specific church. Matters of reinterpretation can be addressed by looking at these differing pathways of appropriation.

Succinctly stated, the case study churches were reinterpreting the use of liturgical prayer in a very obvious way for both emphasis and investment of innovative theological content. When respondent comments turned to matters of liturgical prayer, they retained a strong focus on the anchor of community, but they did move away from an emphasis on rhythm to a closely related theological emphasis of connection to all other Christians. Demonstratively, appropriation of liturgical prayer was in part due to the sense of communal connection as described by Interviewee 37 below.

> For me, the lectionary is a space where, regardless of how disconnected I am from belief or prayer or whatever, a bunch of other Christians worldwide are connected through a similar Scripture on a similar day. This stuff is important and has been important, and how I feel about it in the moment, whether I believe it or not, doesn't really matter.

The theological weight placed on the value of community comes into sharp relief through the foregoing comment. This interviewee noted the strength of empathic connection she felt with other members of the entire Christian community in a way that transcends empirical experience, such as geographic distance. While this theme is not alien to most of the Christian church, it does represent a significant departure from the EC participants' previous evangelical context.

Innovative theological investment begins even within participant comments concerning issues of emphasis. For instance, as noted by Interviewee 37 above, the emphasis on connection to other Christians through liturgical prayer can even trump a value placed on theological belief or present feelings of the moment. This observation in interviewee comments comes into even starker relief upon investigation of liturgy creation within CitC. Community becomes the primary anchor by which the actual words of appropriated liturgy are changed to reflect a gender inclusive position. While this aspect of appropriation and reinterpretation will also be considered in connection with the anchor of experimentation, it is important to note here that reinterpretation of liturgical prayer is conducted for the express purpose of *building community* with those traditionally alienated by Christian theological boundaries. So, through emphasis and innovation, the anchor of community was more important to interviewees than other theological boundaries. This importance, particularly with regard to the issue of boundaries, was also noted when interviewees discussed the meaning behind appropriating the practice of fasting.

Fasting was appropriated by emergent case study churches in three principal forms for three particular situations, as noted in chapter five. The three forms line up on a continuum of discipline or sacrifice with the most rigorous discipline shown in complete abstention from all food. However, few participants practiced fasting to this extent; instead, they favored partial abstentions either through a Daniel fast or simply giving up a favorite food or activity. These differing ways to fast were appropriated within the case study churches for three types of circumstances. First, fasting was advocated by the leadership of a church when seeking an answer from God on a particular question. Second, fasting was often connected with the season of Lent. Finally, fasting was used for personal reasons by multiple respondents. This final situation for fasting mapped chiefly to the anchor of experimentation, but other reasons and times for fasting were connected by EC participants to the anchor of community.

Particulars of EC appropriation of fasting display the level of reinterpretation under which this practice is placed. Notably, the connection of fasting to community was more subtle than practices already considered because interpretative focus remained firmly on the side of *emphasis* with respect to community. While fasting might logically favor a personal emphasis, interviewees often appropriated this practice on the basis of larger community emphases, highlighting the EC tendency to subsume the theological placement of personal practice within the anchor of community. The most foundational example of how this relationship operated in the case study churches was through a communal purpose in fasting. This community connection with fasting was especially noted by RCC, who was in the habit of calling numerous community-wide fasts with a common purpose in mind. Therefore, it is unsurprising that the majority of participants who saw a communal connection with fasting came from RCC. For instance, Interviewee 5 noted the purpose of fasting as prompting, "the Spirit flow throughout the church rather than just through one individual or another because they were looking for answers about where they wanted to move the location of the church to." This role of fasting for community purposes was also noted by Interviewee 6 through semantic focus on the term *community*: "I think there's been a couple of community-wide fasts. I'm even saying 'community.' We used to say 'church-wide,' but in the emerging church, they call it 'community.'" It is noteworthy that Interviewee 6 has strongly recognized the terminological push within his church to utilize language in keeping with their high value on community. In fact, Interviewee 6 noted that this theological anchor had been invested into the practice by his emergent church, and he had assimilated this idea into his way of speaking even though he was not entirely in accord with this change, showing the level of reinterpretation an individual is willing to make in order to appropriate these practices within the community.

As another example of relative emphasis, community was also noted as a theological anchor in connection with fasting when coupled with the use of the liturgical calendar. For instance, one respondent highlighted this emphasis by contrasting the Lenten practice of his current EC context with the evangelical context in which he was raised.

> We just didn't do Lent in the church I grew up in, and when I joined Church in the Cliff, and I've been through three Lenten seasons now; there's just this sense of the tradition. That there's this weight behind it [that] makes me feel like part of this community, and not just the Church in the Cliff community, but the 2,000-year-old Christian community. (Interviewee 29)

This quotation shows both the emphasis of community in fasting and the liturgical calendar. Here, fasting has become a gateway for Interviewee 29 to feel a communal connection to the 2,000-year-old Christian community through his participation in Lent. Therefore, fasting is valuable for EC participants because of the communal aspects connected to it through liturgical prayer. Additionally, while this theological investment is a matter of emphasis, it is still noteworthy to mention a nuance of innovation because Interviewee 29 is mapping Lenten fasting to the scope of Christian community throughout the ages, not to the traditional process of preparation for confession and repentance leading up to remembrance of the Crucifixion and the subsequent celebration of the Easter season. So, while the theological anchor of community is invested in minor ways with respect to appropriation of the practice of fasting, community is a driving theological piece for interview participants nonetheless. Ties to the anchor of community are also evident in practices located within the category of divergent minor practices.

Divergent Minor Practices

In a similar pattern to divergent major practices, divergent minor practices appeared in the survey data as minor practices, but diverging definitions were offered for these practices in actual interviews. Divergent minor practices of the Jesus Prayer and fixed-hour prayer were appropriated by participants on the basis of community as a theological anchor for the EC. While the adoption of divergent minor practices was not particularly prevalent in studied emergent churches, the EC focused appropriation and reinterpretation of the practices on the *purpose* of community. The Jesus Prayer and fixed-hour prayer display how individual practices fit into a larger communal purpose. Concerning divergent minor practices, many participant comments that focus on the anchor of community interpret community in the direction of an individual person relating to a larger group. Interviewee comments concerning reasons for appropriation illustrate this specific pathway of interpretation.

Two divergent minor practices, the Jesus Prayer and fixed-hour prayer, which interviewees appropriated through the theological anchor of community, were rather surprisingly mapped to a communal emphasis. The Jesus Prayer followed the typical pattern of divergent minor practices in suffering from a multiplicity of definitions among respondent remarks. In this case, the Jesus Prayer was understood by interviewees variously as the Lord's Prayer, generally praying to Jesus, or the Jesus Prayer as developed in the Eastern Orthodox Church. Fixed-hour prayer suffered from an even greater multiplicity of specific definitions because its vagueness resulted in being associated for most respondents with a regular prayer time in one's day. While the Jesus Prayer also mapped to the anchor of experimentation, fixed-hour prayer only mapped to the anchor of community. The very situation of how these practices were appropriated according to a high value on community displays the interesting juxtaposition by which they were reinterpreted in case study churches.

Reinterpretation on the basis of emphasis and investment of innovative theological content is evident in the appropriation of these mystic practices. Particularly, utilization of the Jesus Prayer and fixed-hour prayer were typically appropriated on the basis of the communal value of the practices used by an individual when alone. In other words, the appropriation of these practices on the basis of community occurred through interpretation of an individual as essentially a part of a community, whether the community was present or not. With respect to the Jesus Prayer, Interviewee 26 noted the ways in which this prayer shapes the individual for relationship with others. "It's not about me and my wants. It really is this universal prayer that it was true hundreds of years ago, when it was first written. It's still true now, and it will remain true, and it will remain a prayer that we will continually pray." Here, it can be seen that communal purpose was invested into this prayer even though it was typically not practiced together in the case study churches.

Fixed-hour prayer was seen very similarly by participants who integrated this mystic practice into their spirituality. For instance, Interviewee 20 viewed fixed-hour prayer as "a habitual time [that] we're all going to spend morning, noon, evening spending doing this reading the same things, getting connected in that way." Here again, interviewees stressed the anchor of community because they interpreted fixed-hour prayer according to the purpose of interacting spiritually with others. This progression of appropriation and reinterpretation is most notable in moving beyond areas of emphasis to investment of theological innovation because fixed-hour prayer is traditionally practiced in a community context, but the case study churches did not utilize it in this manner, except to introduce the practice. Such a situation is unsurprising in light of how fixed-hour prayer was interpreted very widely by the EC, which also placed it in the same context as the analogous evangelical practice of a "quiet time." As a result of this evangelical connection, more striking community possibilities for fixed-hour prayer were not overtly evident to interviewees. However, the assertion of community value for preparing an individual through both the Jesus Prayer and fixed-hour prayer brilliantly displays how strong the anchor of community is in this context. In other words, the reasoning behind the appropriation of these practices shows that even when it's not community in the EC, it still is. So, whether the community was large or small or a practice was conducted in solitude or multitude, the EC invested the Jesus Prayer and fixed-hour prayer with a *communal* orientation, emphasizing relationship. In the final category of practices of passing familiarity, interviewees also found ways to connect the appropriation of mystic practices to the theological anchor of community.

Practices of Passing Familiarity

As discussed within the last chapter, there were several mystic practices that were only appropriated in the most cursory way by the emergent churches studied. As a result of this marginal integration, respondents understandably made fewer comments outlining the process of appropriating these practices according to particular theological anchors, and, when they did so, few specifics were noted beyond simply referring to community in passing. However, interviewees still had some remarks that expressed theological reinterpretation and investment of community among these practices.

For instance, *lectio Divina* was appropriated in part on the basis of the anchor of community even though it also mapped to other anchors. As described in the previous chapter, *lectio* was implemented occasionally in a corporate church context, but it was more often appropriated on a personal basis. Whether used communally or personally, *lectio* was viewed as an opportunity to engage with Scripture in ways beyond historical readings, specifically moving to imaginative and meditative perspectives of the Bible. While *lectio* was appropriated and reinterpreted more directly through other anchors, connection can still be glimpsed with respect to community. Illustratively, Interviewee 30 noted that part of what she felt during this practice was still communal: "I sort of feel like I'm breathing it, and then it becomes part of me in a different way, and then I'm able to sense [that] I can hear the community's voice, almost, filtered through that." So, theological investment of community is so pervasive that even in a practice which would seem only to involve an individual and God, the whispers of the people are still present.

In a more typically communal direction, the stations of the cross were appropriated into EC spirituality partially through this anchor as well. Chapter five presented the appropriation of the stations of the cross as an outgrowth of the liturgical observances surrounding the preparation for Easter, but the ways in which case study churches appropriated this practice showed a strong emphasis on creativity and personal expression. While matters of creativity will be discussed fully with respect to the anchor of experimentation, it is still important to note at this juncture that innovative appropriations of the stations of the cross tended to connect to local community contexts for interviewees. This aspect was particularly notable with respect to ERC inviting their founding church and surrounding community to share in a celebration of the stations as well as how CitC modified the stations of the cross to be performed in the very public setting of the train stations of the DART system. These examples of appropriation hint strongly at the extent of reinterpretation that EC participants used in connection with the stations of the cross, but the reasoning behind such reinterpretation became evident in interviewee explanations.

While in the most literal sense, the stations of the cross are usually experienced in the presence of others, EC interviewees emphasized communal participation in their interpretation of the practice. Interviewee 21 gave representative voice to this viewpoint by saying, "I do them [the stations] as part of the community, because I think it's special, in a way, to engage with Christ in the same ways that other people have. I think it builds tolerance." Interestingly, this engagement with others, as an interpretive emphasis, and tolerance of other's traditions took center-stage for many interview participants over against any historical significance of the stations of the cross. Consequently, this is a clear example of appropriation leading to reinterpretation with a value on community as paramount.

In an additional means of connection with others, practitioners who utilized icons within their prayers invested the value of community into their appropriation of this mystic practice. Concerning appropriation, the discussion in the previous chapter stated the appropriation of the use of icons according to two paths in the case study emergent churches: a background for worship services and personal experimentation. While this division of appropriation naturally maps to a theological reinterpretation and investment based on the anchor of experimentation, EC participants made slight connections with reinterpreting this practice according to community as well. Particularly, Interviewee 23 related the following theological interpretation undergirding his use of icons:

> This is a person who has gone before me that's part of my family, that's still in some ways, still present, because I believe that the curtain between this world and the next is a lot thinner than a lot of people think, and so thinking of them in terms of this is a way for me to communicate in one way, but also just celebrate and appreciate those that have gone before me, the cloud of witnesses and put an image to that.

Icons, in this perspective, had the primary purpose of connecting the individual in the EC with the larger faith community, including those members of the community who were no longer alive. While this theological nuance is not absent in the traditional use of icons, EC practitioners emphasized this connective aspect.

Use of the rosary was appropriated on a similar basis to icons. While this practice was typically a carryover from childhood religious traditions, the anchor of community was utilized to reinterpret the rosary in its new context as well as allow for its appropriation through valuing what an individual participant brings with him/her spiritually to the EC conversation. Use of the rosary connected the individual to the larger faith community, but the community was reinterpreted, as in the words of Interviewee 27, to include God as well: "It's [the purpose of the rosary is] still that relationship. Everything we do is to build relationship with God and then to others." Again, the rosary became a tool for the investment of community. So, while interviewees did not make extended remarks concerning the rosary or any of the practices of passing familiarity, they were still investing them, when appropriated, with the theological anchor of community.

As seen in this section, one of the major theological anchors of EC spirituality is a high value on community. This particular anchor meshed with the case study churches in such a way as to allow for the appropriation and reinterpretation of mystic practices from every category discussed in the interviews. Specifically, fourteen of twenty-one practices surveyed were tied by interview respondents to community in some way. Several of these practices had a natural connection to this theological anchor, so appropriation and reinterpretation was a matter of emphasis as well as innovative reinterpretation. For example, Holy Communion, spiritual direction, the liturgical calendar, liturgical prayer, and stations of the cross require some type of communal context in order to be utilized. However, the communal contexts of these practices were heightened beyond the confines of the evangelical tradition. Additionally, mystic practices, such as centering prayer or fasting, that would typically be used by an individual alone were often reinterpreted for use in communal settings. In retrospect, empirical research supports the assertion of EC literature that community is an essential theological anchor for appropriating mystical practices and investing them with EC theological content, such as the primacy of relationships, the breadth of community, and the purpose of community. With the next theological anchor, however, this correlation between literary and empirical research begins to diverge.

Experimentation

While the theological anchor of community maps neatly between literary research and empirical results, the second theological anchor to emerge from empirical research displays some subtle divergences from its analogous theological theme in EC literature. Within EC literature, authors prominently discuss appropriation and reinterpretation of mystic practices through an emphasis on the literary anchor of relevance over tradition. This literary anchor is not entirely absent from the case study churches, but it did not appear in exactly the same form. Precisely, the EC literary anchor of relevance over tradition is more properly termed *experimentation* within empirical findings. While this change may seem only to be semantic, it brings to light an important difference. In EC literature, mystic practices were often introduced for appropriation with at least some measure of historical comment on origin and development before proceeding to a discussion of how that practice could be appropriated by EC Christians. Among the case study churches, I did not find any strong correlation with tradition although there were occasional vague references to a particular practice as "traditional" or diverging from evangelical tradition. Therefore, emphasis for the anchor of experimentation is not a balance between two theological concepts, that is relevance and tradition; rather, it is a singular focus on experimentation. Additionally, within the context of the interviews, this theological anchor actually appeared to be the *strongest* theological anchor mapped to practices for the purposes of both appropriation and reinterpretation through investment of EC theological content. While interviewees more often mentioned the term *community*, their descriptions of the use of mystic practices displayed a higher regard for experimentation, at least in connection with the mystic practices explicitly noted on the spiritual practices questionnaire. With this perspective in mind, interviewees very readily described their experimentation with specific practices within all categories of usage.

Major Practices

Concerning the major practices used in the case study emergent churches, there was an interesting inverse relationship between those mapped to the theological anchor of community and those mapped to the anchor of experimentation. This relationship also highlights an important factor with regard to interviewee remarks. Participants tended to map the anchor of experimentation *only* to practices that had not been appropriated in previous contexts. As an example, while all of the churches were experimenting with the practice of Holy Communion in some way, they did not view it as mapped to this anchor because they had utilized the practice in previous contexts. Silence, solitude, and meditation came within the purview of experimentation more directly for interviewees, for they had not practiced them in other churches. In this sense, these mystic practices were not so much viewed as reinterpreted by EC practitioners as interpreted by them for the first time. Consequently, specific minor nuances of theological content are not as clearly visible as with the anchor of community; rather, a general trend of appropriation, reinterpretation, and investment through experimentation can be glimpsed with highly individualized results for each participant.

As noted within the fifth chapter, silence and solitude can be considered together because they were often inextricably linked for interviewee practitioners. Several were quick to point out that one could be silent in a group, but, in their actual spirituality, silence appropriated in a spiritual manner always required some measure of solitude as well. Additionally, interview respondent comments grouped together to present these practices as primarily contextual for other practices, noting that many other appropriated mystic practices needed silence and solitude to be implemented fully. They also remarked concerning the timing of this practice as much less structured than other practices. These qualities of appropriation offer insight concerning whether the case study churches and interviewed individuals reinterpreted silence and solitude.

Due to the expansive nature in which silence and solitude were appropriated in these EC contexts, there was little possibility that they would not be reinterpreted in an equally extensive way. Notably, these practices were reinterpreted in interviewee remarks through the *intentionality* of appropriating the practices for oneself. Interviewee 31 provides a striking example of this trend.

> [Silence and solitude are] also pretty counter-cultural. We're in such a loud culture at this stage of humanity. I almost feel like

it's a way to say "Nope, there's other ways." So, that's obviously, I think, most people think that's just bizarre, but it also kind of changes the way I can look at the world and changes the way that I come back to being verbal with people. I guess it's renewing.

While not directly using the term *experimentation*, Interviewee 31 aptly described the appeal for the appropriation of silence in connection to resistance to present culture. In this way, she reinterprets the seemingly passive actions or situations of silence and solitude to be active forms of personal expression and even as forms of social activism in rejecting an aspect of the larger Western culture. Interviewee 11 also echoes this attitude in her conversation concerning the interpretation of silence and solitude as spiritual practices:

> I tend to reflect a lot on why I would use these [practices of silence and solitude], so I tend to have more of a thoughtful like "Oh, there's an ecumenical value here." But, it's interesting to see how little that plays into people's choices, I think, of spiritual disciplines. I find more and more that it tends to be like "This seems to work for me." So, [people respond more] like, "We're sticking to that," and less "Oh, I've always been curious to see what the Anglicans do."

As seen in this comment, while other purposes might be investigated, the theological anchor which maps most directly to the interpretation of silence and solitude for this interview participant is experimentation. As an incisive representative example, Interviewee 11 articulates the value of the anchor of experimentation for the EC through this exact lens of "This seems to work for me." Therefore, the EC process of appropriation of silence and solitude, as well as for other mystic practices, can be elucidated in the following manner: the task of the individual is to experiment with a wide variety of spiritual and/or mystic practices with the specific intent of finding his or her own best mix of practices that express a highly personalized spirituality. This reinterpretation has a wide application for the EC in appropriating and reinterpreting mystic practices, but it is particularly evident here due to the contextual nature of the practices of silence and solitude.

This focus on experimentation with the intent to customize spirituality was not limited to silence and solitude. Meditation was also appropriated on this basis. An extended section on this practice was necessary in the previous chapter to portray adequately the different connections which were subsumed under this term. Specifically, meditation was used by interviewees with communal, personal, and singular connotations. With respect to communal connotations, some interview participants

THEOLOGICAL REINTERPRETATION OF MYSTIC PRACTICES 213

mentioned specific moments in corporate worship gatherings for limited meditation usually under the moniker of "reflections" or "guided meditation" in which the attendees were enjoined to think deeply on a subject. Personal connotations were discussed in terms of passive understandings, such as moments of "being still" before God, and active understandings, such as combining meditation with various everyday activities. A final connotation provided the central bonding agent for various understandings of meditation among interviewees. Succinctly stated, meditation was seen by EC practitioners to require a singular focus of thought whether that focus was Scripture, a literary character, or nature. From this understanding(s) of meditation, it is quite evident that the case study churches were appropriating this practice on the basis of experimentation, and interviewee comments also provided an answer to whether this appropriation was coupled with subsequent reinterpretation.

Concisely, meditation was not only appropriated but also reinterpreted according to the anchor of experimentation. This reinterpretation was particularly expansive and not simply limited to matters of emphasis. As a very visible example, meditation was interpreted on the basis of experimentation through its *combination* with various practices. Indeed, this practice proved to be a very fertile ground for combination with other practices due to the semantic range of the term. For instance, Interviewee 30 experimented with combining Christian meditation with forms of meditation which arose in other religious traditions.

> To me, meditation goes with yoga, not exclusively, but I do the two together, as much as I can. I first got exposed to it, trained in it, when I was studying abroad in London. I went to the homeopathic hospital there, and I did some meditation. I did some yoga and meditation there by someone who was really on their own path and had a teacher and really integrated the body movement with the part at the end where we would meditate. So, I really learned a lot, and I even remember one time we were there, and the sirens went by outside, and this idea [of] notice the sound, how you can't control it. It comes and moves and leaves. Things that sort of really actually help you step over this chasm of realizing you're not in control of most things, all things. I think that's what meditation is. It's a container to help ease that realization into your consciousness.

So, as is evident from this extended comment, the reinterpretation of the practice of meditation mapped strongly to the theological anchor of experimentation for interviewees. In fact, the theological investment of experimentation extended further than the traditional boundaries of specific belief systems, so EC practitioners of Christian meditation were free also to appropriate aspects from Buddhist meditation as well as religious forms of yoga. In other words, the anchor of experimentation is displayed in the practice of meditation as even superseding the traditional limits of Christian faith and practice. Whether through combination or intention, theological experimentation took a central role in the reinterpretation of major mystic practices appropriated by the EC. Emphasis on experimentation is also clearly displayed in the theological underpinnings which interviewees mapped to practices in the divergent major category.

Divergent Major Practices

To reiterate from the previous chapter, the practices of centering prayer, contemplative prayer, and spiritual direction were placed in this divergent category as a result of the multiplicity of definitions assigned by interview respondents to these terms without any major point of contact connecting disparate views. Specifically, centering prayer was interpreted in a tripartite division among interviewed individuals. Some interviewees viewed centering prayer as simply praying silently, others understood this practice as a means to pray through one's actions (linking it to the similar concept of meditation explained previously), and still other interviewees defined centering prayer as any prayer that is essentially characterized by listening to God rather than speaking or asking. Contemplative prayer similarly suffered from contrasting definitions. Definitions of contemplative prayer coalesced into the categories of intense concentration in prayer, a context for other practices, or an event rather than a practice. Spiritual direction diverged in semantic branches based on whether one preferred the term *spiritual direction* or *spiritual friendship*. These disparate definitions bear the marks of appropriation through experimentation, proceeding from many possible origins, but these semantic issues also inform one toward accurate understanding of reinterpretation with respect to these practices.

In a way, EC participants are indeed *not* reinterpreting centering prayer and contemplative prayer by investing a high regard for experimentation into the theological underpinnings of the practices. This is only the circumstance because they are using experimentation to interpret these practices for the *first* time in their own context and understanding, which often led to definitional confusion as the previous chapter demonstrated. Participant discussion concerning centering prayer and contemplative prayer highlights this progression. To begin with, respondents perceived vast areas of overlap among the practices of centering prayer, contemplative prayer, and meditation although none desired to treat them as entirely synonymous when queried concerning this possibility. Partially as a result of this ambiguity, the same avenue of appropriation through experimental *combination* with other practices has application for centering prayer and contemplative prayer. Interviewee 30 representatively illustrated this line of reinterpretation in tying Buddhist meditation to Christian meditation, centering prayer, and contemplative prayer.

> I claim a "Buddheo-Christian" perspective. So, I have had more instruction in meditation from that [Buddhist] perspective. And, I would put centering prayer as what I think I'm doing when I meditate, which is a kind of emptying out in noticing the thoughts and letting them pass, and then it's this deepening down to the bottom of the river experience, and that's maybe one part of it. I don't know if I would call that "centering prayer." I'd probably call it "meditating" or "contemplative prayer."

While the theological connections with meditation led in the direction displayed above to discuss centering prayer and contemplative prayer in the same inter-faith context, other interviewees invested an even wider scope for experimentation in these practices. When asked concerning the criteria for combining differing practices, Interviewee 23 succinctly stated that he combined practices from Christianity or other religions, simply "as I see them fit together." This perspective draws close to the "what-works" mentality invested into the major practices which guides the theological anchor of experimentation.

Other respondents appropriated centering prayer and contemplative prayer because of other means of experimentation. For instance, Interviewee 21 mapped contemplative prayer simply to the purpose of gaining a new perspective: "Sometimes, it enlightens me, helps me view something in a different aspect I hadn't seen before." Interviewee 21 is guided in the exercise of reinterpretation through this experimentation. Interviewee 10 takes up this interpretation, particularly concerning contemplative prayer, and generalizes even further. "I don't get hung up in definitions. I don't get hung up in doctrine. I just know what I feel and what he [God] leads me to." Interviewee 10, then, is guided in his appropriation of practices by what he feels in his different acts of experimentation. As illustrated in the above quotes, the process of reinterpretation can extend all the way to the very definition of a practice so that the definition of centering prayer or contemplative prayer becomes whatever an individual desires.

Experimentation formed half of the basis for appropriating spiritual direction in the investigated EC contexts. As noted within the fifth chapter, the practice of spiritual direction divided unevenly into two categories among interviewees centered on whether they focused on *spiritual direction* or *spiritual friendship* since both terminological variants were offered on the spiritual practices questionnaire. When interviewees mapped the practice to the term *spiritual friendship*, appropriation and reinterpretation was principally achieved in connection with the theological anchor of community. Conversely, when interviewees connected with the term *spiritual direction*, they saw it in terms of experimentation. Spiritual direction was understood as a one-on-one relationship that was viewed as a formal mentor and disciple bond. As this practice was appropriated on the basis of experimentation, it was also reinterpreted according to this anchor.

While any appropriation of a formal process of spiritual direction might rightly be termed as an illustrative example of reinterpretation, innovative investment of the anchor of experimentation was evident in EC practitioner responses. Particularly, spiritual direction mapped to experimentation for interviewees through its value for experimenting with other practices. Notably, Interviewee 38 recognized this relationship and denoted it in stating, "It's not counseling necessarily. It's about helping you to develop a spiritual practice." She then went on to explicate her meaning fully through an anecdote of how a spiritual director aided her in investing the practice of meditation with her personal love for music. So, by using this anecdote to explain her understanding, Interviewee 38 displayed that "developing" a spiritual practice really meant experimenting with various spiritual practices to find one(s) that fit best personally. Freedom to experiment truly reaches its apex with regard to divergent major practices, but this same freedom is still evident in matters of appropriating more uniformly defined practices, such as those in the category of minor practices.

Minor Practices

Minor practices which interviewees mapped to the theological anchor of experimentation were the liturgical calendar, liturgical prayer, and fasting. By close inspection of the reasoning behind appropriating these practices, a progression emerges from a disenchantment with history to a strong investment of the aforementioned "what-works" theological perspective. As treated in chapter five, discussions of the liturgical calendar and liturgical prayer tended to weave in and out from one practice to the other, as interviewees viewed an inextricable link between the two practices. Additionally, liturgical prayer was occasionally considered under the moniker of the lectionary. Respondents came the closest at any point to deliberation on history or tradition with these practices since they were quite aware that these practices had a long history in other Christian traditions. While the history of these practices became a point of celebration and connection under the anchor of community, matters of history and tradition were not appropriated wholly. Specifically, the limiting boundaries of tradition associated with the liturgical calendar and liturgical prayer were entirely subjugated to the anchor of experimentation when appropriating these practices, as seen in the representative example from the pastor of ERC below.

> We recognize we're in the season of Pentecost. We talk about that, but I'm doing a sermon series that isn't necessarily going along with the lectionary, and I think that's okay. I recognize, hey, we have a leading to go in this direction, so we'll do that, but we also recognize the rhythms of our faith. So, we're trying to find this third way where I don't have to preach the lectionary every week, but it's there.

This quote beautifully illustrates the value placed on experimentation in connection to liturgical prayer and the liturgical calendar. To state it concisely, EC Christians are appropriating practices and ideas from different traditions, but they do not feel bound to keep what they are appropriating in exactly the same shape as they first found it. They feel perfectly at ease with taking what they want and leaving what they do not want, all the while reinterpreting for their own practical benefit.

Interviewees reported varying levels of this experimental type of reinterpretation. On one end of the spectrum, participants held a high value for history in some sense because of the community which they fit with that tradition, and, on the other end of the spectrum, appropriated mystic practices became simply a jumping-off point for very expansive reinterpretations. The scope of reinterpretation is quite vivid within interviewee comments as seen with regard to liturgical prayer as a personal devotional option, in Interviewee 21, or with regard to the selective and creative adaption of the liturgical calendar in the words of Interviewee 31.

> I just do it [liturgical prayer]. It's an easy way instead of opening my Bible and finding a random passage. I can have something concrete to think about throughout the day. (Interviewee 21)

> We had a party for the feast day of Mary Magdalene, and it definitely was a party. We had a talk about Mary Magdalene, but we also had glitter eye shadow that we were putting on. So, we were

dressing up as the caricatures of Mary Magdalene. And then, doing the historical work of understanding who Mary Magdalene might have been. (Interviewee 31)

This same level of connecting appropriation to reinterpretation through experimentation is also evident among interviewee comments on the practice of fasting.

As noted in chapter five, fasting was appropriated within the case study emergent churches in three types and in three major contexts. Specifically, fasting could entail complete abstention from food, a Daniel fast, or giving up a favorite food or activity. With respect to context, interviewees practiced fasting as part of church-wide called fasts, Lenten observances, or personal reasons. While fasting often mapped to the theological anchor of community, this connection existed primarily for church-sponsored fasts or those which followed the liturgical calendar. When fasting was appropriated for personal reasons, it much more clearly mapped to the anchor of experimentation, as demonstrated by Interviewee 3, in saying "For me, the fasting is a time of refocusing. It's trying to change your usual patterns, so maybe you can look at things a little bit differently. It's a practice that *is what you make it*" [Emphasis added]. As displayed in the above quote, it is easy to note that this interviewee interprets the purpose of her personal fasting to "refocusing," yet she grounds this personal purpose for an appropriated practice within the overall context of her theology through the anchor of experimentation, as noted in her tagline statement at the end of the quote. Specifically, fasting, for her, "is what you make it," reflecting back to a "what-works" theological emphasis. This sense of customization invested through the anchor of experimentation permeated interviewee comments with regard to multiple practices as already seen above, and this connection only becomes more pronounced as participants moved to consider practices that were enacted on a more personal and occasional basis.

Divergent Minor Practices

To reiterate the definition of the category of divergent minor practices from the previous chapter, this category contains practices which appeared to be appropriated in a minor way within the case study emergent churches, but, on closer inspection, they were difficult to chart due to differences in definition. As a result of this categorical issue, it is no surprise that the practices herein map to the anchor of experimentation, for they were usually only appropriated as the subject of experimentation within the EC contexts under observation. Specifically, interviewees mapped the practices of the Jesus Prayer and pilgrimage to the anchor of experimentation. While fixed-hour prayer was definitely the subject of experimental application within the case study churches, no interview respondent made this particular connection with regard to the purpose for appropriating and reinterpreting that practice. However, with the other divergent minor practices, the anchor of experimentation interacted with appropriation and reinterpretation on multiple fronts.

The Jesus Prayer was appropriated in part through its relation with the theological anchor of experimentation. As noted above, the Jesus Prayer was defined variously as the Lord's Prayer, generally praying to Jesus, or the Eastern Orthodox Jesus Prayer. When principally considering the Eastern Orthodox Jesus Prayer, which was less familiar to participants, a slight connection to the anchor of community was made because participants were often introduced to the Jesus Prayer in a community context, but from that point this practice maps solely to experimentation. In an example of appropriation according to experimentation leading to reinterpretation, the Jesus Prayer was specifically introduced for appropriation in the communal context of ERC for the purpose of allowing congregants to experiment with the practice on a personal level. Following that communal introduction, interviewees typically experimented with the Jesus Prayer similarly to Interviewee 23 who remarked, "I don't know that it will be a regular practice for me. I have no problem with it, but there's just [something]. I don't know that you have to practice all of them. I think there's just certain ones that some of us are more inclined towards." As with many practices, the Jesus Prayer was invested with the characteristic of choice because it was available for use, or not, depending on *an individual's preferences*.

Pilgrimage was also appropriated on the basis of the anchor of experimentation. As with other divergent minor practices, pilgrimage was categorized in this way in light of the fact that interviewees were quite divided on how they defined the term. With pilgrimage, respondents divided in three ways on the basis of whether they considered pilgrimage as primarily an issue of place, group, or time. One should also remember from chapter five that responses might have been slightly skewed since ERC refers to all of their official church retreats or trips as "pilgrimages." However, the practical divisions of place, group, and time offered a tangible initiation point for EC participants to appropriate pilgrimage and then leap off in experimentation from this foundational platform.

In terms of reinterpretation, the practice of pilgrimage maps strongly to the anchor of experimentation through what interviewees individually interpreted to be the central elements of the practice. For instance, Interviewee 16 emphasized greatly that neither the destination nor the reasons for pilgrimage were primary; rather, the central element is that "the journey becomes the most important thing." Interviewee 38 invested a similar viewpoint by noting that her primary criterion for pilgrimage was personal change. As seen in these interviewee perspectives, the relationship between an appropriated practice and experimentation was reinterpreted through shifting the locus of meaning for the practice to an aspect which could only be divined personally. In this way, all other aspects of the practice could be the subject of significant reimagining. These participant perspectives outline the contours of how certain mystic practices could be reinterpreted not only according to the anchor of experimentation but also as inextricably linked to an experimental context; therefore, experimentation became the primary theological content invested into these practices as well as the anchor which allowed for initial appropriation. Interestingly, this anchor relationship was extended by interviewees to the point of viewing experimentation as the *overriding* component of the appropriation process when commenting on practices of passing familiarity.

Practices of Passing Familiarity

In much the same vein as the previous section, the appropriation of practices from this category was done on the basis of the anchor of experimentation. However, not all practices in this category were directly linked to this anchor by interviewees themselves. As a result, theological consideration of the use of prayer labyrinths and the rosary will be conducted in connection with other anchors. With respect to the anchor of experimentation, respondents noted particular links to use of *lectio Divina*, stations of the cross, and icons. In fact, interviewees hinted at the primacy of an experimental context for *any* level of appropriation of these mystic practices within their church contexts.

Lectio Divina was discussed in connection with the previous theological anchor of community on the basis that this practice was occasionally implemented in communal church contexts. However, the principal context for the appropriation of *lectio* was more individualistic, particularly in how individual EC participants engaged with Scripture in imaginative and meditative ways. With this emphasis for appropriation, reinterpretation of *lectio* became indispensable in order to fit it within its new EC environment. The strong correlation between experimentation and the interpretation of *lectio* can be seen in participant statements regarding the purpose of appropriating the practice. Interviewee 23 provides a representative example of such a statement.

There's all kinds of possibilities that come out of this scriptural story. So, for me, it's [the purpose of *lectio Divina* is] saying "Okay, I'm willing to go to some of those other levels that maybe I wouldn't have before." And so, I think there's lots of things that come out of that.

While this statement does not mention experimentation specifically, it illustrates the high level of importance placed on this anchor through new levels sought in Scripture. Interviewee 23 comments positively on the context of experimentation at the center of appropriation of *lectio* because it results in a focus on possibilities of interpretation for the practice. It is through comments of this type that one can ascertain just how vital reinterpretation through experimentation is to EC appropriation of *lectio*.

Comments concerning the purpose of other practices center extensively on placing a high value on personal creativity. As mentioned concerning the previous anchor, appropriation of the stations of the cross connected to the anchor of community because this practice was conducted in communal church contexts at specific times of the church year, but stations of the cross map more strongly to the anchor of experimentation in their reinterpretation. The range of interpretation for this practice is evident in the various ways that it was appropriated by the case study churches. RCC did not use this practice communally, ERC would celebrate the stations but give congregational artists great freedom in interpreting stations, and CitC reimagined the practice of the stations of the cross almost entirely by celebrating them in the context of train stations in the DART system. These forms of appropriation answer in a strongly affirmative way whether the case study churches were reinterpreting the stations of the cross according to the anchor of experimentation.

For instance, with respect to innovative ways in which the case study churches reinterpreted the stations of the cross, interviewees connected all statements of theological investment to creativity and personal expression. Interviewee 20 noted these connections while also linking creativity to community in mentioning, "Within the stations of the cross, expressing your creativity and understanding that God is the ultimate creator and this is a way that we can express that aspect of ourselves through our community." This primacy of creativity, innovation, and personal expression mapped deeply for interviewees with the anchor of experimentation with respect to the stations of the cross. In addition, traditional theological connections with the stations of the cross were strikingly de-emphasized. This de-emphasis can be seen in a progression of stress on theological content away from sin and purgation to creatively entering into the story of Jesus Christ, as first observed in the previous chapter. So, whether through personal expression or personal engagement, stations of the cross were reinterpreted by EC interviewees to have a strongly experimental element, but it was not the only practice mapped in such a way.

Appropriation of icons was also interpreted as having a primarily experimental purpose on the basis of personal expression. To briefly reiterate, case study churches reported that this mystic practice was appropriated by participants in two main ways: as a background for communal worship and as a means for personal spiritual expression. As one might easily suspect, the second avenue for appropriation mapped most directly to the anchor of experimentation. Interviewee 29 pointed out this relationship in describing his use of icons.

> I honestly have no idea how they're used in the Eastern church. I shouldn't say I have no idea; I've read about it, But, it's not something I get. But, something about contemplating the icon, it's like it opens a door in my mind somehow, and sometimes I try to always know the story behind whatever is depicted. So, sometimes, that's what I don't want to say "ruminate" on because it's not like I'm sitting there thinking about it, but I just sort of imbibe the stories and live with them, just sit with them for a while, and the icon helps me focus on that.

So, while this respondent was aware of other contexts and purposes for this practice, they had little bearing on his appropriation and reinterpretation; rather, personal value for the practice that had proven useful through experimentation took the center place of attention in a description of purpose. As a result, experimentation allowed Interviewee 29 to appropriate the use of icons, but this anchor also was invested by him into the practice to give it theological meaning. With discussion of these practices of passing familiarity, experimentation has moved fully from a theological anchor which *allows* for appropriation and reinterpretation to the central reason that interviewees felt they *should* reinterpret practices that have been appropriated for their spirituality.

The relationship between EC appropriation of mystic practices and the anchors of community and experimentation have some similarity but even greater differences. EC interviewees mapped fourteen of the twenty-one mystic practices surveyed to the theological anchor of experimentation in varying levels of necessity. While this numerical aspect is equal between the anchors of community and experimentation, notable differences arise at this point as well. First, interviewee comments emphasize experimentation in the process of appropriating mystic practices. While community is perhaps a more vital anchor for the EC social context as a whole, the specific engagement which the EC case study churches had with mystic practices is shaped more deeply by experimentation. This factor was quite evident even in chapter five through the fact that none of the practices were appropriated in an "untouched" form. Every mystic practice was really the subject of the anchor of experimentation. Second, while the anchor of community allowed for mystic practices to be understood in new ways, the anchor of experimentation often allowed, and even urged, the appropriation and interpretation of *entirely new* practices into EC contexts, often practices which would not have found any application in the sociological environment of evangelicalism from which the EC developed. Third, interview participant remarks concerning this theological anchor highlighted the beginning of a gap between the anchors emphasized in EC literature and the anchors displayed in actual emergent churches. Specifically, the anchor of experimentation replaces empirically the anchor of relevance over tradition. While these anchors are not entirely distinct, the shift in terminology is necessary to make manifest a shift in theological focus for empirical respondents. Succinctly stated, interviewees appropriated practices on the basis of experimentation and curiosity with little concern for where those practices originated or to what theological ideas they had previously been connected. Investment of the anchor of experimentation progresses naturally from this disconnection. Specifically, when disconnected from historical provenance, these practices become valuable on the basis of what a practitioner can invest into them. Therefore, the theological anchor of experimentation stands as the *primary* point of conceptual reasoning for EC spiritual borrowing of mystic practices. Still, other theological anchors mapped to appropriation of practices in lesser ways.

Embodied Spirituality: Social Action

As first considered within the third chapter, one of the major innovative theological anchors to which emergent churches are mapping their spirituality is the anchor of embodied spirituality. In fact, this term originated within sociological literature as a neologism intended to describe the growing sense observed in the EC that spirituality should be vitally concerned with this present world rather than focused chiefly on life after death.[2] One of the understandable issues of coining a new term is the immediate need to define it. In this light, literary sources approached this term and concept as being

2. Flory and Miller, *Finding Faith*, vii.

concerned with a tangible level of spirituality on two fronts: an engagement with the secular world and a literal focus on the human body. When studied empirically, the emergent case study churches also evinced a significant relationship with the theological anchor of embodied spirituality; however, the ways in which this anchor supported the appropriation and reinterpretation of mystic practices necessitated a separation of its two emphases into two separate anchors for consideration. Consequently, interviewee comments can be discussed in relation to the theological anchor of embodied spirituality through social action and in relation to the theological anchor of embodied spirituality through physicality. Additionally, the theological anchor of contemplation with action, as introduced in chapter three, was not considered independently from embodied spirituality through social action since "action" in distinction from "contemplation" was interpreted by interview respondents as social action. As noted at the end of the previous section, these two anchors of embodied spirituality were engaged with mystical appropriation to a lesser degree for many interview participants. While interviewees were very vocal about a strong emphasis on social action in their churches, this emphasis was often viewed *in opposition to* the appropriation of mystic practices unless practices could be reinterpreted to be less "passive" in nature. Therefore, the practices in this category were invested with a strong theological focus on social action.

Major Practices

A high value on social action naturally fit into participant conversations concerning the theological anchor of community as well as embodied spirituality. In this sense, the anchor of embodied spirituality through social action was invested by interviewees primarily as a theological widening of the boundaries of community in the reinterpretation of major practices, particularly Holy Communion and solitude. While Holy Communion was anchored most strongly to community through the commonality of the practice (95% of all interviewees utilized it), the frequency of observance, and the variety of modes for appropriation, connection to the anchor of social action also mapped to this practice through reinterpretation of those who could be, or should be, involved in this community ritual. While interviewees from each church made this connection, Interviewee 32 speaks directly to this widening in saying, "The major value for Church in the Cliff is inclusivity. And, that this is God's table, and all are welcome. And so, that gives us a chance to practice that, and I think everyone loves the words 'whether you believe a little or a lot or not, come, because all things are ready.'" For multiple interviewees, social action began for them in the inclusion of those traditionally considered to be the "other" into the rituals of the community. In other words, this theological widening allowed social action to begin at "home" for these churches rather than going to help "them" as a discrete separable unit. Interestingly, this incorporation of immediate local community into the practice of Holy Communion did not always stop at inclusion of participants. Specifically, the elements used in Holy Communion at CitC always came from locally grown food sources as a further act of social interaction with the local community. So, participants mapped their church's emphasis on Holy Communion to an embodied spirituality through social action in which the theological understanding of the term *community* was reinterpreted.

In contrast to how Holy Communion maps to both community and embodied spirituality, the practice of solitude *unexpectedly* maps to the anchor of embodied spirituality through social action as well. As noted in the fifth chapter, solitude was appropriated on an as-needed basis by most interviewees, and, consequently, the time and place of the practice varied widely. However, respondents also displayed a marked preference for viewing solitude as a contextual practice, and it was through this contextual perspective that social action connected for appropriation and reinterpretation. Specifically, Interviewee 23 makes the connection between solitude and social action through reference to his personal experiences.

> Again, my own internal struggle is in a reaction to individualism. Sometimes, I've emphasized the "communal" so much that I even [forget the individual]. When I did my spiritual formation classes in grad school was one of the first premises I came in with, and I told the teachers, "This is incredibly hard for me, because it's hard for me to think about my own individual spiritual journey because I've seen that abused so much that all that I want is 'Well, how do we as a community experience this? How is this a communal experience?'" But, it's been helpful for me to go, "Okay, the two aren't necessarily divorced." Thomas Merton has been helpful for me because he was a social activist, social justice activist, but had a huge value for solitude and silence, and it wasn't in a sense of "We've got these two separate things, and they're both important" [to Merton]. It was [a sense of] "These two are actually integrated, and how I am by myself has a huge impact on how I am in the world and vice versa." So, yeah, that's redeemed the element of solitude.

While this interview participant does diverge from others in noting a more defined historical sense of the mystic practice of solitude, he opens a window through this comment to his own internal thought process of how some mystic practices which seem to be incredibly individualistic can actually be integral to a life of social action, preparing an individual for meaningful social interactions or concerns. This comment displays a vital link of appropriation, reinterpretation, and investment for this particular participant, but few others made this type of connection. For other respondents, individualistic practices were not appropriated for the purpose of social action because they did not make a connection between practices perceived as individualistic and the theological anchor of embodied spirituality through *social* action. In light of this circumstance, no interviewees commented on divergent major practices as mapping to this anchor either. They once again broached theological discussions of purpose in terms of social action with minor mystic practices which more naturally fit with that social context.

Minor Practices

While minor practices (confession, liturgical calendar, liturgical prayer, fasting, and making the sign of the cross) were not appropriated preeminently on the basis of the anchor of embodied spirituality through social action by interviewees, use of the liturgical calendar and fasting did receive respondent remarks that displayed points of contact and theological investment. Social action was held so strongly that the practices of confession, liturgical prayer, and making the sign of the cross displayed lesser usage in connection to this anchor, which is logical since there is less potential reinterpretation of these practices on a social basis. This anchor also did not map as strongly to appropriation here because several minor practices could be interpreted "passively" which this anchor sought to avoid.

The liturgical calendar did map to the anchor of embodied spirituality through social action although this practice was primarily appropriated and reinterpreted on the basis of the anchor of community. However, there are points of connection with social action and the liturgical calendar through a widening sense of Christian community *in time*. This progression allows for a subtle reinterpretation of the practice according to social action. Connection between the liturgical calendar and social action is shown in who is focused on for inclusion. Specifically, celebration of certain church holidays and feasts was tied to identifying with the plight of the oppressed and neglected in Christianity. Interviewee 31 commented on this connection at length.

> We've typically celebrated the feast days of women because there's not a lot of space for that in the traditional liturgical calendar.

THEOLOGICAL REINTERPRETATION OF MYSTIC PRACTICES   227

> Since I've been at Church in the Cliff, we've done Hildegard of Bingen. We've done the rags in the trees [for] St. Brigit. Anyway, I'm probably forgetting some of the other ones we've done, but we do that fairly consistently, at least a couple times a year, we'll celebrate some of the feast days of our lady saints.

So, for this interviewee, the extent to which the liturgical calendar was appropriated became a theological investment of connecting with those who have been subjected to gender prejudice and exclusion. Similar connections can be made concerning the appropriation and reinterpretation of fasting.

As stated in the previous chapter and foregoing sections of this chapter, fasting was appropriated for use in multiple contexts, principally church-called fasts, Lenten fasts, and personal fasts. While community fasts connect strongly to other anchors, personal fasting as an appropriated practice necessitates individual interpretation. Occasionally, in respondent comments, noted purposes moved to a social action focus. While this interpretation occurred on an individual level, it had social implications as noted in the following response: "What I give up [in fasting] is always somehow tied to a larger issue. And, for me, food and food justice are such big issues for me" (Interviewee 29). While the quote concerning the liturgical calendar displays how the anchor of embodied spirituality through social action can reinterpret a mystic practice with respect to its depth of implementation, the interviewee comment on fasting shows how the investment of this anchor into a practice can reinterpret a personal practice into one which is focused on others, particularly others who are less fortunate. Fasting and the liturgical calendar show how mystic practices can be tailored to emphasize EC theological themes, such as an emphasis on the marginalized in society whether through economic or gender exclusion.

Divergent Minor Practices

Only one divergent minor practice, practicing the presence of God, mapped to the anchor of embodied spirituality through social action for appropriation and reinterpretation, and it connected in a unique way. Explanation of how practicing the presence of God mapped to this anchor requires a brief revisit to the discussion of chapter five for disambiguation. Specifically, interviewees interpreted this practice through two divergent definitions. First, many individuals connected this mystic practice to Brother Lawrence and his introduction of the practice through the writings collected as *The Practice of the Presence of God*. Second, other interview participants interpreted the meaning of this practice as a "feeling" of God's presence. While distinct processes for feeling God's presence could be articulated by respondents, this definition did not connect with the anchor of embodied spirituality through social action. On the other hand, connection between this anchor and the Brother Lawrence definition of the practice was evident, but a difficulty still remained. Notably, multiple EC interviewees shrewdly observed that practicing the presence of God, as described by Brother Lawrence, is not exactly a discrete practice, so it is a bit more difficult to trace lines of appropriation, reinterpretation, and investment than with other practices.

The previous considerations of other practices often display how embodied spirituality through social action can be used to invest new facets and angles into mystic practices which were appropriated through greater emphasis on other anchors, but this anchor actually provided the chief impetus for interviewees who appropriated practicing the presence of God into their spirituality. To illustrate this strong correlation, when Interviewee 32 was queried concerning the purpose behind practicing the presence of God, she artfully described the essential link between the mystic practice and the theological anchor of embodied spirituality through social action in describing its purpose as "Recognizing that God just isn't in the four walls of a church or in our little prayer closet, but that God is living and active in the world." So, while this theological anchor was not the most significant conceptual point of connection for appropriation and reinterpretation of most mystic practices among interviewees, occasionally it provided the driving force behind the entire process of appropriation, reinterpretation, and investment. However, in view of the relative lack of emphasis on this anchor in comparison with the two previous theological anchors, a legitimate question can be raised concerning the centrality of this anchor for EC spirituality in relation to mystic practices. Concerning this line of questioning, it may indeed be the *lack* of mystic practices mapped to this anchor which actually serve to explain its value.

Other Practices

The theological anchor of embodied spirituality through social action was not mapped by interview participants to any practices contained within the categories of divergent major practices or practices of passing familiarity. This lack of connection might seem to suggest the exclusion of this theological anchor as a major point of connection to EC spirituality and spiritual borrowing. While such a conclusion would seem logical at first glance, it does not take into account a vital element. It is a high value on social action which explains the relative lack of connection among respondents from mystic practices to this anchor. Succinctly stated, focus on social action often meant *not* appropriating certain mystic practices for interviewees. An inverse relationship is most visible in light of which practices were not appropriated by many participants in the case study emergent churches. For instance, few practices in the categories of divergent minor practices and practices of passing familiarity required a social action component. This reasoning was most clearly highlighted in some brief comments by Interviewee 35 on why he does not participate in mystic practices (other than those utilized in worship services): "I'm more interested in an active Christianity of going out and doing, following Christ's teachings rather than spirituality and contemplation and meditation and silence and prayer and all that stuff." While this participant stated matters most concisely, other respondents also noted favoring spiritual practices that engage with larger society than mystic practices that might be perceived as only turned inward. To state the relationship in more positive terms, an integral link between EC spirituality and social action resulted in a marked preference for appropriating and reinterpreting mystic practices with strong social and communal connotations. In a contrasting manner, the final theological anchor of embodied spirituality through physicality was directly related to the appropriation, reinterpretation, and theological investment of certain practices in a very individualistic fashion.

Embodied Spirituality: Physicality

Multiple mystic practices were mapped by interviewees to the theological anchor of embodied spirituality through physicality. While the previous embodied spirituality category dealt with social justice issues and matters of community involvement, this anchor connects theologically to appropriation of mystic practices that literally require some measure of physical activity on the part of the individual in appropriating the practice. This category was first described by EC authors, though named by sociologists, as a reaction to overly intellectualized approaches to spirituality that were favored within the evangelical context from which the EC emerged. In other words, EC Christians often expressed a desire for a more physical component to their spirituality, and this need formed a specific purpose in looking for practices to appropriate from other Christian traditions that carried a physical component or could possibly be invested with a physical component. Empirical research results buttressed this literary assertion. Observably, this theological anchor has the benefit of clarity in reasoning, for interviewees mapped embodied spirituality through physicality to the appropriation of mystic practices which had an overtly physical component. Interviewees often noted that their first interest in a particular mystic practice was through physical actions that surrounded that practice. While they often went on to tie reinterpretation of mystic practices to other theological anchors, physical aspects of spirituality retained this introductory and initial appropriating position.

Major Practices

Two major practices which interview participants mapped to the theological anchor of embodied spirituality through physicality were Holy Communion and meditation. While Holy Communion is such a significant mystic practice that it maps to multiple anchors, the primary anchor for this practice was community. However, Holy Communion also found points of contact with an embodied spirituality through physicality. As noted previously, Holy Communion was performed more frequently in the case study emergent churches than in their originating evangelical tradition, and various modes of practice were utilized. Yet, the most preferred mode of intinction highlights the reinterpretation of Holy Communion through physicality as one of *emphasis*. Specifically, intinction stresses physical actions such as processing in a line, being served bread, dipping/handing over the bread for dipping, and having the server speak the words of institution specifically to each person in line. These physical qualities were present in the practice as appropriated but emphasized by the case study churches through frequent practice.

Additionally, interviewee comments emphasized physical connections to the entire process of celebrating Holy Communion.

> One of the things that I was really challenged by early on was if the only thing that's really important is how meaningful it is in our brains to us, then maybe we're missing something, because I think there's times when you can take in the Eucharist, and it's not necessarily an intellectual, meaningful experience, but just the act of participating in it really does something. (Interviewee 23)

> There's a personal sense of what it means. You are what you eat, and we eat the Christ mystery again and again and again, and then we become more Christlike and more comfortable with mystery. (Interviewee 30)

While these interviewees approach the purpose of Holy Communion from two very different angles, they both interpret the physicality of this practice as an integral quality. Whether it's through the term *participation* or the trite cliché "you are what you eat," they are both hitting upon the tangibility of this practice. Holy Communion requires certain physical actions that one must go through, and interviewees communicated the essential nature of physical action for their reinterpretation of this practice. This type of appropriation is easy to glimpse in a practice with specific actions associated with it, but the theological anchor of embodied spirituality through physicality also allows appropriation and reinterpretation of practices which are optionally physical.

Meditation, unlike Holy Communion, does not absolutely require a physical component for practice, but interview participants often focused their comments on appropriating this practice through linked physical actions with spiritual endeavor. As mentioned previously, interview respondents interpreted meditation variously, but interviewee definitions followed three main avenues of delineation: communal, personal, and singular (focus for thought). While most definitional emphases map to the anchor of experimentation for the appropriation and reinterpretation of the practice of meditation, the anchor of physicality also provides a point of contact for interpreting "active" personal understandings of meditation. Following this semantic path, meditation was viewed as a mystic practice which allowed easy combination with other practices from many contexts.

Illustratively, meditation was mapped by multiple EC conversationalists to inter-faith possibilities with Buddhist forms of meditation and religious forms of yoga. Interview participants also touched upon the theological anchor of embodied spirituality through physicality with reference to possible areas of theological investment of Christian meditation into yoga. For instance, Interviewee 21 connected meditation and yoga in the following way.

> Whenever I do yoga, I do it as a physical exercise, but I find at the very end after being quiet or after being very active, if you sit down and you're quiet, I feel that a lot of the issues and worries I'd been thinking about they come to the forefront, and I get clarity about them. If there was a problem I was thinking about, I find the solution really fast. So, right after yoga, I'll just lie down quietly and I'll think about spiritual issues or issues in my own life.

While connections between yoga and meditation in the foregoing comment definitely provide a physical connection to embodied spirituality, other respondents noted additional forms of "physical" meditation by connecting it with activities like gardening or composing music. So, while interviewees did not explicitly state that meditation *required* a physical component, they offered many examples of reinterpretation of this mystic practice with overt physical elements.

Experimentation *allows* for a wideness of interpretive possibilities and combination with other practices, and physicality *emphasizes* certain practices for potential combination by EC practitioners. The inclusion of meditation in connection to embodied spirituality through physicality might be a result of the wideness of potential reinterpretation of this practice, yet this potential ambiguity did not result in similar connections of this anchor to the divergent major practices of centering prayer and contemplative prayer. Other practices in categories of lesser usage adhered more closely to this anchor when a physical component was *not* optional.

Minor Practices

Within the previous chapter, appropriated mystic practices which the EC case study churches integrated in a minor way included confession, the liturgical calendar, liturgical prayer, fasting, and making the sign of the cross. While all of these practices might result in certain physical actions, fasting and making the sign of the cross are tied to specific physical actions in an essential way. The practice of fasting is significant for this study in that it was the only mystic practice which interview respondents mapped to all four theological anchors. As a result of such levels of linkage, interviewees tended to focus their comments on fasting through the theological anchors which seemed more conceptually abstract and, therefore, easier to overlook as part of the appropriation and reinterpretation process. Conversely, the physical component of fasting seems quite apparent as part of the practice itself. As a result, few respondents spoke at length on this aspect of the practice.

When remarking on the personal value of fasting, as opposed to called or Lenten communal fasts, participants did, however, map it to the anchor of embodied spirituality through physicality. Interviewee 5 mapped fasting in this way: "I think a lot of people do fasting to get some spiritual enlightenment. For me, it's more of a need to put myself above that, and I'm in control of this." The previous quote highlights how the interviewee interpreted the physical aspect of fasting as essential to investing this practice with a concern for balance. Inclusion of this perspective in a discussion of fasting emphasized the emergent impulse that one's spirituality should extend beyond the bounds of specifically religious acts to physical acts done for a spiritual purpose or spiritual acts done for a physical purpose. This same theological investment of embodied spirituality through physicality also allowed interview participants to appropriate physical religious acts into their spirituality which arose in a tradition separate from their own.

The other minor practice which interviewees appropriated according to the theological anchor of embodied spirituality through physicality was making the sign of the cross. While the physical actions taken in making the sign of the cross were quite simple and took much less effort and sacrifice than fasting, multiple interview participants noted the theological interpretations and investments they made through this small, yet very physical, act. Interviewee 24 zeroed in on this viewpoint by saying, "It's [making the sign of the cross is] just something tangible in a way. It's a physical act in accordance with spiritual reality. Something to put wheels on what I believe and what I'm doing." EC practitioners of the sign of the cross were looking for every possible way to make their spirituality tangible, and the sign of the cross was, indeed, a small way to "put wheels" on that theological anchor. Notably, this mystic practice was appropriated by interview participants in both sacred and secular settings. A high theological value for embodied spirituality allowed for appropriation and urged reinterpretation of these practices into a spirituality of everyday life, and this way of interpreting embodied spirituality was also prevalent in discussions concerning the one divergent minor practice connected to this anchor.

Divergent Minor Practices

While chapter five included the Jesus Prayer, practicing the presence of God, pilgrimage, and fixed-hour prayer within the category of divergent minor practices, only the practice of pilgrimage was appropriated by interviewees according to the theological anchor of an embodied spirituality through physicality. Reasoning for the lack of connection between this theological anchor and other divergent minor practices principally refers back to the observation that interviewees tended to map this anchor *only* to practices with the potential for overt physical components. Pilgrimage, in its most literal sense, requires some type of physical journey from one destination to another, and, therefore, it came within the purview of this theological anchor for EC respondents.

While interviewees noted the primacy of *spiritual* journey in pilgrimage with regard to interpretation according to the theological anchor of experimentation, there was still a vital *physical* link to appropriating the practice. Appropriation of pilgrimage through the anchor of physicality also cleared the path for reinterpretation of the practice to apply to nontraditional activities and locations. By way of illustration, interviewees often reinterpreted pilgrimage according to embodied spirituality through their choices of what to offer as examples of potential pilgrimages, which can be seen in the representative quotes below.

> I try to do that a couple times a year. Usually, I'll go camping, or I'll take a bike trip for a long weekend, and I think those are also pilgrimages for me, defining [it] as a journey in my heart. (Interviewee 8)

> For me, pilgrimage in the past has taken on [camping], and I enjoy nature too, so I'll do a camping trip. I'll get out. I'll go somewhere. I'll camp with dedication, set aside to maybe tackle a particular issue that God has brought to my attention. (Interviewee 24)

Evidently, interviewees viewed a significant aspect of pilgrimage as camping, or more generally being in nature, when reinterpreted into their personal spiritualities. Additionally, this practice was reinterpreted according to embodied spirituality through ancillary advantages noted as part of the purpose for appropriating pilgrimage into one's life. Specifically, Interviewee 8 noted that "it's [pilgrimage is] a way that I feel rested, refueled, the release of anxiety, the release of control over things. It really, really helps me in those areas." It is notable that these advantages are closely related to a physical understanding of rest, i.e., bodily rest.

Through these specific connections, one can view how an appropriated mystic practice which has a physical component, like pilgrimage, is reinterpreted conceptually by the EC to allow for appropriation. Interestingly, these purposes, as stated by interviewees, lacked an overt theological investment component; it is likely that theological connections remained mapped to the anchor of experimentation to which participants also connected pilgrimage. Also, practices of lesser usage which have physical components find a home in the EC context through the theological anchor of an embodied spirituality through physicality.

Practices of Passing Familiarity

Interestingly, while all the practices contained within this category have potential for physical applications, participants only noted overt connections for the appropriation and reinterpretation of *lectio Divina*, prayer labyrinths, and the stations of the cross to the theological anchor, or theme, of embodied spirituality through physicality. While the use of icons and the rosary require physical *objects*, interviewees did not map their use directly to physical *actions* which must be taken by a practitioner.

Lectio Divina mapped very uniquely to the anchor of embodied spirituality through physicality. As a brief reminder, *lectio* was appropriated in the emergent case study churches in an occasional communal context, but it was principally utilized on an individual basis. Within a personal context of appropriation, *lectio* was reinterpreted as experimental ways to engage with Scripture imaginatively or meditatively, thereby connecting to the anchor of experimentation. *Lectio* was also discussed by interviewees in connection with physicality, but interviewees reinterpreted it according to this theological anchor through a metaphorical emphasis. Interviewee 30 provided a characteristic description of this physical metaphor by admitting, "I sort of feel like I'm breathing it [Scripture], and then it becomes part of me in a different way, and then I'm able to sense. I can hear the community's voice, almost, filtered through that, and I also almost filter my own voice." This participant approached the appropriation of *lectio* through the metaphorical image of "breathing" in order to reinterpret this practice according to an embodied spirituality through physicality. While the literal physical component of this practice involves reading and speaking, these metaphorical connections allowed for the emergent case study churches to conceive of *lectio* as a strongly physical practice rather than simply a spiritual one; perhaps, this practice was only connected to physicality due to its relative physical emphasis in distinction from evangelical non-physical emphases on devotional reading of Scripture. In a decidedly unmetaphorical turn, the final two practices mapped to this theological anchor require obvious physical actions.

Use of prayer labyrinths was appropriated only according to the theological anchor of an embodied spirituality through physicality. Within the previous chapter, the level of appropriation of prayer labyrinths in the case study churches was delineated and described. To briefly reiterate, labyrinths were walked on a sporadic basis by individuals who were seeking them out occasionally. Usually, this situation resulted in labyrinths appropriated only on a personal level of emphasis; however CitC created temporary labyrinths as aids to a topical issue or conversation. It is likely that this greater emphasis in CitC is due to the pastor's interest in labyrinths being much greater than the interest of other interview participants in this mystic practice.

EC interviewees generally noted some spiritual value in appropriating labyrinths in an infrequent and cursory way, but when connections were made, they proceeded in a predictable fashion. Unsurprisingly, labyrinth users that were interviewed focused on spiritual connections to the physical act of *walking* a labyrinth. This kinetic quality was a notable aspect for interviewed individuals who wished to invest their spirituality with a very basic physical activity of human experience. In this sense, interviewees valued prayer labyrinths as a means to connect physical and spiritual aspects of themselves on this basic level.

As a second emphasis, some respondents noted the physical suitability of appropriating prayer labyrinths according to their personalities. Interviewee 11 provided a representative example of this type.

> The prayer labyrinths, for me, the beneficial thing there is doing something while you're praying, like, moving. It helps to walk around [be]cause I'm hyperactive, so getting out and walking around or running while I'm praying or something like that is effective. Any sort of movement of the labyrinth, stepping and focusing on walking around and praying is just helpful.

While interviewees were also quick to note that other practitioners might not make this particular physical connection, they personally interpreted the connection to the body allowed by walking prayer labyrinths as a means of focusing and relieving anxiety. It is likely that this value stood out because prayer labyrinths offered an obviously physical way to pray, and other forms of prayer did not often have a required physical component. The final practice to be discussed in connection with the theological anchor of embodied spirituality through physicality also requires an extent of walking, but that was not the primary physical connection which interviewees made.

Multiple respondents connected embodied spirituality through physicality to their appropriation and reinterpretation of the stations of the cross as part of their spirituality as an EC Christian. As noted in chapter five and in the community and experimentation sections of this chapter, emergent case study churches appropriated the practice of the stations of the cross (although usually only twelve stations) as part of Holy Week celebrations. Appropriation of this mystic practice occurred on the basis of multiple theological anchors, but a theological concern for the investment of physicality informed reinterpretation among EC practitioners in matters of emphasis and investment of entirely new theological content and expression.

While participation in the stations of the cross required the physical movement of going from one station to the other, physical connections truly shone through interviewee comments in ways that the content of these stations was thoroughly reinterpreted through the unique contexts in which they were practiced in each church investigated. Occasionally, interview respondents would only touch upon this connection, such as Interviewee 29 who summed up the purpose of stations of the cross as a "very visceral" way of reminding Christians of the sacrifice of Jesus Christ. However, other respondents went into more detail of how the reinterpretation of the stations of the cross invested a deeper degree of physicality to their spirituality. Interviewee 26 provided an extended comment from this perspective.

> The different stations were set up, and they were interactive stations in the sense of let's see, there was, for example, there was one where we smelled perfume, and we sat and prayed. It was this remembrance of Mary Magdalene who washed the feet of Christ with the perfume and this idea of "How much are we willing to sacrifice?" [There is] So much of this sensory stuff that we don't really think about. We don't know what's that going to sound like, or we don't think about somebody doing this to somebody's hand [referring to a station where nails were hammered into a board]. Oh, my goodness. Again, just acknowledging the pain and suffering that he [Jesus Christ] experienced for me.

Through this detailed comment, it is quite apparent that interviewees were able to map the stations of the cross to a heightened level of embodied spirituality because they were heightening the physical aspects of utilizing the stations of the cross. In other words, EC practitioners of the stations of the cross were not just engaging the story of the crucifixion with their eyes, as is the traditional method; rather, they were engaging this mystic practice with all of their senses.

While the reinterpretation of stations of the cross to include all the senses is a notable emphasis that EC practitioners invest into this practice, they also go beyond matters of emphasis to total reinterpretation. Manifestly, CitC reinterpreted the stations of the cross to be not only fully engaged with an individual's sense but also moved this practice to the context of complete bodily interaction through the element of movement and the addition of the local non-participating community as part of the context of practice in the DART stations of the cross. For interviewees from CitC, this unique celebration of the stations of the cross was deeply meaningful to participants on the level of physicality of participation, freshness of perspective, and connection to local city context. In these multiple levels of meaning, interviewees from CitC asserted that this practice had great value for an embodied spirituality.

Unlike the previous theological anchor considered, the theological anchor of embodied spirituality through physicality was linked for EC interviewees in an almost entirely predictable way to the appropriation of particular mystic practices. The previous anchor mapped to few mystic practices and, in fact, led many interviewees away from integrating mystic practices on the basis of perceived passive facets of these practices. In distinction, embodied spirituality through physicality buttressed any theological justification needed in the case study churches for appropriating physical emphases and reinterpretations of Holy Communion, meditation, fasting, the sign of the cross, pilgrimage, *lectio Divina*, prayer labyrinths, and the stations of the cross. While the anchors of community and experimentation supported practices from a more central place in EC theology, embodied spirituality through physicality connected significantly to appropriation on the basis of its visibility, tangibility, and ease of comprehension in how practices could map to this anchor. In fact, many of the physical aspects noted above appear quite obvious when stated, and this self-evident quality strengthened a rationale for acceptance for those in the EC context with a primary theological value attached to a "whatever works" mentality.

Summary of Chapter

Within the scope of this chapter, discussion has developed with respect to interviewee comments on the twenty-one mystic practices investigated. While these comments were also the subject of the previous chapter, focus moved here from questions of *how* each practice was appropriated to questions of *why* that practice was appropriated, reinterpreted, and invested with new theological content. Care has been taken to present explanations of purpose and rationale in the exact terms offered by interview respondents. As a consequence, categorical divisions became quite necessary on multiple levels. Categories of usage, as introduced in chapter five, have been useful to order information about appropriated practices within larger categories, but the principal classifying units of this chapter have been the theological anchors, or unique themes, under which interviewee comments can be grouped and explicated. These anchors were community, experimentation, embodied spirituality through social action, and embodied spirituality through physicality.

The anchors identified within the range of this chapter are distinctive themes within the theology of the EC; however, they are not the only themes present within EC theology or, even, the only themes which interview participants connected to implementation of particular practices. By way of clarification, the vital *distinction* of these anchors is that they are unique theological themes that are present within the EC that specifically allow for the appropriation of mystic practices from other traditions and that encourage reinterpretation for the EC social context. Additionally, EC participants were reinterpreting practices principally by investing them with the very theological themes which allowed for appropriation. These anchors arose within the context of empirical study in both expected and unexpected ways.

As noted in the general flow of discussion on specific practices, expected and unexpected features arose concerning how individuals correlate practices with theological anchors. Precisely, some practices mapped to a particular theological anchor in an anticipated way. For instance, the practice of Holy Communion was connected deeply to the theological anchor of community. As another example, the practice of walking prayer labyrinths was predictably related to the anchor of embodied spirituality through physicality. On the other side of this observation, multiple practices were surprisingly mapped by interviewed individuals to anchors that would not naturally seem to offer such a relationship. As an illustration, the practice of solitude would not seem to be very connected to social action or community, but some respondents made these links. Additionally, *lectio Divina* might not be predictably correlated with an enhanced focus on physicality within spirituality, yet interviewees made this connection anyway. Expected and unexpected developments arose on the practice-by-practice level as a result of the major anchor relationship to which interviewees tied the entire appropriation and reinterpretation process. Precisely, the task of the individual EC spiritual practitioner was to experiment with a wide variety of spiritual and/or mystic practices with the specific intent of finding his or her own best mix of practices that express a highly personalized spirituality. In other words, *experimentation was the primary theological anchor* for respondents interviewed in the empirical research phase of the study, and experimentation led to innovative behavioral modifications and conceptual connections to other theological anchors.

Although noted at the outset of the chapter, it is helpful to reiterate before closing that EC theological anchors which connect to spiritual borrowing of mystic practices have points of similarity and difference from EC literature to empirical results. There are definite points of contact, as one might expect. The degree to which the anchor of community is stressed in EC literary conversations naturally leads one to expect this value to be prominent in actual churches as well. This expectation was fulfilled. In fact, the term *community* was prominent in all areas of discussion within interviews. Additionally, both literature and empirical research revealed an abiding concern among EC adherents for an embodied spirituality. However, significant divergences from EC literature also appeared in the analysis of empirical data. Notably, two categories delineated from EC authors, mystery and contemplation with action, were not significant theological anchors for interviewees. Additionally, the anchor of embodied spirituality required a full separation between different definitions, a distinction not shown to be so strong within EC literature. Also, a singularly focused anchor of experimentation replaced the split focus of relevance and tradition. While considerable comment has been offered on how theological anchors map to the appropriation, reinterpretation, and theological investment of practices, discussion now needs to progress to compare and contrast literary and empirical findings in the final chapter with a particular eye turned toward conclusions which can be delineated for contribution to larger areas of research.

7

Conclusions, Contributions, and Recommendations

THE PURPOSE OF THIS book has been to investigate the veracity of the research claim: *the emergent church is appropriating Christian mystical practices by investing these practices with their own theological content.* This claim has been thoroughly investigated on literary and empirical bases, and the overall conclusion of this study rests on analysis and interpretation of findings discovered in the research process concerning EC theological anchors which are invested in the practices through appropriation and reinterpretation. In this light, direct comparison and contrast of theological anchors will display the logic with which this study reaches a final conclusion. From the basis of this conclusion, final comments can be offered with respect to the areas of contribution for this research study as well as areas of recommendation for further research. To state the matter simply, a comparison between EC literary theological anchors and empirically researched theological anchors will answer the question, "What has really been learned in the research process?" The answer to this question provides an answer to the research claim and serves as a conclusion for the study. From this point, however, another question is raised, "What is the significance of this conclusion?" Answering this question sheds light on the areas of contribution for this piece of research. Additionally, matters of contribution lead to one final area of investigation which can be encapsulated in the question, "Where should research proceed from this point?" So, this final chapter will answer these three questions of conclusion, contribution, and recommendation.

Emergent Church Theological Anchors from Literature

EC theological anchors were first considered and classified within chapter three as part of an overall explanation of themes within EC literary discussions. The term *anchor* was employed in explication of these theological themes for two reasons. First, the term *anchor* was utilized by an actual interviewee to describe his most important theological beliefs, supporting the phenomenological focus of the study. Second, the term *anchor* artfully expresses the tenuous relationship which EC participants have with the nonnegotiable overtones present in traditional evangelical terms, such as *belief, proposition,* or *fundamental*. Specifically, five anchors were identified within literary sources: community, relevance over tradition, mystery, contemplation with action, and embodied spirituality. Each of these five observed anchors requires a short, succinct summation with particular focus on its logical impact on the appropriation and reinterpretation of mystic practices within EC contexts.

First, community was offered as a primary theological anchor for all points of the EC conversation. As Kathy Smith succinctly expressed, "For emergent communities, relationship supersedes everything else."[1] Such an emphasis on community was held in tension with a focus on the individual. This empirical finding followed in a predictable line from the sociological location of the EC as first identified and discussed in chapter two. Stress on community was due in part to the rejection of intense concentration in evangelical sources on an individual's one-on-one relationship with God. Departing from this evangelical context, EC authors stressed the role of the community in their spirituality and theology. In this way, the subject of the *extent* of the Christian community, i.e., all the denominations and branches of Christian faith, became a major topic of discussion for EC literary participants. Consequently, many EC voices argued for a wide sense of Christian tradition with permeable boundaries among traditions. According to this pattern of reasoning, looking at other Christian traditions for practices to appropriate was *allowed*, which was a permission that was not granted within evangelical spirituality. Along with this allowance, the theology of community was not only useful for appropriation, but it was also invested in practices through stress on social connections and the view that theological boundaries are not insurmountable. Similarly, the next literary anchor dealt with issues of permission.

---

1. Smith, "Training Wheels," 19.

The second EC literary anchor that was identified was a value of relevance over tradition. With regard to a literary conversation, EC adherents considered and discussed the issue of postmodernity. They were vitally interested in how much Western society has changed with the shift to postmodernity, and they continually grapple with what that change means for Christianity. Considerations of relevance were often verbalized by EC authors in comparison with considerations of faithfulness to Christian tradition. This anchor was characterized by the tension between these two expansive areas which required, in EC thinking, a new balance in which relevance gained the upper hand over tradition although not to the complete dissolution of all traditional categories and perspectives. Through this aspect of conversation between relevance and tradition, EC literary participants again focused on this aspect as *allowing* appropriation. As a direct relationship, each new practice appropriated from the mystical tradition was invested with an ability to be reshaped in order to serve relevance. Apparently, the need for two theological anchors, community and relevance over tradition, to support the same point of *allowing* appropriation shows the strength of prohibition for appropriating mystic practices that existed in their previous evangelical environments. So, with permission given to look at other traditions and some measure of freedom to appropriate and reinterpret granted, EC literary conversation could then proceed to discuss appropriation from a positive stance. In other words, once they answered the question of why one *might* be allowed to appropriate, they moved to issues of why one *should* appropriate.

Following the same line of logical progression, EC literary conversationalists were next led to the category of mystery. In brief summation, they had recognized from their own experience that there were many aspects of God, Christian faith, and practice that were inexplicable. Coming out of an evangelical tradition which EC authors perceived as oblivious to such difficult issues, they advocated a reaction to evangelical avoidance by embracing mystery. As mystic practices were perceived in literary discussions to deal most directly with the unknown aspects of God, they became not only allowable but *attractive*. So, the act of embracing mystery attracts EC individuals to mystic practices, according to EC literature. In fact, this love for mystery is stressed to such an extent that Leonard Sweet, a prolific EC author, turns to a recent neologism by which to denote this development: *mysterian*.[2] As practicing *mysterians*, in literary understandings, EC participants are attracted to spiritual practices that do not shy away from mystery, and they find a ready supply of such thinking and acting in mystic practices.

2. Sweet, *Learn to Dance the Soul Salsa*, 67.

As part of the process of reinterpretation, EC participants then moved from the attractiveness of mystery already present in some of the appropriated practices to carving out a place for mystery in practices that did not originally emphasize this theological theme and/or emphasize the *unanswerable* nature of the questions which mystery might raise.

A fourth anchor was not as directly stated within EC literature; rather, it was present through the logical underpinning of appropriating mystic practices. Precisely, the fourth theological theme for EC mystic practice appropriation, demonstrated by literary conversations, was contemplation *with* action. While the juxtaposition of contemplation and action in some way is quite common to discussions of mystic practices and the mystical tradition, EC literary comments focused on the necessary change from conjunction to preposition, from *and* to *with*. Particularly, EC writers strongly emphasized that contemplation and action should be viewed as complementary categories, each needing the other. In this sense, the logical progression of thought moves from *allowing* through *attracting* to *urging*. To clarify, appropriation of mystic practices is allowed through community and relevance, they become attractive through mystery, and they become urgent matters for appropriation and reinterpretation with this anchor. As noted in considerations of evangelical distinctives, *activism* is a peculiar trait of this Christian tradition.[3] So, EC Christians primarily arise out of a social and theological context which urges action; however, they were dissatisfied with being, in their perception, urged to action without any depth of spirituality undergirding that action. As a result, EC authors saw mystic practices and the perspective which they may bring as a potential means of balancing action and adding spiritual depth to the willingness to act. According to this way of thinking, one can logically understand why it might actually be better to term this anchor *action with contemplation* in order to note the balance of theological emphasis. So, while this anchor allows for the appropriation of mystic practices, it also directs the practitioner to invest these practices with a theological viewpoint that highly values action. With this anchor, appropriation of practices had a completed basis in EC literary discussions to move into integration of the major noted theme of EC spiritual theology.

Within the purview of EC literature, an innovative category for EC spiritual theology was embodied spirituality. This term differs from previous terms for theological anchors because it did not originate in the EC conversation. Sociologists Richard Flory and Donald Miller coined this term specifically to describe EC spirituality through its participatory focus

---

3. Bebbington, Noll, and Rawlyk, "Introduction," 6.

on how a Christian should live spiritually from day to day rather than focus principally on attaining a desired afterlife situation.[4] According to EC literary output, it was this embodied impulse which tied most directly to the appropriation and reinterpretation of mystic practices. Literary discussions also tended to split this anchor into a twin focus of embodied spirituality on a social level and a personal level. In order to find a range of spiritual practices to fulfill this twin focus, appropriation was not only allowed, attractive, or urged, but it became *necessary*. So, while not only limited to mystic practices, the appropriation and reinterpretation of mystic practices in the EC followed a logical progression of theological anchors of community and relevance *allowing* appropriation and reinterpretation, through mystery *attracting* appropriation and reinterpretation, through contemplation with action *urging* appropriation and reinterpretation, to the final end result of embodied spirituality *necessitating* appropriation and reinterpretation. While this progression provides an easily comprehensible basis for assimilation of mystic practices by the EC, it also raises issues, as noted at the start of chapter four, whether such a progression is actually so straightforward in real-life social interactions. Typically, literary output displays the long process of reflection which tends to simplify progressions which are often more complex empirically. Therefore, empirical research can be used to validate the simplicity or complexity of literary explanations as well as serve as an instrument of research and discovery in its own right. As discovered in empirical research, the progression of reasoning for appropriation and reinterpretation was in fact a bit more circuitous.

Emergent Church Theological Anchors from Empirical Research

In order to investigate independently the theological anchors noticed in EC literature, I employed a phenomenological method of empirical research among three case study emergent churches. This research consisted primarily of lengthy qualitative interviews. As a result of these research methods, considerable data was gathered concerning the appropriation, implementation, and reinterpretation of twenty-one mystic practices. From the findings and analysis of this data, notable qualities concerning theological anchors were uncovered which compare and contrast to the aforementioned literary themes. Before proceeding to an anchor-by-anchor discussion, it should be noted that the research results were intended to provide thick qualitative description rather than quantitatively-based statistics. Understandably, these

4. Flory and Miller, *Finding Faith*, vii.

findings may not be generalizable to every local permutation of the EC; however, there are potential generalization possibilities for churches which are similar to the case study churches. Also, the multifaceted differences among case study churches, as outlined in chapter four with respect to the continuum aspect of how strongly each church identified with the emergent conversation, does lend support for generalization prospects. With this caveat in mind, the theological anchors delineated from empirical research results were community, experimentation, embodied spirituality through social action, and embodied spirituality through physicality. Each of these anchors requires some comment concerning appropriation and reinterpretation of mystic practices.

To begin, the first anchor that was empirically discerned mapped rather neatly to the first literary anchor. Simply put, whether viewed literarily or empirically, EC participants are interested in community. While interviewed and observed individuals did value community over individuality similarly to what was described in literary discussions, the role of this anchor in the appropriation of mystic practices became more clear. Empirically, a high theological value on community *allowed* for looking at other traditions, but the actual process of appropriation was performed practically through the individual EC participants in a congregation. To clarify, the theological anchor of community *allowed* for looking at other traditions specifically through tolerance of and interest in what each individual *brought to* the EC. This progression was not as fully defined in EC literature, and it may seem to be a minor difference, yet it sheds light on why the EC appropriates mystic practices in the eclectic ways which they do.[5] Mystic practices are appropriated when, where, and how individual participants view them as valuable. So, while this anchor definitely maps to mystic practice appropriation on the basis of *allowing*, it offers more information concerning exactly how such theological permission leads to theological reinterpretation.

With the second empirically observed theological anchor, differences between literary and empirical research begin to become noticeable. Distinctively, case study churches emphasized greatly an anchor of theological experimentation rather than relevance over tradition. While there are definite points of contact between these two anchors, the balance of emphasis is shifted. Rather than presenting a tension in which relevance was held slightly higher than tradition, interviewees remarked that relevance was strongly ascendant over any other conceptual relationship. Interviewee 11 gave a representative articulation of this viewpoint by saying,

5. This tendency was often referred to obliquely in the literature: "Everyone is encouraged to bring their own background, experience, and understanding to the mix, enriching and deepening communal identity." Smith, "Training Wheels," 19.

> I tend to reflect a lot on why I would use these [practices of silence and solitude], so I tend to have more of a thoughtful like "Oh, there's an ecumenical value here." But, it's interesting to see how little that plays into people's choices, I think, of spiritual disciplines. I find more and more that it tends to be like "This seems to work for me." So, [people respond more] like, "We're sticking to that," and less "Oh, I've always been curious to see what the Anglicans do."

As this quote illustrates, EC interviewees were not wholly unaware or specifically rejecting the historical provenance of mystic practices, but tradition and history were not the primary issues. Most likely, this situation was a result of the freedom they felt to reinterpret practices to fit their own needs in an entirely new social context. This tendency has also been illustrated in previous chapters in which individuals expressed within an interview context that spiritual practice appropriation did not just occur for them from among Christian traditions. They also felt free to assimilate practices from religious traditions outside the umbrella of Christianity. So, in denoting the logical progression of thought glimpsed through phenomenology, the anchor of community *allows* appropriation of practices and the anchor of experimentation *necessitates* appropriation. Additionally, as mentioned in the previous chapter, the anchor of experimentation mapped more strongly than any other anchor to the process of spiritual borrowing. While community and experimentation may seem to provide a simple line from allowance to necessity, empirical research results also offered insight into how the progression from allowance to necessity proceeds through additional theological anchors.

While the anchors of community and experimentation offer the beginning and end for empirical findings on mystic practice appropriation in case study churches, there remains the need for some comment concerning anchors supporting the middle of a logical progression for appropriation and reinterpretation. As noted in the previous chapter, the anchors of mystery and contemplation with action did not map significantly in the minds of interview respondents to the reasoning behind utilizing mystic practices. While this surprising lack of connection shortened the list of theological anchors which could be empirically considered, it also allowed for a more detailed consideration of the anchor of embodied spirituality. Embodied spirituality was discussed in the section above in terms of EC emphasis on a spirituality that is decidedly "this-world" in its orientation. This facet of embodied spirituality was stressed very heavily by interviewees, leading to a series of surprising results.

First, interview participant remarks concerning the reasoning behind connecting mystic practice appropriation and embodied spirituality necessitated a complete separation between the anchor of embodied spirituality through social action and the anchor of embodied spirituality through physicality. This distinction became necessary on the basis of how each emphasis mapped to appropriation. The second result proceeds from this distinction because individuals who placed a high value on embodied spirituality through social action noted that this value actually led them *away* from appropriating several mystic practices, perceiving them to be inapplicable to an active spirituality. Finally, individuals who placed a high value on embodied spirituality through physicality tended to mention influence from this anchor only when particular practices would necessarily have physical actions tied to them. In other words, the physicality of spirituality was not the primary motivation for the appropriation of most mystic practices; rather, it was viewed as an unexpected fringe benefit.

So, while interviewees noted several theological themes that fit under the category of embodied spirituality, this anchor was usually notable as an *enriching* perspective in the process of reinterpretation once a participant had already appropriated a practice on the basis of the theological anchors of community and/or experimentation. While a few practices were appropriated solely on the basis of these anchors, empirical findings displayed that individuals in the case study churches were logically viewing the typical process of spiritual borrowing in the following theological manner: community *allowed* for the appropriation and reinterpretation of mystic practices, experimentation *necessitated* the appropriation and reinterpretation of mystic practices, and the twin anchors of embodied spirituality *enriched* the reinterpretation of mystic practices. In light of the difference in logical progression of reasoning for appropriation and reinterpretation between EC literature and empirical study, some conclusions of comparison and contrast can be drawn.

Conclusions

An overall conclusion concerning the research claim of the study can only be approached through consideration of the minor conclusions which can be drawn when literary and empirical anchors are compared and contrasted. As an initial minor conclusion, the strongest point of connection between literary and empirical investigations is the theological anchor of community. While literary sources organized their discussions in such a way that it appeared that impartial, objective appropriation of practices was occurring, empirical research discovered that actual appropriation was proceeding on a practice-by-practice basis, depending on how a practice(s) was valuable to an individual in an EC community. This interaction between literary and empirical findings follows in a direct line from the sociological location of the EC conversation in the larger developments of religious resistance to institutionalization through an innovative balance between the worth of the community and the importance of the individual. In conclusion, concerning the first anchor, *appropriation first became theologically valuable because each person who aligns with an EC community is viewed as a valuable combination of experience and knowledge.* Reinterpretation then proceeded on this basis of personal value over theological consistency. It is important to note at this initial step of logical progression towards a conclusion that individuals bring *whatever* their experience reflects to the process of spiritual borrowing. Mystic practices are only one possible group for appropriation. The next conclusion builds on this basis.

The second conclusion of comparison and contrast is the crux of the reasoning behind mystic practice appropriation for the EC as empirically investigated. While EC literary conversationalists would term this theological anchor as relevance over tradition, the interviewed practitioners displayed the ascendancy of relevance through an anchor of experimentation. Freedom in spiritual borrowing and reinterpretation was based on the theological anchor of experimentation as *primary* for spiritual borrowing, and it is best encapsulated in the "whatever works" mentality noted above by Interviewee 11. This point is in direct contrast to EC literary output which viewed the primary anchor as embodied spirituality. However, this drive to customize one's spiritual experience fits neatly with the value of each individual as noted in the first anchor. In conclusion, *mystic practices were appropriated on the basis of experimentation through a perspective that EC practitioners are appropriating a practice as a container which can then be "emptied" of old theology and "filled" with new content which reflects EC theological distinctives.*

Anchors of mystery and contemplation with action, while notable in the literature, were not major points of contact for interviewed EC individuals. While this lack of linkage should not be utilized to invalidate the applicability of the EC literary discussion, it does display a notable disconnect between how literary sources perceive EC theology and how EC participants express their theology. Therefore, some minor conclusions can be suggested on the basis of a lack of connection. While these conclusions will not be indisputable because they are based at least in part on silence, they offer notable insights for the overall progression of thought leading from the consideration of individual anchors to the overall conclusion of the book. With respect to the third literary anchor, one minor conclusion is that *mystery is a possible attractor to mystic practices, but it might be an attractor based only on one's personal value for mystery*. In this way, the third conclusion really is an extension of the second conclusion's tendency toward customization. Contemplation with action similarly can be regarded as an extension of another conclusion. With regard to a minor conclusion concerning the fourth literary anchor, it may be noted that *contemplation with action can be subsumed under the category and reasoning of embodied spirituality, particularly as it is understood through the aspect of social action*. These minor conclusions are a result of the observed circumstance that the anchors of mystery and contemplation with action were not present in empirical case studies as separate anchors. Therefore, they are not as primary for the EC conversation, at least in the case study churches, as the literature seeks to display.

Embodied spirituality, in all of its permutations between literary and empirical research, offered many aspects of comparison and contrast. While all aspects of emphasis on this anchor map to a concern for creation of a "this-world" spirituality, the manner in which such a spirituality interacts with spiritual borrowing appears differently when comparing literature to empirical case studies. In the literature, this anchor is singled out as primary rather than the anchor of experimentation which was primary in empirical investigation. Additionally, focus on social action and physicality respectively receive varying degrees of interest and separation between literary and empirical sources. Specifically, these foci are fully separate in empirical results as reasons which lead to different levels of appropriation and reinterpretation. In literary conversations, these foci are simply different sides of the same coin. While all of these points from the foregoing discussion weigh into a conclusion, they also illustrate where the area of confusion arises. Specifically, as a fifth conclusion, *the anchor of embodied spirituality was not unequivocally the principal point of connection for the appropriation and reinterpretation of mystic practices*. To clarify, embodied spirituality appeared to be the major anchor for appropriation in the literature because it was discussed as the major anchor for EC spiritual endeavor in general. It was only with close empirical investigation that it became apparent that this anchor was less central than the anchor of experimentation for the task of spiritual borrowing in the case study churches.

Therefore, conclusions drawn from literary and empirical observations lead to offer an important insight for the entire research study. This insight is that in actual permutations of emergent churches the appropriation of mystic practices proceeds from a foundation built on experimentation, not embodied spirituality, with the supporting logic that mystic practices are

CONCLUSIONS, CONTRIBUTIONS, AND RECOMMENDATIONS   251

independent containers that are not connected inseparably to any particular theological content; rather, they are perceived as neutral vessels which can be filled with "whatever works." Consequently, the research claim of the study that *the emergent church is appropriating Christian mystical practices by investing these practices with their own theological content* can be affirmed. Additionally, it is evident empirically that the EC is investing these borrowed mystic practices with the *very theological content* which allowed for their appropriation. Interestingly, while this overall conclusion can be glimpsed on the basis of literary research alone,[6] the actual mechanics of this process become clear in empirical investigations. Indeed, the research claim becomes even stronger in light of the fact that empirical research uncovered that the primary anchor of EC spiritual borrowing is the drive for experimentation. On the foundation of this conclusion, several comments can be approached concerning the areas of contribution for this research study as well as recommendations for potential areas of further research.

Contributions

To return to the three major questions stated at the beginning of this chapter, the previous section offered an answer to the question, "What has really been learned in the research process?" On the basis of that answer, the next question, "What is the significance of this conclusion" can be approached. The largest area for contribution from this research study is the sociology of religion. It is unsurprising that this area would receive the lion's share of contribution due to the shape of the study as a sociology of theological developments. Particularly, this piece of research contributes to the field of sociology in two ways. First, contribution occurs through thick description of the process of mystic practices moving from one religious tradition to another. A detailed analysis of the process of appropriation and reinterpretation of mystic practices has displayed the phenomenological relationship between the practices themselves and the theological beliefs tied to them. Furthermore, this process of spiritual borrowing demonstrates how a mystic practice can be changed when divested of theological content then

---

6. As an example, John Drane predicts this conclusion in the following comment using the evangelical designation of "spiritual disciplines" instead of mystic practices: "Spiritual disciplines will be adopted from across the spectrum with scant regard for their origins, and will be merged to form new ways of expressing faithful discipleship. This is likely to take place not only across theological traditions but also across the boundaries of time and space, so that insights from the Celtic saints will be seamlessly melded with notions from medieval monasticism, alongside biblical passages and insights from contemporary artists and musicians." Drane, *After McDonaldization*, 52.

filled with new theological content. As a specific example, it is theologically valuable to map scientifically how the traditional mystic practice of the stations of the cross is appropriated by CitC and reinterpreted as an expressive, physical means of reaching out to others (i.e., the DART stations of the cross) with emphases on community and experimentation overshadowing, or completely replacing, themes of sin, guilt, suffering, and sacrifice. Even the number of stations was changed from fourteen to twelve in order to better suit the new purpose for their practice. At the end of reinterpretation, few points of connection are left unchanged other than the time at which these stations would be practiced.

Demonstrations of the process of spiritually borrowing mystic practices from one tradition to another lead back to the metaphor utilized within the first chapter of the research project. To reiterate, a study of mystic practices moved from one social/religious context to another can be likened to the scientific study of particular "microbes" being moved from one "solution" to another for the express purpose of investigating the changes which occur in the microbes as a result of being placed in a new environment. As noted in chapter one, when the microbes begin to adapt to this new environment, a researcher can observe whether they take on the characteristics of their new solution (i.e., EC social and theological culture) and/or retain previous environmental traits (i.e., Christian mystical context). At the end of this study, an answer can be approached concerning this issue. In short, it appears that the microbes have taken on the characteristics of their new solution. To be circumspect, this conclusion was hinted at in a general way within EC literary conversations.

Despite all of the talk about worship styles in the emergent church— the return of ancient, Celtic prayers; the grungy music; the dialogical sermons—it's really the theology underneath the styles that is most important and provocative. Indeed, the emergent innovations in worship rarely raise an eyebrow among the critics. What's really intriguing about emergent Christianity? The theology. For several years now, two camps have formed in the movement. Among some who are emerging, the methods of Christianity have become irrelevant and they must change. But for this group, the message of the gospel is unchanging—it's been figured out, once and for all, never to be reconsidered. But to another group, the methods *and* the message of Christianity are bound to be reconceived over time. Indeed, if one changes the methods, one will inevitably change the message. Another way of saying this is that the Christian gospel is always enculturated, always articulated by a certain people in a certain time and place. To try to freeze one particular articulation of the gospel, to make it timeless and universally applicable, actually does an injustice to the gospel. This goes to the very heart of what emergent is and of how emergent Christians are attempting to chart a course for following Jesus in the postmodern, globablized, pluralized world of the twenty-first century.[7]

As Tony Jones points out, the EC was and is concerned with reevaluating the methods of Christianity, which leads to appropriation of mystic practices which traditionally had lain outside of the scope of evangelical spirituality, their originating tradition. Additionally, Jones goes further to emphasize that the message of Christianity is a subject for reinterpretation which, in turn, opens the door for the reinterpretation of the borrowed practices. If such is the case, it raises the question of why empirical research was required at all. Doesn't EC literature present the case for spiritual borrowing clearly? The answer to this question is both yes and no due to the nature of the EC conversation itself. Some voices, like Jones, in EC literature are very clear, but underneath the surface EC spirituality can seem vague and indistinct. This circumstance was also present in empirical research through interviewee variance in defining spirituality, mysticism, and the EC itself. Lack of consensus haunts the EC conversation and necessitates multiple research perspectives in order to verify observations and insights. This development is indicative of why the EC requires the designation of *conversation* rather than the clearer label of *movement*.

The plurality of perspectives is celebrated within the EC as illustrative of all persons and viewpoints as inherently valuable, even if the resulting lack of consensus makes academic study difficult. Still, the findings of this study have corroborated Jones' comments and shown that this change extends from methods to message and even back to those "new" methods which the EC appropriate for themselves. In fact, this progression of thought leads unsurprisingly to the characteristic among interviewees of considerable confusion, ambiguity, and overlap in their definitions of mystic practices because this trait also reflects EC variance. According to EC literary proponents as well, this quality of flux is preferable as a recognition of the inherent changeability of belief.[8] So, the other contribution of the study is that the process of appropriation and reinterpretation displays that a change in interpretive framework leads to a change in the practice itself. In other words, this book provides *an extended example of the interpenetrating influence of belief and behavior in the process of spiritual borrowing.*

---

7. Jones, *New Christians*, 96.
8. Ibid., 112.

Recommendations for Further Research

With questions of "what has really been learned" and "why is it significant" now answered, discussion can now proceed to the final question of this chapter, "Where should research proceed from this point?" Multiple avenues for further research present themselves based on reference to the areas of contribution noted above. First, concerning the conclusion of this study that emergent churches are, indeed, appropriating Christian mystical practices by investing these practices with their own theological content can be the basis for widening the scope of investigation to spiritual borrowing of mystic practices by other traditions. To extend directly from the subjects involved in this study, one could, for instance, research borrowing of mystic practices by the charismatic tradition or within evangelical spirituality. These possibilities are examples of research on spiritual borrowing that is only one step removed from the social context of the EC. Possibilities for examination of the process of spiritual borrowing could extend in quite a few directions.

As a second avenue of research, one could move from the subject and perspective of this study to examine other aspects of the EC in order to create thick description for qualitative analysis of this fascinating religious tradition. A researcher could even follow the spiritual borrowing emphasis of this study to take the next logical step in studying the EC—sociological investigation of spiritual borrowing of mystic practices from religious traditions *outside Christianity*. In fact, from the basis of the data, this step would already have a starting point because several interview respondents from these specific case study churches noted the influence of non-Christian religious traditions in discussion of the reinterpretation of Christian mystic practices. Notably, multiple participants remarked concerning the influence of Judaism, Buddhism, and Hinduism (through yoga) on their personal spiritualities. In retrospect, while either of these recommended directions for further research have great promise, they can only be built on the basis of what has been concluded in this study: *the emergent church is appropriating Christian mystical practices by investing these practices with their own theological content.*

Appendix A

Spiritual Practices Questionnaire

- centering prayer (wordless prayer)
  - ☐ used personally in the last 12 months
  - ☐ used in a group in the last 12 months
  - ☐ used as a regular group practice
- communion/Eucharist/Lord's Supper
  - ☐ used personally in the last 12 months
  - ☐ used in a group in the last 12 months
  - ☐ used as a regular group practice
- confession
  - ☐ used personally in the last 12 months
  - ☐ used in a group in the last 12 months
  - ☐ used as a regular group practice
- contemplative prayer
  - ☐ used personally in the last 12 months
  - ☐ used in a group in the last 12 months
  - ☐ used as a regular group practice
- Daily Office/fixed-hour prayer
  - ☐ used personally in the last 12 months
  - ☐ used in a group in the last 12 months
  - ☐ used as a regular group practice
- fasting
  - ☐ used personally in the last 12 months
  - ☐ used in a group in the last 12 months
  - ☐ used as a regular group practice
- icons
  - ☐ used personally in the last 12 months
  - ☐ used in a group in the last 12 months
  - ☐ used as a regular group practice
- Jesus prayer
  - ☐ used personally in the last 12 months
  - ☐ used in a group in the last 12 months
  - ☐ used as a regular group practice
- *lectio divina/*
  - ☐ used personally in the last 12 months
  - ☐ used in a group in the last 12 months
  - ☐ used as a regular group practice
- liturgical calendar
  - ☐ used personally in the last 12 months
  - ☐ used in a group in the last 12 months
  - ☐ used as a regular group practice
- liturgical prayer (e.g., the Book of Common Prayer)
  - ☐ used personally in the last 12 months
  - ☐ used in a group in the last 12 months
  - ☐ used as a regular group practice
- meditation
  - ☐ used personally in the last 12 months
  - ☐ used in a group in the last 12 months
  - ☐ used as a regular group practice
- pilgrimage
  - ☐ used personally in the last 12 months
  - ☐ used in a group in the last 12 months
  - ☐ used as a regular group practice
- practicing the presence of God (following the teachings of Brother Lawrence)
  - ☐ used personally in the last 12 months
  - ☐ used in a group in the last 12 months
  - ☐ used as a regular group practice
- prayer labyrinth
  - ☐ used personally in the last 12 months
  - ☐ used in a group in the last 12 months
  - ☐ used as a regular group practice
- rosary
  - ☐ used personally in the last 12 months
  - ☐ used in a group in the last 12 months
  - ☐ used as a regular group practice
- making the sign of the cross
  - ☐ used personally in the last 12 months
  - ☐ used in a group in the last 12 months
  - ☐ used as a regular group practice
- silence
  - ☐ used personally in the last 12 months
  - ☐ used in a group in the last 12 months
  - ☐ used as a regular group practice
- solitude
  - ☐ used personally in the last 12 months
- spiritual direction/spiritual friendship
  - ☐ used personally in the last 12 months
  - ☐ used in a group in the last 12 months
  - ☐ used as a regular group practice
- stations of the cross
  - ☐ used personally in the last 12 months
  - ☐ used in a group in the last 12 months
  - ☐ used as a regular group practice

- other, please specify

_____
_____
_____

Would you be willing to be contacted about the possibility of further participation in this research project?

☐ Yes   ☐ No

If yes, then please provide any necessary information on how you would prefer to be contacted:

_____
_____

Thank you very much for taking the time to complete this questionnaire!

Appendix B

Interview Questions[1]

Note: Follow-up questions are noted for purposes of clarification. It is unlikely that all follow-up questions will be asked for any particular question. Major interview questions are italicized.

Opening Comment: This interview is part of doctoral research which I am conducting on the Emergent Church. I am studying the use and reasons for the use of particular spiritual practices by the Emergent Church. This interest arises from observations that the Emergent Church utilizes spiritual practices that arise out of ancient Christian traditions.

1. General Questions

- *Would you tell me a little about why you first started attending the church in which you are now involved?*
  - Follow-up: What was your religious background prior to involvement?
  - Follow-up: How are you now involved in the Emergent Church?
  - Follow-up: Are you involved in any other churches at the moment? If so, how are you involved in these other churches?
- *How would you describe the Emergent Church?*
  - Follow-up: What is distinctive about the Emergent Church?
- *How would you describe the distinctive perspective on Christian spirituality that is expressed by the Emergent Church?*

---

1. Follow-up questions only appeared on the interviewer copy of the interview schedule.

– Follow-up: How would you describe the Emergent Church's particular approach to being spiritual?

2. Definitions

- *How would you define/describe the term "spiritual" or "spirituality?"*
    - Follow-up: If someone were to say the word "spiritual," what image would pop into your head?
    - Follow-up: What does this term have to do with being a Christian?
- How would you define/describe the term "mystical" or "mysticism?"
    - Follow-up: If someone were to say the word "mystical," what image would pop into your head?
    - Follow-up: What does this term have to do with being a Christian?
- How would you define/describe the term "mystery" in the context of Christian faith?
    - Follow-up: How does the concept of "mystery" figure into being a Christian?

3. Spiritual Practices (from Questionnaire)

- *How do you use the practice of _____?*
    - Follow-up: What are the physical actions you take when you practice _____?
    - Follow-up: Could you describe the last time you practiced _____?
    - Follow-up: Do you practice _____ in a group or individually?
    - Follow-up: Where do you use this practice?
    - Follow-up: When do you use this practice?
- *Why do you use the practice of _____?*
    - Follow-up: Where did you first learn about this practice?
    - Follow-up: How did you begin using this practice?
    - Follow-up: Are there any specific resources (authors, speakers, historical figures) which help you to practice _____?

- Follow-up: Why do you like this practice as a way to worship God?
- *Follow-up: Do you connect this practice with any specific belief?*
- Follow-up: If so, what?
- Follow-up: Have you ever wondered why you do this practice?
- Follow-up: If so, how have you tried to figure out why you use this practice?
- Follow-up: What does God do in this practice?

Closing

- *In light of the previous questions and answers, how would you characterize the relationship between the Emergent Church and your use of these spiritual practices?*
  - Follow-up: Is there a connection?
  - Follow-up: Would you do the same things in a different kind of church?
  - Follow-up: Why or why not?
- Is there anything we have not discussed that you would like to bring up at this time?
- Do you have any questions you would like to ask me?
- Are there any questions that you would recommend to be changed/re-worded?
  - Follow-up: How should they be changed?

Demographic

- Would you mind if we ended with some demographic information?
  - age
  - education level (highest attained)
  - ethnicity
  - gender
  - economic status
- profession/occupation

- income level
- perceived economic status (lower, middle, or upper class)
  - marital status
  - children (number, gender, age)

Appendix C

Participant Information Sheet

Thank you for your time and consideration in being a part of this research project. To offer a little background, my name is Dann Wigner, and I am a student at the University of Durham (UK). For my doctoral thesis, I am conducting research on the emerging church with particular attention to the spiritual practices which are used in emerging churches. I also intend to relate the emerging church to precedents in Christian history, especially to see if their spiritual practices might be set in a broader theological context. In order to further this research, I am interested in talking to those who are involved in an emerging church or who identify as an "emerging" or "emergent" Christian. Through a conversational interview process, I hope to learn more about what spiritual practices are essential and distinctive for you and your church and what they mean to you.

Each interview is designed to last between half an hour and an hour. I have several primary questions which I would like to ask you, but these questions can be answered in any order. Particular questions can also remain unanswered if you desire. These questions serve the purpose of getting a conversation started about your church as an emerging church, the spiritual practices that occur at your church, and your own spiritual practices. Some of these areas of discussion may be personal, and I do not ask you to answer any question with which you are uncomfortable. Please also feel free to comment on any question that you think might be confusing, unclear, or less applicable to the topic.

If you would allow, I would like to audio record and take notes on our conversation for purposes of later consideration and analysis. This information, whether recorded or written, will remain confidential. I am planning to utilize analyzed inferences, personal observations, and verbatim quotes from interviews in my doctoral thesis, but I will not identify you by name in any reference to our conversation. I would also like to keep my notes and recordings for possible future publications on this topic, and I will not identify you by name in any of these potential materials either.

Appendix D

Ethical Consent Form

ETHICAL CONSENT FORM

TITLE OF PROJECT: The Spirituality of the Emerging Church

(The participant should complete the whole of this sheet himself/herself)

Please circle answer

Have you read the Participant Information Sheet?	YES / NO
Have you had an opportunity to ask questions and to discuss the study?	YES / NO
Have you received satisfactory answers to all of your questions?	YES / NO
Have you received enough information about the study?	YES / NO

Who have you spoken to?   Dr/Mr/Mrs/Ms/Prof. ....

Do you consent to participate in the study?	YES / NO
Do you consent to your interview being audio or video recorded?	YES / NO
Do you consent to allowing the data from this interview to be used by the researcher for a doctoral thesis and possible future publications	YES / NO

Do you understand that you are free to withdraw from the study:

* at any time and
* without having to give a reason for withdrawing and
* (if relevant) without affecting your position in the University?   YES / NO

Signed ....   Date ....

(NAME IN BLOCK LETTERS) ....

Bibliography

Ammerman, Nancy T., Jackson W. Carroll, Carl S. Dudley, and William McKinney. "An Invitation to Congregational Study." In *Studying Congregations: A New Handbook*, edited by Nancy T. Ammerman, Jackson W. Carroll, Carl S. Dudley, and William McKinney, 7–21. Nashville, TN: Abingdon, 1998.

Baum, George R. "Emerging from the Water." In *Stories of Emergence*, edited by Mike Yaconelli, 193–203. El Cajon, CA: Emergent YS, 2003.

Beaudoin, Tom. *Virtual Faith: The Irreverent Spiritual Quest of Generation X*. San Francisco: Jossey-Bass, 1998.

Bebbington, David. *Evangelicalism in Modern Britain: A History from the 1730s to the 1980s*. London: Unwin Hyman, 1989.

Bebbington, David, Mark A. Noll, and George A. Rawlyk. "Introduction." In *Evangelicalism: Comparative Studies of Popular Protestantism in North America, the British Isles, and Beyond, 1700–1990*, edited by David W. Bebbington, Mark A. Noll, and George A. Rawlyk, 3–15. New York: Oxford University Press, 1994.

Bell, Rob. *Love Wins*. New York: HarperOne, 2011.

———. *Velvet Elvis: Repainting the Christian Faith*. Grand Rapids, MI: Zondervan, 2005.

Bellah, Robert N., Richard Madsen, William M. Sullivan, Ann Swidler, and Steven M. Tipton. *Habits of the Heart: Individualism and Commitment in American Life*. Berkeley: University of California Press, 1985.

Berger, Peter, Grace Davie, and Effie Fokas. *Religious America, Secular Europe? A Theme and Variations*. Aldershot, UK: Ashgate, 2008.

Bielo, James S. *Emerging Evangelicals: Faith, Modernity, and the Desire for Authenticity*. New York: New York University Press, 2011.

Boss, Pauline, Carla Dahl, and Lori Kaplan. "The Use of Phenomenology for Family Therapy Research: The Search for Meaning." In *Research Methods in Family Therapy*, edited by Sidney M. Moon and Douglas H. Sprenkle, 83–106. New York: Guildford, 1996.

Brasher, Brenda E. *Give Me that Online Religion*. San Francisco: Jossey-Bass, 2001.

Bregman, Lucy. "Defining Spirituality: Multiple Uses and Murky Meanings of an Incredibly Popular Term." *The Journal of Pastoral Care & Counseling* 58 (Fall 2004) 157–67.

Browning, Don S. *Practical Theology: The Emerging Field in Theology, Church, and World*. San Francisco: Harper & Row, 1983.

Burke, John. "The Emerging Church and Incarnational Theology." In *Listening to the Beliefs of Emerging Churches*, edited by Robert E. Webber, 39–69. Grand Rapids, MI: Zondervan, 2007.

———. *No Perfect People Allowed: Creating a Come as You Are Culture in the Church*. Grand Rapids, MI: Zondervan, 2005.

Burke, Spencer. "From the Third Floor to the Garage." In *Stories of Emergence*, edited by Mike Yaconelli, 27–39. El Cajon, CA: Emergent YS, 2003.

Burke, Spencer, and Barry Taylor. *A Heretic's Guide to Eternity*. San Francisco: Jossey-Bass, 2006.

Burke, Spencer, and Colleen Pepper. *Making Sense of Church: Eavesdropping on Emerging Conversations about God, Community, and Culture*. El Cajon, CA: Emergent YS, 2003.

Byassee, Jason. "Emerging from What, Going Where?: Emerging Churches and Ancient Christianity." In *Ancient Faith for the Church's Future*, edited by Jeffrey P. Greenman and Mark Husbands, 249–63. Downers Grove, IL: InterVarsity Academic, 2008.

Carson, D. A. *Becoming Conversant with the Emerging Church: Understanding a Movement and Its Implications*. Grand Rapids, MI: Zondervan, 2005.

Claiborne, Shane. "Mark 2: Sharing Economic Resources with Fellow Community Members and the Needy among Us." In *School(s) of Conversion: 12 Marks of a New Monasticism*, edited by The Rutba House, 26–38. Eugene, OR: Cascade, 2005.

Clark, Jason. "The Renewal of Liturgy in the Emerging Church." In *Church in the Present Tense: A Candid Look at What's Emerging*, edited by Jason Clark, Kevin Corcoran, Scot McKnight, and Peter Rollins, 75–87. Grand Rapids, MI: Brazos, 2011.

Cleaveland, Adam Walker. "Presbymergent: The Story of One Mainliner's Quest to Be a Loyal Radical." In *An Emergent Manifesto of Hope*, edited by Tony Jones and Doug Pagitt, 119–27. Grand Rapids, MI: Baker, 2007.

Clément, Olivier. *The Roots of Christian Mysticism: Text and Commentary*. Translated by Theodore Berkeley and Jeremy Hummerstone. Hyde Park, NY: New City, 1995.

Cole, Neil. *Organic Church: Growing Faith Where Life Happens*. San Francisco: Jossey-Bass, 2005.

Conder, Tim. *The Church in Transition: The Journey of Existing Churches into the Emerging Culture*. Grand Rapids, MI: Zondervan, 2006.

Congar, Yves. "Theology: Christian Theology." In vol. 13 of *Encyclopedia of Religion*, edited by Lindsay Jones, 9139. 2nd ed. Detroit: Thomson Gale, 2005.

Creps, Earl. "Worldview Therapy." In *Stories of Emergence*, edited by Mike Yaconelli, 147–60. El Cajon, CA: Emergent YS, 2003.

Day, Abby. *Believing in Belonging: Belief and Social Identity in the Modern World*. Oxford: Oxford University Press, 2011.

de Guibert, Joseph. *The Theology of the Spiritual Life*. Translated by Paul Barrett. New York: Sheed and Ward, 1953.

DeNavas-Walt, Carmen, Bernadette Proctor, and Jessica Smith. *Income, Poverty, and Health Insurance Coverage in the United States: 2011*. Washington, DC: US Census Bureau, 2012.

Dey, Ian. *Qualitative Data Analysis: A User-Friendly Guide for Social Scientists*. London: Routledge, 1998.

Dorrien, Gary. *The Remaking of Evangelical Theology*. Louisville, KY: Westminster John Knox, 1998.

Drane, John. *After McDonaldization: Mission, Ministry, and Christian Discipleship in an Age of Uncertainty.* Grand Rapids, MI: Baker Academic, 2008.

———. *Do Christians Know How to Be Spiritual? The Rise of the New Spirituality, and the Mission of the Church.* London: Darton, Longman and Todd, 2005.

Driscoll, Mark. *Confessions of a Reformission Rev: Hard Lessons from an Emerging Missional Church.* Grand Rapids, MI: Zondervan, 2006.

———. "A Pastoral Perspective on the Emergent Church." *Criswell Theological Review* 3 (2006) 87–93.

Engel, James F. "A Search for Christian Authenticity." In *Stories of Emergence*, edited by Mike Yaconelli, 117–31. El Cajon, CA: Emergent YS, 2003.

Erdman, Chris. "Digging Up the Past: Karl Barth (the Reformed Giant) as Friend to the Emerging Church." In *An Emergent Manifesto of Hope*, edited by Doug Pagitt and Tony Jones, 235–43. Grand Rapids, MI: Baker, 2007.

Flanagan, Kieran. "Visual Spirituality: An Eye for Religion." In *A Sociology of Spirituality*, edited by Kieran Flanagan and Peter C. Jupp, 219–49. Aldershot, UK: Ashgate, 2007.

Flory, Richard W. "Toward a Theory of Generation X Religion." In *GenX Religion*, edited by Richard W. Flory and Donald E. Miller, 231–49. New York: Routledge, 2000.

Flory, Richard W., and Donald E. Miller. *Finding Faith: The Spiritual Quest of the Post-Boomer Generation.* New Brunswick, NJ: Rutgers University Press, 2008.

Foster, Richard. *Celebration of Discipline: The Path to Spiritual Growth.* San Francisco: HarperSanFrancisco, 1998.

Frost, Michael. *Exiles: Living Missionally in a Post-Christian Culture.* Peabody, MA: Hendrickson, 2006.

Frost, Michael, and Alan Hirsch. *ReJesus: A Wild Messiah for a Missional Church.* Peabody, MA: Hendrickson, 2009.

———. *The Shaping of Things to Come: Innovation and Mission for the 21st-Century Church.* Peabody, MA: Hendrickson, 2003.

Garrigou-Lagrange, Reginald. *The Three Ages of the Interior Life: Prelude of Eternal Life.* Translated by M. Timothea Doyle. Vol. 1. New York: Herder, 1947.

———. *The Three Ages of the Interior Life: Prelude of Eternal Life.* Translated by M. Timothea Doyle. Vol. 2. New York: Herder, 1947.

Gay, Doug. *Remixing the Church: The Five Moves of Emerging Ecclesiology.* London: SCM, 2011.

Gibbs, Eddie. *Churchmorph: How Megatrends Are Reshaping Christian Communities.* Grand Rapids, MI: Baker Academic, 2009.

———. *ChurchNext: Quantum Changes in How We Do Ministry.* Downers Grove, IL: InterVarsity, 2000.

———. "Church Responses to Culture Since 1985." *Missiology* 35 (2007) 157–68.

Gibbs, Eddie, and Ryan K. Bolger. *Emerging Churches: Creating Christian Community in Postmodern Cultures.* Grand Rapids, MI: BakerAcademic, 2005.

Grenz, Stanley J. *A Primer on Postmodernism.* Grand Rapids, MI: Eerdmans, 1996.

Grenz, Stanley J., and John R. Franke. *Beyond Foundationalism: Shaping Theology in a Postmodern Context.* Louisville, KY: Westminster John Knox, 2001.

Guder, Darrell L. "The Church as Missional Community." In *The Community of the Word*, edited by Mark Husbands and Daniel J. Treier, 114–28. Downers Grove, IL: InterVarsity, 2005.

———, ed. *Missional Church: A Vision for the Sending of the Church in North America.* Grand Rapids, MI: Eerdmans, 1998.

Guest, Mathew. *Evangelical Identity and Contemporary Culture: A Congregational Study in Innovation.* Studies in Evangelical History and Thought. Milton Keynes, UK: Paternoster, 2007.

Hammersley, Martyn. *What's Wrong with Ethnography?: Methodological Explorations.* London: Routledge, 1992.

Hansen, Colin. "Pastor Provocateur: Love Him or Hate Him, Mark Driscoll is Helping People Meet Jesus in One of America's Least Churched Cities." *Christianity Today* 51 (2007) 44–49.

Hart, D.G. "The Church in Evangelical Theologies, Past and Future." In *The Community of the Word*, edited by Mark Husbands and Daniel J. Treier, 23–40. Downers Grove, IL: InterVarsity, 2005.

———. *Deconstructing Evangelicalism: Conservative Protestantism in the Age of Billy Graham.* Grand Rapids, MI: Baker Academic, 2004.

Haselmayer, Jerry, Brian D. McLaren, and Leonard Sweet. *A Is for Abductive: The Language of the Emerging Church.* Grand Rapids, MI: Zondervan, 2003.

Hatch, Nathan O. *The Democratization of American Christianity.* New Haven: Yale University Press, 1989.

Henderson, Jim, and Matt Casper. *Jim & Casper Go to Church: Frank Conversation about Faith, Churches, and Well-Meaning Christians.* Carol Stream, IL: Tyndale, 2007.

Hendricks, William D. *Exit Interviews.* Chicago: Moody, 1993.

Hirsch, Alan. *The Forgotten Ways: Reactivating the Missional Church.* Grand Rapids, MI: Brazos, 2006.

Howard, Ken. "A New Middle Way? Surviving and Thriving in the Coming Religious Realignment." *Anglican Theological Review* 92 (Winter 2010) 103–10.

Hübner, Shane. "'X' Marks the Spot? How Generational Theory Can Help the Emerging Church." *St. Mark's Review* 193 (2003) 3–10.

Hudson, Winthrop S. "Denominationalism." In vol. 4 of *Encyclopedia of Religion*, edited by Lindsay Jones, 2286. 2nd ed. Detroit: Thomson Gale, 2005.

Hunter, Todd D. *Giving Church Another Chance: Finding New Meaning in Spiritual Practices.* Downers Grove, IL: InterVarsity, 2010.

Introvigne, Massimo. "Cults and Sects." In vol. 3 of *Encyclopedia of Religion*, edited by Lindsay Jones, 2084. 2nd ed. Detroit: Thomson Gale, 2005.

Jamieson, Alan. *A Churchless Faith: Faith Journeys Beyond the Churches.* London: SPCK, 2002.

———. "Post-Church Groups and Their Place as Emergent Forms of Church." *International Journal for the Study of the Christian Church* 6 (2006) 65–78.

Jenkins, Julian. "Postmodern Evangelicalism: Painting a Picture of an Emerging Movement in the Church." *Lucas: An Evangelical History Review* 33 & 34 (2003) 181–93.

Jones, Susan R. "Becoming Grounded in Grounded Theory Methodology." In *Qualitative Research in Practice: Examples for Discussion and Analysis*, edited by Sharan B. Merriam, 175–77. San Francisco: Jossey-Bass, 2002.

Jones, Tony. *The Church Is Flat: The Relational Ecclesiology of the Emerging Church Movement.* Minneapolis, MN: JoPa Group, 2011.

———. *The New Christians: Dispatches from the Emergent Frontier*. San Francisco: Jossey-Bass, 2008.
———. *The Sacred Way: Spiritual Practices for Everyday Life*. Grand Rapids, MI: Zondervan, 2005.
Keel, Tim. *Intuitive Leadership: Embracing a Paradigm of Narrative, Metaphor, and Chaos*. Grand Rapids, MI: Baker, 2007.
Kelley, Dean M. *Why Conservative Churches Are Growing: A Study in the Sociology of Religion*. New York: Harper & Row, 1972.
Kenney, Maria Russell. "Mark 3: Hospitality to the Stranger." In *School(s) of Conversion: 12 Marks of a New Monasticism*, edited by The Rutba House, 39–54. Eugene, OR: Cascade, 2005.
Keuss, Jeff. "The Emergent Church and Neo-Correlational Theology after Tillich, Schleiermacher, and Browning." *Scottish Journal of Theology* 61 (2008) 450–61.
Kimball, Dan. *The Emerging Church: Vintage Christianity for New Generations*. Grand Rapids, MI: Zondervan, 2003.
———. "The Emerging Church and Missional Theology." In *Listening to the Beliefs of Emerging Churches*, edited by Robert Webber, 81–105. Grand Rapids, MI: Zondervan, 2007.
———. *They Like Jesus, but Not the Church: Insights from Emerging Generations*. Grand Rapids, MI: Zondervan, 2007.
King, James. "Emerging Issues for the Emerging Church." *The Journal of Ministry & Theology* 9 (2005) 24–62.
Larson, Bruce, and Ralph Osborne. *The Emerging Church*. Edited by Richard Engquist. Waco, TX: Word, 1970.
Lee, Shayne, and Phillip Luke Sinitiere. "A New Kind of Christian: Brian McLaren and the Emerging Church." In *Holy Mavericks: Evangelical Innovators and the Spiritual Marketplace*, 77–105. New York: New York University Press, 2009.
Leedy, Paul D., and Jeanne Ellis Ormrod. *Practical Research: Planning and Design*. 7th ed. Upper Saddle River, NJ: Merrill Prentice Hall, 2001.
Liederbach, Mark, and Alvin L. Reid. *The Convergent Church: Missional Worshipers in an Emerging Culture*. Grand Rapids, MI: Kregel, 2009.
Long, Jimmy. *Emerging Hope: A Strategy for Reaching Postmodern Generations*. Downers Grove, IL: InterVarsity, 2004.
Louth, Andrew. *The Origins of the Christian Mystical Tradition*. Oxford: Clarendon, 1981.
Luckmann, Thomas. *The Invisible Religion: The Problem of Religion in Modern Society*. New York: Macmillan, 1967.
Lyon, David. *Jesus in Disneyland: Religion in Postmodern Times*. Cambridge: Polity, 2000.
Malloy, Patrick L. "Rick Warren Meets Gregory Dix: The Liturgical Movement Comes Knocking at the Megachurch Door." *Anglican Theological Review* 92 (Summer 2010) 439–53.
Mann, Alan. *Atonement for a "Sinless" Society: Engaging with an Emerging Culture*. Milton Keynes, UK: Paternoster, 2005.
Marti, Gerardo, and Gladys Ganiel. *The Deconstructed Church: Understanding Emerging Christianity*. Oxford: Oxford University Press, 2014.
Mason, Jennifer. *Qualitative Researching*. London: Sage, 1996.

McGinn, Bernard. *The Flowering of Mysticism: Men and Women in the New Mysticism (1200–1350)*. Vol. 3, *The Presence of God: A History of Western Christian Mysticism*. New York: Crossroad, 1998.

———. *The Foundations of Mysticism*. Vol. 1, *The Presence of God: A History of Western Christian Mysticism*. New York: Crossroad, 1992.

———. *The Growth of Mysticism*. Vol. 2, *The Presence of God: A History of Western Christian Mysticism*. London: SCM, 1995.

———. *The Harvest of Mysticism in Medieval Germany*. Vol. 4, *The Presence of God: A History of Western Christian Mysticism*. New York: Crossroad, 2005.

McGuire, Meredith B. *Religion: The Social Context*. Belmont, CA: Wadsworth, 1981.

McKnight, Scot. "Five Streams of the Emerging Church: Key Elements of the Most Controversial and Misunderstood Movement in the Church Today." *Christianity Today* 51 (2007) 34–39.

McLaren, Brian D. "Church Emerging: Or Why I Still Use the Word *Postmodern* but with Mixed Feelings." In *An Emergent Manifesto of Hope*, edited by Doug Pagitt and Tony Jones, 141–51. Grand Rapids, MI: Baker, 2007.

———. *The Church on the Other Side: Doing Ministry in the Postmodern Matrix*. Grand Rapids, MI: Zondervan, 2000.

———. *Everything Must Change: Jesus, Global Crises, and a Revolution of Hope*. Nashville: Thomas Nelson, 2007.

———. *Finding Our Way Again: The Return of the Ancient Practices*. Nashville: Thomas Nelson, 2008.

———. *A New Kind of Christian: A Tale of Two Friends on a Spiritual Journey*. San Francisco: Jossey-Bass, 2001.

———. *The Secret Message of Jesus: Uncovering the Truth that Could Change Everything*. Nashville: Thomas Nelson, 2006.

———. *Why Did Jesus, Moses, the Buddha, and Mohammed Cross the Road?: Christian Identity in a Multi-Faith World*. New York: Jericho, 2012.

McLaren, Brian D., and Tony Campolo. *Adventures in Missing the Point: How the Culture-Controlled Church Neutered the Gospel*. El Cajon, CA: Emergent YS, 2003.

McManus, Erwin. "The Global Intersection." In *The Church in Emerging Culture*, edited by Leonard Sweet, 235–63. El Cajon, CA: Emergent YS, 2003.

Merriam, Sharan B. "Case Study." In *Qualitative Research in Practice: Examples for Discussion and Analysis*, edited by Sharan B. Merriam, 178–80. San Francisco: Jossey-Bass, 2002.

———. "Grounded Theory." In *Qualitative Research in Practice: Examples for Discussion and Analysis*, edited by Sharan B. Merriam, 142–44. San Francisco: Jossey-Bass, 2002.

———. "Phenomenological Research." In *Qualitative Research in Practice: Examples for Discussion and Analysis*, edited by Sharan B. Merriam, 93–95. San Francisco, CA: Jossey-Bass, 2002.

Metz, Johann Baptist. *The Emergent Church: The Future of Christianity in a Postbourgeois World*. Translated by Peter Mann. New York: Crossroad, 1981.

Miller, Donald E. *Reinventing American Protestantism: Christianity in the New Millennium*. Berkeley: University of California Press, 1997.

Miller, Donald E, and Arpi Misha Miller. "Understanding Generation X: Values, Politics, and Religious Commitments." In *GenX Religion*, edited by Richard W. Flory and Donald E. Miller, 1–12. New York: Routledge, 2000.

Mitchell, Nathan D. "Religious Communities: Christian Religious Orders." In vol. 11 of *Encyclopedia of Religion*, edited by Lindsay Jones, 7721. 2nd ed. Detroit: Thomson Gale, 2005.

Moon, Sidney M., and Terry S. Trepper. "Case Study Research." In *Research Methods in Family Therapy*, edited by Sidney M. Moon and Douglas H. Sprenkle, 393–410. New York: Guildford, 1996.

Moritz, Joshua M. "Beyond Strategy, Towards the Kingdom of God: The Post-Critical Reconstructionist Mission of the Emerging Church." *Dialog: A Journal of Theology* 47 (2008) 27–36.

Moynagh, Michael, and Philip Harrold. *Church for Every Context: An Introduction to Theology and Practice*. London: SCM, 2012.

Nash, Robert N. *An 8-Track Church in a CD World*. Macon, GA: Smyth & Helwys, 1997.

Nelson, Thorana S. "Survey Research in Marriage and Family Therapy." In *Research Methods in Family Therapy*, edited by Sidney M. Moon and Douglas H. Sprenkle, 447–68. New York: Guildford, 1996.

Newbigin, Lesslie. *Proper Confidence: Faith, Doubt, and Certainty in Christian Discipleship*. Grand Rapids, MI: Eerdmans, 1995.

Noll, Mark A. *American Evangelical Christianity: An Introduction*. Oxford: Blackwell, 2001.

———. "Revolution and the Rise of Evangelical Social Influence in North Atlantic Societies." In *Evangelicalism: Comparative Studies of Popular Protestantism in North America, the British Isles, and Beyond, 1700–1990*, edited by David W. Bebbington, Mark A. Noll, and George A. Rawlyk, 113–36. New York: Oxford University Press, 1994.

———. *Scandal of the Evangelical Mind*. Grand Rapids, MI: Eerdmans, 1994.

Olson, Roger E. *How to Be Evangelical without Being Conservative*. Grand Rapids, MI: Zondervan, 2008.

Packard, Josh. *The Emerging Church: Religion at the Margins*. Boulder, CO: First Forum, 2012.

Pagitt, Doug. *A Christianity Worth Believing: Hope-Filled, Open-Armed, Alive-and-Well Faith for the Left Out, Left Behind, and Let Down in Us All*. San Francisco: Jossey-Bass, 2008.

———. *Community in the Inventive Age*. Minneapolis, MN: Sparkhouse, 2011.

Pearson, Geoffrey. "Foreword: Talking a Good Fight: Authenticity and Distance in the Ethnographer's Craft." In *Interpreting the Field: Accounts of Ethnography*, edited by Dick Hobbs and Tim May, vii–xx. Oxford, UK: Clarendon, 1993.

Penning, James M., and Corwin E. Smidt. *Evangelicalism: The Next Generation*. Grand Rapids, MI: Baker, 2002.

Perriman, Andrew. *Otherways: In Search of an Emerging Theology*. [S.l.]: Open Source Theology, 2007.

Pettegrew, Larry D. "Evangelicalism, Paradigms, and the Emerging Church." *Master's Seminary Journal* 17 (2006) 159–75.

Pew Forum on Religion and Public Life. *U.S. Religious Landscape Survey*. Washington, DC: Pew Forum on Religion and Public Life, 2008.

Piatt, Christian, and Amy Piatt. *MySpace to Sacred Space: God for a New Generation*. St. Louis, MO: Chalice, 2007.

Putnam, Robert D. *Bowling Alone: The Collapse and Revival of American Community*. New York: Simon and Schuster, 2000.

Rabey, Steve. *In Search of Authentic Faith: How Emerging Generations Are Transforming the Church.* Colorado Springs, CO: WaterBrook, 2001.

Rafuls, Silvia E., and Sidney M. Moon. "Grounded Theory Methodology in Family Therapy Research." In *Research Methods in Family Therapy*, edited by Sidney M. Moon and Douglas H. Sprenkle, 64–80. New York: Guilford, 1996.

Raschke, Carl. *The Next Reformation: Why Evangelicals Must Embrace Postmodernity.* Grand Rapids, MI: Baker Academic, 2004.

Riis, Ole Preben. "Methodology in the Sociology of Religion." In *The Oxford Handbook of the Sociology of Religion*, edited by Peter B. Clarke, 229–244. Oxford: Oxford University Press, 2009.

Roberts, Bob. *Glocalization: How Followers of Jesus Engage a Flat World.* Grand Rapids, MI: Zondervan, 2007.

Robinson, Martin, and Dwight Smith. *Invading Secular Space: Strategies for Tomorrow's Church.* Oxford, UK: Monarch, 2003.

Robson, Colin. *Real World Research: A Resource for Social Scientists and Practitioner-Researchers.* 2nd ed. Oxford, UK: Blackwell, 2002.

Rollins, Peter. *How (Not) to Speak of God.* Brewster, MA: Paraclete, 2006.

———. *Insurrection.* New York: Howard, 2011.

Scandrette, Mark. "A Week in the Life of a Missional Community." In *The Relevant Church*, edited by Jennifer Ashley, 131–45. Lake Mary, FL: Relevant, 2004.

Scott, Eleonora L. "A Theological Critique of the Emerging, Postmodern Missional Church/Movement." *Evangelical Review of Theology* 34 (October 2010) 336–45.

Seay, Chris, and Greg Garrett. *The Gospel Reloaded: Exploring Spirituality and Faith in "The Matrix."* Colorado Springs, CO: Piñon, 2003.

Sheldrake, Philip. *A Brief History of Spirituality.* Malden, MA: Blackwell, 2007.

———. "Introduction." In *New Westminster Dictionary of Christian Spirituality*, edited by Philip Sheldrake, vii–ix. Louisville, KY: Westminster John Knox, 2005.

Shibley, Mark A. *Resurgent Evangelicalism in the United States: Mapping Cultural Change since 1970.* Columbia: University of South Carolina Press, 1996.

Silverman, David. *Interpreting Qualitative Data: Methods for Analyzing Talk, Text and Interaction.* 3rd ed. London: SAGE, 2006.

Sine, Tom. *The New Conspirators: Creating the Future One Mustard Seed at a Time.* Downers Grove, IL: InterVarsity, 2008.

Smith, Christian. *American Evangelicalism: Embattled and Thriving.* Chicago: University of Chicago Press, 1998.

———. *Christian America? What Evangelicals Really Want.* Berkeley: University of California Press, 2000.

Smith, Christian, and Patricia Snell. *Souls in Transition: The Religious & Spiritual Lives of Emerging Adults.* New York: Oxford University Press, 2009.

Smith, James K. A. "The Economics of the Emerging Church." In *The Devil Reads Derrida and Other Essays on the University, the Church, Politics, and the Arts*, 93–96. Grand Rapids, MI: Eerdmans, 2009.

Smith, Kathy. "Training Wheels." *Congregations* 39 (2012) 18–20.

Smith, R. Scott. *Truth and the New Kind of Christian: The Emerging Effects of Postmodernism in the Church.* Wheaton, IL: Crossway, 2005.

Snider, Phil. "Introduction." In *The Hyphenateds: How Emergence Christianity is Re-Traditioning Mainline Practices*, edited by Phil Snider, xv–xxiii. St. Louis, MO: Chalice, 2011.

Snider, Phil, and Emily Bowen. *Toward a Hopeful Future: Why the Emergent Church Is Good News for Mainline Congregations.* Cleveland: Pilgrim, 2010.

Stetzer, Ed, and David Putman. *Breaking the Missional Code: Your Church Can Become a Missionary in Your Community.* Nashville: Broadman & Holman, 2006.

Stoner, Timothy J. *The God Who Smokes: Scandalous Meditations on Faith.* Colorado Springs, CO: NavPress, 2008.

Stringer, Martin D. *On the Perception of Worship: The Ethnography of Worship in Four Christian Congregations in Manchester.* Birmingham: University of Birmingham Press, 1999.

Sweet, Leonard. *A Cup of Coffee at the Soul Café.* Nashville: Broadman & Holman, 1998.

———. *FaithQuakes.* Nashville: Abingdon, 1994.

———. *I Am a Follower: The Way, Truth, and Life of Following Jesus.* Nashville: Thomas Nelson, 2012.

———. *Learn to Dance the Soul Salsa: 17 Surprising Steps for Godly Living in the 21st Century.* Grand Rapids, MI: Zondervan, 2000.

———. *Quantum Spirituality: A Postmodern Apologetic.* Dayton, OH: Whaleprints, 1991.

Taylor, Steve. *The Out of Bounds Church: Learning to Create a Community of Faith in a Culture of Change.* El Cajon, CA: Emergent YS, 2005.

Tickle, Phyllis. *The Great Emergence: How Christianity Is Changing and Why.* Grand Rapids, MI: Baker, 2008.

Tipton, Steven M. *Getting Saved from the Sixties: Moral Meaning in Conversion and Cultural Change.* Berkeley: University of California Press, 1982.

Tomlinson, Dave. *The Post-Evangelical.* Grand Rapids, MI: Zondervan, 2003.

Towns, Elmer L., and Ed Stetzer. *Perimeters of Light: Biblical Boundaries for the Emerging Church.* Chicago: Moody, 2004.

Webber, Robert E. *Ancient-Future Faith: Rethinking Evangelicalism for a Postmodern World.* Grand Rapids, MI: Baker, 1999.

———. *The Divine Embrace: Recovering the Passionate Spiritual Life.* Grand Rapids, MI: Baker, 2006.

———. "Introduction: The Interaction of Culture and Theology." In *Listening to the Beliefs of Emerging Churches*, edited by Robert E. Webber, 9–18. Grand Rapids, MI: Zondervan, 2007.

———. *The Younger Evangelicals: Facing the Challenges of the New World.* Grand Rapids, MI: Baker, 2002.

Weber, Max. *The Protestant Ethic and the Spirit of Capitalism.* Translated by T. Parsons. New York: Scribner, 1958 [1904].

Weiss, Robert S. *Learning from Strangers: The Art and Method of Qualitative Interview Studies.* New York: Free Press, 1994.

Wells, David. "On Being Evangelical: Some Theological Differences and Similarities." In *Evangelicalism: Comparative Studies of Popular Protestantism in North America, the British Isles, and Beyond, 1700–1990*, edited by David W. Bebbington, Mark A. Noll, and George A. Rawlyk, 389–410. New York: Oxford University Press, 1994.

Wells, David F. *Above All Earthly Pow'rs: Christ in a Postmodern World.* Grand Rapids, MI: Eerdmans, 2005.

Wessinger, Catherine. "New Religious Movements: An Overview." In vol. 10 of *Encyclopedia of Religion*, edited by Lindsay Jones, 6513. 2nd ed. Detroit: Thomson Gale, 2005.

Whitesel, Bob. *Inside the Organic Church: Learning from 12 Emerging Congregations.* Nashville: Abingdon, 2006.

Willard, Dallas. *The Spirit of the Disciplines: Understanding How God Changes Lives.* San Francisco: HarperSanFrancisco, 1991.

Williams, Rowan. *Christian Spirituality: A Theological History from the New Testament to Luther and St. John of the Cross.* Atlanta: John Knox, 1980.

Wilson-Hartgrove, Jonathan. "Mark 12: Commitment to a Disciplined Contemplative Life." In *School(s) of Conversion: 12 Marks of a New Monasticism,* edited by The Rutba House, 162–72. Eugene, OR: Cascade, 2005.

Wuthnow, Robert. *After the Baby Boomers: How Twenty- and Thirty-Somethings Are Shaping the Future of American Religion.* Princeton: Princeton University Press, 2007.

Zinnbauer, Brian J., et al. "Religion and Spirituality: Unfuzzying the Fuzzy." *Journal for the Scientific Study of Religion* 36 (December 1997) 549–64.

Index

Acacia group(s), 133, 180
accountability, 152-53, 157-58, 200
Advent, 160-61, 163, 202
alt.worship, 42
ancient-future, 34n74, 71, 271
Anglican, xiii, 42n117, 61-62, 167, 190, 212, 247
Antony of Egypt, 6
anxiety, 138, 143, 145, 234, 236
apophatic, 75, 87
art station(s), xix, 115
artistic expression, 76, 117
Artwalk, 68
awe, 57, 65, 150, 160

Baby Boomer(s), 26-27, 29, 30-31
belief and behavior, xiv, 20, 253
Bell, Rob, 15, 54, 56, 62, 65, 86
Benedict of Nursia, 65
Bielo, James, 44, 68, 80, 91, 109
blog(s), 2, 14, 18, 54, 104, 108, 110, 123, 125, 127, 129n1, 173
Book of Common Prayer, The, 163, 181
boundary(ies), xiv, 13-15, 17, 25, 36, 44, 46, 49, 52, 62, 67, 97, 104, 124, 129, 144, 194, 203, 214, 217, 224, 242, 251n6
bounded system, 17, 98, 103
bricolage, 33, 33n69, 67
Brigit (St.), 161, 227
Brother Lawrence, 63-64, 174-76, 227-28
Buddheo-Christian, 120, 144, 215
Buddhist, 15, 76, 140, 144, 214-15, 231

Burke, Spencer, 54, 63, 86

camping, 179, 234
Carter, James, 23
Cassian, John, 6, 71
Catholic (church), xiii, 1n3, 6, 40, 61-62, 67, 79, 113, 156, 161, 169, 172, 180, 190-91
childhood, 156, 190-91, 209
Claiborne, Shane, 109
club culture, 41
Cloud of Unknowing (The), 71
contextualization, 14-15, 35, 38-39, 45, 53
continuum, 110-11, 115, 121, 203, 246
counterculture, 29

Daily Office, The, 70, 163, 179, 181
Daniel fast, 165, 204, 218
DART Stations of the Cross, 187, 237, 252
Day, Dorothy, 65
deconstruction, 38, 87, 124
deconversion, 85
desert fathers, 65, 79
divergent categories, 130, 192
Divine Hours, The, 181
doubt(s), xvi, 34, 36, 63, 112
Drane, John, 34, 251n6

eclecticism, 66-67, 70, 87, 93, 119-20, 180, 191
Emerson, Ralph Waldo, 34, 48

273

INDEX

Episcopal (church), 108–9, 156, 169, 190
ethnography, 17, 96, 98, 102, 105, 107
evangelical spirituality, 62, 88, 94, 242, 253–54
evangelical theology, 65, 80, 85
experiencing God, 68–69, 119

Fenelon, François, 64
Flory, Richard, 36, 49–51, 81, 90, 244
Foster, Richard, 16, 59
Francis of Assisi, 65
Fresh Expressions, 43–44
Frost, Michael, 42, 54, 63, 73, 77
Fundamentalism, 23, 25, 56

Ganiel, Gladys, x, xxi, 12, 44–48, 81
gardening, 139, 231
Gay, Doug, 40
Generation X, 28, 30
Graham, Billy, 26
Gregorian chant, 1
Gregory of Nyssa, 15, 65
grounded theory, 18, 96, 101–2, 104, 193

Hebrew Root (movement), 111, 113
Hildegard of Bingen, 161, 227
Hindu, 15, 43, 67, 76, 254
Hirsch, Alan, 42, 73
holistic spirituality, 67, 94
Holy Spirit, xvi, 8, 25, 68, 126, 143, 150, 171
Holy Week, 80, 149, 236
home group(s), 112, 145
hospitality, 64, 83, 88, 125–26
Hunter, Todd, 54, 65, 72, 92

identity, ix–x, 34, 52, 78, 122, 124–25, 127, 197
Ignatius of Loyola, 75, 83
illumination, 4–5
imagination/imaginative, 40, 61, 65, 73, 75, 147, 183–84, 207, 220, 235
immanence, 69
inclusion/inclusivity, xiv, xvii, 46, 49–50, 54, 120, 124, 161–62, 164, 201–3, 224–26, 232

inner self, 74
institutionalism, 21, 45–46, 48
institutionalization, 45–48, 51–53, 249
intinction, xx, 133, 135, 196, 230
isomorphism, 46

James, William, 34, 48
Jewish, 15, 67, 113, 115, 125, 161, 177
John of the Cross, 71, 272
Jones, Tony, 16, 54, 60–61, 67, 71–73, 75–80, 82, 88–89, 253
journaling, 68, 76, 149, 185

Keating, Thomas, 71, 142–43

lectionary, 75n85, 160, 162, 184, 202–3, 217
Lent, 160, 163, 166–67, 172, 188, 202, 204–5, 218, 227, 232
Life Connection, The (church), 114, 116–17
Life of Moses, The, 15, 65
Lord's Prayer, The, 170–72, 180, 190, 206, 219
Luther, Martin, 7

Maproom, 68, 80
Mars Hill (church), 29
Marti, Gerardo, x, 12, 44–48, 81
Mary Magdalene, 161, 217–18, 237
McLaren, Brian, 14, 39, 43–44, 54, 64–65, 67, 69, 73, 75, 83, 85, 87–89
meditation, active, 138–40
meditation, guided, 138, 140, 213
meditation, passive, 138
megachurch(es), ix–x, 26
Meister Eckhart, 63
Merton, Thomas, 225
Methodist (church), 44, 111, 114, 119, 132, 161
microbe(s), 2–4, 9, 19, 21, 52, 110, 252
microcosm, 78, 139, 155
Millennial(s), 30
Miller, Donald, 36, 49–51, 81, 90, 244
Mosaic (church), xviii, 29
modernism, 23–24, 33–34, 61
multiculturalism, 109

music, xx, 1n3, 35, 70, 74, 77, 92, 119, 126, 137, 139, 150, 216, 231, 252
mysterian(s), 87, 243
mystical experience(s), 57, 66, 68–70, 73, 93
mystical theology, 1, 3, 6, 57

neo-charismatic movement, xvi, 25
Neo-Evangelical(s), 22–27
neo-monastic, 88n138, 109–10
Newbigin, Lesslie, 28n39, 31n61, 42–43
NewSong (church), 29
non-denominational, 116

organic theologian, 81
Orthodox (church), xiii, 1n3, 6, 61–62, 67, 79, 82, 170–72, 190, 206, 219

Packard, Josh, 11, 44, 46–49, 51
Pagitt, Doug, 10, 54, 69, 84, 92
paradox(es), 10, 45, 60, 66, 87, 93–94
participant observation, 95–96, 98–102, 105–7, 110, 127, 129n1
Pennington, M. Basil, 71, 142
Pentecostalism, 25, 41
perichoresis, 82
Peterson, Eugene, 16n35, 59
phenomenological interview(s), 18, 95–96, 99–100, 105, 107, 118, 129n1, 193, 200
phenomenology, 101–2, 105–6, 132, 247
plumcot, 10
podcast(s), 2, 18, 108, 129n1, 147
poetry, 117, 119, 188
Post-Baby Boomer(s), 29
post-evangelical(s), 24, 27, 42
postmodernism, xvi–xvii, 14, 25, 33–35, 39, 82
postmodernity, ix, xvi, 12–13, 15, 33, 35–36, 110, 124, 243
Practice of the Presence of God, The, 63, 173–74, 227
pragmatic evangelical(s), 24, 26–28, 32, 48
Pray as You Go, 148
prayer rope, 78n101, 172, 190
Protestant ethic, 51–52
Protestant Reformation, 7, 22

purification, 4–5
Putnam, Robert, 30n51, 37

Quantum Spirituality, 42

reenchantment, 57
relationship with God, 55, 149, 195, 209, 242
retreat(s), 65, 137, 178, 185, 219
rhythm(s), 83, 143, 159–62, 164, 202–3, 217
Rollins, Peter, 54, 60, 63
Romanticism, 34
Rule (monastic), xv, 67

sacrament(al), xv, xix–xx, 62, 72, 115, 132, 156
sacred space, 76, 169
Sacred Way (The), 54n1, 75
secularity, 32, 91
secularization, 24, 26, 41
seeker(s), 26, 29, 79
self-evaluation, 148–49
Sheilaism, 51
sin, 6, 155, 158–59, 200–201, 221, 252
social justice, xvii, 64, 88, 91, 117, 120, 225, 229
Solomon's Porch (church), xviii, 10, 83
solution, 3–4, 9, 19, 21, 52, 110, 252
Southern Baptist (church), ix, 108, 121
spiritual disciplines, 16, 59–60, 62, 65, 212, 247, 251n6
spiritual formation, 67, 79, 83, 115, 145, 159, 163, 225
Sweet, Leonard, 42, 54, 69, 73–74, 87, 243
symbol(s), 62, 72–73, 75, 133

Taylor, Steve, 42
Teresa of Avila, 66, 71
Theresa of Calcutta, 65
thick description, xvi, 4, 17, 97–98, 103–04, 109, 251, 254
this-world spirituality, 247, 250
Thoreau, Henry David, 34
threshold experience, 69
Tomlinson, David, 42
unchurched, 41, 46

union, 4–6, 8
unknown, 56, 60, 70, 87, 243
usage ranges, 130

Velvet Elvis, 15
Virgin Mary, 90, 161

Walk to Emmaus (conference), 178
Wesley, Charles, 22
Wesley, John, 22, 165
what-works mentality, 15, 127, 173, 215–16, 238, 249, 251

Whitefield, George, 22
Whitman, Walt, 34, 48
Willard, Dallas, 16, 59
wordless prayer, 141–42, 148

yoga, 67, 72, 76, 140, 144, 213–14, 231, 254
Young Leader's Network, 43

Zander, Dieter, 29

www.ingramcontent.com/pod-product-compliance
Lightning Source LLC
Chambersburg PA
CBHW061433300426
44114CB00014B/1659